ÌSARÀ

ÌSARÀ

A Voyage Around "Essay"

WOLE SOYINKA

Random House New York

Library of Congress Cataloging-in-Publication Data

Soyinka, Wole.
Ìsarà, a voyage around "Essay" / by Wole Soyinka.
p. cm.
ISBN 0-394-54077-8
1. Soyinka, Wole—Biography—Family.   2. "Essay."   3. Fathers and
sons—Nigeria—Biography.   4. Authors, Nigerian—20th
century–Biography.   I. Title.
PR9387.9.S6Z466 1989
822—dc20   87-42670   89-3944
[B]

Manufactured in the United States of America
24689753
First Edition

Author's Note

I have borrowed *Ìsarà*'s subtitle from John Mortimer's play *A Voyage Round My Father*. The expression captures in essence what I have tried to do with the contents of a tin box which I opened some four years ago, that is, about two years after *Aké* was written. The completion of that childhood biography, rather than assuage a curiosity about a vanishing period of one's existence, only fuelled it, fragments of an incomplete memory returning to haunt one again and again in the personae of representative protagonists of such a period. Of course my own case may have been especially acute; I was in political exile when "Essay" died. All plans to return home for the funeral were abruptly cancelled when I received a message from the "Wild Christian" urging me to return home indeed if I wished to bury her with her lifelong partner. I recorded a message, which was played at the funeral, and stayed put in an indifferent clime.

Years later, I opened the metallic box, scraped off the cockroach eggs, and browsed through a handful of letters, old journals with marked pages and annotations, notebook jottings, tax and other levy receipts, minutes of meetings and school reports, programme notes of special events, and so on. A tantalising experience, eavesdropping on this very special class of teachers of our colonial period; inevitably I would become drawn to attempting to flesh out these glimpses on a very different level of awareness and empathy from that of *Aké*.

I have not only taken liberties with chronology, I have deliberately ruptured it. After all, the period covered here actively is no more than fifteen years, and its significance for me is that it represents the period when a pattern of their lives was set—for better or worse—under the compelling impact of the major events in their times, both local and global, the uneasy love-hate relationship with the colonial presence, and its own ambiguous attitudes to the Western-educated elite of the Nigerian protectorate.

Life, it would appear, was lived robustly, but was marked also by an intense quest for a place in the new order, and one of a far more soul-searching dimension than the generation they spawned would later undertake. Their options were excruciatingly limited. A comparison between this aspect of their time and their offsprings', when coupled with the inversely proportionate weight of extended family demands and expectations, assumes quite a heroic dimension.

Ìsarà then is simply a tribute to "Essay" and his friends and times. My decision not to continue with real names, as in *Aké*, except in a few cases, is to eliminate any pretence to factual accuracy in this attempted reconstruction of their times, thoughts, and feelings. Like most voyages, this one has not followed the itinerary I so confidently mapped out for it; indeed it proved an almost impossible journey which came close to being abandoned more than once. "Ilesa" is of course not simply one such institution nor Ìsarà one such community. I hope the surviving "ex-Ilés" all over the nation will understand this compulsion to acknowledge in some form, and however tenuously, their seminal role in the development of present-day Nigerian minds, and will overlook the obvious lapses and areas of dissatisfaction.

W. S.
November 1988

I

EX–ILÉ

Ashtabula! Soditan eased out the envelope with foreign stamps, addressed in a bold, sweeping cursive. It was already slit open, and as he released the neatly folded sheets, his spare frame responded to the emerging treat and he visibly relaxed. The luxury of reading and re-reading his private correspondence was one in which he indulged whenever possible in the privacy of Ìsarà, especially when he returned there out of season. Season was New Year, Harvest, or Easter; or whenever the ex-Ilés agreed to meet in the hometown for a special occasion, usually a wedding, a grand funeral, or a house-warming for one of The Circle who had finally "returned to sender." This meant more than a simple homecoming; it was homecoming in a manner (and on a scale) that finally fulfilled the hopes and prayers, the nursed dreams and burdensome aspirations, of that close community from which they were dispersed to nearly every region of the country. Success, and its embodiment on their natal soil, preferably in the form of a modest but "modern" house, was a "return to sender."

In a seasonal reentry one was never alone; Ado, Ibadan, Jos, Ede, Benin—all places of exile descended on the small community, retailing accounts of the intervening months, swapping anecdotes, doctoring failures, and decking out successes. Off-season visits were peaceful; there were hours of quiet intimacy with Mariam, his mother, and Pa Soditan, his father. Hours to pick his way between recumbent sheep and sunken waterpots which lined the shadowy passages, ducking beneath low trestles from which indigo-dyed cloths would drip on busier days; to acknowledge the few greetings without their usual accompanying impositions, the demands and enquiries. It was as if the town had evolved a tacit understanding: No one bothered "Tisa," or *omo* Josiah, with the casual request for monetary help, a letter of introduction for a job-seeker, assistance with admission to a school—all this was somehow restricted to the seasonal visits. Of course most of the inhabitants were out on their farms, living in makeshift homes for weeks, even months, at a time, or had travelled to Lagos, Ibadan, and Kano farther north on trading forays. No matter, Ìsarà out of season was without the usual incursions on his presence, peaceful, and somewhat lonely, steeped in an unshakable languor which spread even over the marketplace. The Oba's palace, despite the lounging figures of the royal retinue in the verandah and the rare appearance of a brace of chiefs in robes and shawl, appeared curiously untenanted. The few public centres, such as the clinic, tax office, and Native Authority court, exuded a mere symbolic air, languishing for lack of patronage. The gates to the *iledi* would creak open only once or twice; a priest would emerge, shut the gate carefully behind him, and shuffle homewards with eyes cast to the ground, greeted by and greeting none, his silence inviolate as the heart of divination. Only the primary school, St. James's where Akinyode himself began his journey to adulthood, seemed to contest the general lethargy, yet even here the teachers merely led in muted voices their pupils' rote responses, no different from the small clumps of pupils in the open-air Koranic school on the other side of the market from the palace—bored voices, vacant stares, stirring to life only when the *mallam*'s sporadic whip beat a slow tattoo on their docile heads. Nothing really stirred, not the sheep with huge pregnancies hugging the shadows of red mud walls. The solitary hawker made the rounds of the few tenanted passages, her hawking cries more dirged than full-throated, no rousing accent to entice the indifferent. Built into the hillsides of red laterite, Ìsarà at such periods was neither hostile nor welcoming; it was simply indifferent, the stone shrapnels of its walls and rust of corrugated roofs belying the lushness of the valley below, which wove a moist sash round the town on nearly every side. Why, Akinyode sometimes wondered, had his ancestors chosen to build on such inclement soil? Was it a need for safety in those earlier, uncertain times? Yet the town looked exposed to any determined incursion. The wooded valleys were perfect hiding places for an enemy; he could lay indefinite siege to these birdcages tucked precariously against the naked sides and ridges of a nature cantilevered hill.

One did not notice these features when the town came to life in season. Then Ìsarà metamorphosed into a giddy butterfly, and even the harsh-grained walls turned soft and coquettish, overwhelmed by new voices, incessant taps on open doors and the rattle of latches, yells of children and the hum of the lone corn mill. The narrow streets broadened overnight to receive their sons and daughters, heedless of the constant cloud of dust that swiftly coloured their skin, finery, and hair a brilliant red. But that was not now, and the school-teacher did not mind their absence. The distant clang of the black-smith's anvil was truly music to his ears, and his letters kept him company. Contentedly he communed with distant friends while he waited to be summoned for the final rites of the event that brought him unseasonally into town—the "outing" of the first motor lorry to be owned by an indigene of Ìsarà. The pioneer was his father's friend Node, sadly paralysed—by the evil machinations of a treacherous friend, as all Ìsarà knew, but that matter had long been settled, the culprit (or suspect, the teacher persisted in saying) ostracised. It was the least he could do, to be present, since he had himself to blame or praise for bringing the monumental project to fruition. His fellow ex-Ilés would be here as well if Node were of their generation, but Node was a stay-at-home successful farmer of his father's age, illiter-ate but shrewd. Negotiations had begun before his illness and he had relied on the schoolteacher's contacts with the world of forms and legal mazes. The lorry would be used to transport timber—for that he also required a special licence. This was one point on which Akinyode had failed to move him—Node would have nothing to do with passengers. Nor did that parsimonious mind make the mistake of launching his vehicle "in season." He knew what this would have meant—feasting the entire Ìsarà, streams of mendicant drummers and praise-singers, and even uninvited out-of-town well-wishers come to celebrate (and squander) his good fortune. No, a small cere-mony it had to be, *etutu* rituals performed by Jagun, a Christian blessing by Pa Josiah, and a Koranic reading by the imam. The day would be rounded off by a modest feast—just for Node's household and Jagun's and Soditan's families, and of course those whom he had invited to officiate and launch the vehicle into a career of luck and profit.

Even as the schoolteacher settled more snugly into his father's fibre-cane chair, a crude guttural bleat pierced the afternoon haze, and Akinyode, irritated, glanced angrily through the window in the

direction of Node's compound. Again the bleat was repeated, if anything reinforced with a desperate vigour, shattering the accustomed
peace of an unseasonal day. Node would not skimp on the girth and
soundness of the sacrificial ram, the teacher knew, so it was certain
that this bleat, quite unlike the perfunctory sounds that emerged
from the native quadrupeds of Ìsarà, could only be that of the
doomed animal. The schoolteacher chuckled to himself—all right, I
give you till dawn tomorrow; then Node will ride on your back to
Ashtabula!

It had taken quite a while before the schoolteacher brought himself to accept the word as yet another place-name. Like Ìsarà. Or
Kaura Namoda. That had made him pause. What would the natives
of Ashtabula think of that one? Or Olomitutu? How did it sound in
their ears? Even so, as a name for white people—Ashtabula? This
hand from beyond the seas had stretched the bounds of place-
naming beyond easy acceptance. What spirits had presided over the
naming ceremonies of such a place? A settlement was no different
from a child; you recognised its essence in the name. That was the
problem—there was nothing remotely European about the name
Ashtabula! Or were Americans now far removed from white stock
and breeding? And Wade Cudeback—that name was also striking—
rough, rugged, no doubt a disciplinarian of the old school. His handwriting did its best to extend Ashtabula beyond plain images of a
small provincial town—*90 degrees Fahr., whereas our average for this
date is merely 55 degrees.* That reminded Akinyode that he should
take the readings of the school thermometer and barometer and
record them as soon as he returned to Abeokuta. The rain gauge was,
like the school, on pre-harmattan vacation; there would be not one
inch to record for another three months, possibly four. No moisture
but the morning dew.

Cudeback used a thick nib, he noted. And the notepaper? He held
it to his nose—yes, the faint smell was not too dissimilar from that of
his favoured Quink ink. There were suggestions also of pinewood,
river moss, possibly gum arabica. With this last, however, he suspected that he had merely foisted that much-remarked smell from
his own desk in Aké onto a stranger's remote corner of the world. It
was the man's handwriting that evoked such fancies. Each exclamation mark was like the housepost of the *ogboni* shrine, or a Corin-

thian column in the Illustrated Bible (Authorized Version). His *I* had
generous loops both up and down, resulting in a coracle shape, mildly
unbalanced by a wave, akin to a fat cowrie, or a curled-up millipede.
Each *D* was consistently like the cauliflower ear of Osibo, the pharmacist, while the *W* was just like an *abetiaja*,* or the starched,
bristling headgear of the Reverend Sisters from Oke Padi hospital.
And so it went on: The lower-case *y* had its downward tail reversed
and looped so far upwards that it became a hangman's noose, while
an ultimate *t*, contrasted with the ordinariness of his *t* at the start of
a word, was slashed downwards with a vicious, decapitating stroke
which, extended far below the base of the letter, turned it into an
amputee, a cheerful acrobat dancing on its one leg, amusing the rest
of its alphabetic audience with that near-magical turn of the *iguniko*
as it shoots up skywards on one stilt.

The teacher absolved himself of envy. It was a different calligraphy
from his, that was all, not necessarily a better one. It needed no bias
at all to see that his own handwriting was more disciplined, more
consistent. There were some self-indulgent quirks in Cudeback's
penmanship; perhaps it had to do with the sometimes erratic, sometimes magical scenes he described as he proceeded through the vast
continent of America on his restless vacations.

There was this also about the man's narrative: a bias? No, perhaps
a slant, an unintended flavouring, maybe no more than the Ashtabu-
lan essence of the man himself, which brought the schoolteacher
down to the favourite gibe of the ex-Ilés at themselves: "You can take
an Ìsaràman out of Ìsarà, but you cannot take Ìsarà out of an Ìsaràman." Wherever his pen pal went, all through *the four provinces of
Canada and six states of the United States, a scintillating 3,500-mile
trip in my jallopie,* it seemed as if this traveller was never really out
of Ashtabula. How this feat was wrought, Akinyode could not quite
decide, but it seemed Wade Cudeback always humped Ashtabula
with him in his rucksack. . . . *The Thousand Islands Bridge, the
Chateau de Ramezay, a bell which weighed 24,780 pounds and is
probably the largest bell in America, the lowlands and sandstone
landscapes, St. Joseph's shrines where many come to be cured, a
three-mile walled city, upstream tides of the Petitcodiac River* . . .

* A Yoruba dress-cap.

Petitcodiac! And yes, this was the fact that had briefly slipped his mind. The Indians were the real owners of the American continent, and it explained everything, even the name Ashtabula. Little wonder their spirits still roamed the continent at will: Ashtabula was everywhere. Perhaps even in the name Cudeback? No matter, Akinyode settled for a kindred spirit. A teacher too, no wonder at all. Did he suffer from this compulsion to instruct? Mr. Cudeback and his single-spaced seven-page letter filled with rare scenic details would provide a departure in next year's geography classes. Or general knowledge. A passionate traveller, his friend; even as he narrated his adventures of the summer of thirty-seven, he was already planning an excursion for the following year, singing his signature tune:

> I never see a map but I'm away
> On all the errands that I long to do
> Up all the rivers that are painted blue
> And all the ranges that are painted gray . . .

Would they ever meet? And where? Ìsarà or Ashtabula? What had moved the man to send a letter to the *Gazette?* And he in turn, in far-off Ìsarà, had been moved to write—and post (a very different step!)—a reply. Then commenced the exchange of letters, sometimes personal, sometimes, as in the case of these "tales of adventure," circulated among others. Even as he read his letters, Akinyode would begin to compose his reply, mostly laudatory, but with the occasional reprimand. *Sir, how could you devote so many lines to "the famous Montmorency Falls," picturesque and charming though they may be, yet they are but a norm of nature, while the Magnetic Mountain, which deserves to be the Eighth Wonder of the World, is given such scant attention. Perhaps, my dear Mr. Cudeback, such sights are commonplace in Ashtabula (and environs), yet I must tell you that in Ìsarà there are no such wonders seen. I must therefore request that you devote an entire letter to describing again this phenomenon of nature which, I assure you, I shall be hard put to convince my pupils thereof, even as my own circle to whom I read this portion of your letter have expressed the greatest scepticism, suggesting that this is twin-fantasy to the tales of* A Thousand and One Nights *or the* Adventures of Sindbad the Sailor.

Was that last too long a sentence? He would review it later, but first to re-read the passage that had so much whetted his appetite, fired his imagination, and provoked his protest. *From Moncton we drove to Magnetic Hill. To get the thrill of this phenomenon I drove my car down the hill to a certain spot at the foot, shut off the motor, put the gears in neutral, released the brakes, and my car started slowly backing up the hill, gaining speed as it ascended. Thus my car backed up the hill without power!* Nothing more? Tucked within a seven-page letter, tightly spaced? And there was the issue of the quotation marks—what did they signify? Was Cudeback interjecting the experience of some other traveller? Apart from the breathtaking impossibility of this eerie power, there were far too many other questions unanswered. Under no scale of values, even for a society with scientific explanations for every freak of nature, could such a phenomenon be worth less than three exclamation marks! This portion being for circulation to others, it was typed, so perhaps one should not judge Cudeback too hastily. If it had been handwritten, that exclamation mark would perhaps have revealed more of the traveller's state of mind by its girth, by the agitated impression left by Cudeback's favoured nib.

The letter was lavishly interlaced with snippets of verses—were they his own composition? The references to plants and flowers received Akinyode's neat question marks on the margin, betraying none of his inner excitement, for the schoolteacher was a nature fiend. For instance, were his water lilies in Ashtabula the same species as those in Ìsarà's lush vegetation?

> The water lilies beckon in the cove
> I snatch just one, to breathe its heady spice
> For we must on, beyond the point, to find
> A wooded shore all virgin in its solitude
> And skirt the hoary rock that turns around . . .

Even the rocky parsonage at Abeokuta had its share of water lilies. As for Ìsarà, the deepened, walled-in section of the stream where every household fetched its water was filled with ferns and lilies, many of them species unknown in the much-tended gardens of the parsonage. And what a strange man, this Cudeback. *It seems to me that you also are smitten by the travel bug*—that was surely an understatement to bring the year to a close. Was it by chance he brought all Cudeback's letters to Ìsarà to read and re-read even when he had yet no intention of replying? *Take the adventure, heed the call now, ere the irrevocable moment passes. 'Tis but the banging of the door behind you, a blithesome step forward, and you are out of the old life into the new.* Again his friend had placed that in quotation marks—it was frustrating. Were they his words, something he had written before to others? He made a note to demand the source and, if possible, the book from which it had been quoted.

Ashtabula was a private world, one which he kept secure even from the close circle of the ex-Ilés. From time to time he would "lend" them a portion of that world, a portion too immense to keep within Ìsarà. The Magnetic Mountain was one—no one could be expected to guard such a revelation selfishly beneath his pillow. And to Sipe, the other adventurer, the would-be merchant prince, he passed on tidbits that could guide his constant search for new commercial chances. Like the paper mill in Dalhousie, yes, that was something in which he could, as teacher, not now as the business tycoon into which Sipe would convert him, devote his energies and even his school and personal resources. Books. This was where books began, at least the material which made them books, not the mere facts and fancies of nature and experience, of reality and imagination. His neat hand copied the description, eyes aglow with the prospect of a paper mill in his hometown of Ìsarà. Timber was everywhere. The 'Gborobe stream would be dammed—he knew the very spot, just where a tiny waterfall cascaded twenty feet down deep-pocked red-ochre laterite. . . . *Wood supply held nearby, sent to the mill, cut in two-foot lengths, these forced thru crushes by pressure broadside against the face of the wood by rapidly revolving stones. Water is added during the process to reduce the heat created by the friction, and to see the material after the log has been crushed, one would think that hot water had been added, but our guide plainly told us the steam was caused by the friction. The pulp thus made is passed thru screens which remove the coarse particles and then run on rotary screens to allow the water to be drawn off by means of a vacuum suction. Near the end of the process it passes over several rollers for further drying of the pulp and is then rolled, weighed, and bound for shipping.* Akinyode nodded his approval. So simple. What, after all, was the value of all the training at St. Simeon's, whose constant sermon was self-reliance? If they could not now harness their environment to the end of such a basic product, why were they Simeonites? Was all the material needed for that potential industry not already in place in Ìsarà, the stagnant backwater that flung its sons far inland to St. Simeon's Teacher Training Seminary at Ilesa? Another backwater, Ilesa; its sole claim to note was the seminary itself and the young elites it trained.

But now Akinyode re-examined their status—were they really frogs in such inert, anonymous ponds? These places also had their history. The Fulani wars raged through their earth, razing and dividing the old Kingdom of Oyo, pitting warlord against warlord; their petty calculations, greed, ambition, alliances of convenience, the ravages of slavers and fanatic hordes . . . and Ìsarà, harassing and harassed in turn by Egba, Ijaiye, sometimes Ibadan, but never subdued. How else did the town obtain its praise-name, Afotamodi— they whose city ramparts are raised on ammunition? He conceded it—the reminiscences of a Wade Cudeback, strolling through his own history and others', did provoke these envious thoughts. Why, even Mr. Cudeback motoring into a place called Salem—strange, the name should be a prerogative of the Bible—even Cudeback had found, faithfully preserved, the famous Witches' House. If there was one commodity Ìsarà had no shortage of, it was witches! His own grandfather's name translated as "surrounded by sorcerers." So where was Ìsarà's Witches' or Sorcerers' House? Was it by any chance the *iledi?*

That could be, come to think of it, an equivalent of sorts. Akinyode felt slightly relieved, then moved to other paths and monuments of history trodden and touched by his wandering friend. *We saw the Plains of Abraham famed for the battle in 1759 between Wolfe and Montcalm which ended in the defeat of Montcalm and the fall of Quebec. Later we saw Montcalm's house, one of the oldest houses in the city, where he is supposed to have been taken after the battle and which is now used for a souvenir store.* Well, a mere 1759? Ijaiye, Kiriji, Basorun Gaha, those belligerent Aare ona Kakanfo, and Okenla, Lisabi . . . the worthy Dr. Johnson had chronicled their era, and many of these wars were even more recent. The aged survivors—and some not so ancient—would sometimes recount their own participation, bringing the scenes of courage and terror to life. So where were the trails, the spots, the landmarks? Where could he take his senior pupils—assuming he could persuade the mission to such a bold extension of the history classroom? And yet why not? It was the kind of excursion that was endorsed in principle by *The Nigerian Teacher*—so where could he take even a handful of pupils on such an exercise? Then sit them down to write the story of their passage among the ghosts of their own history. He would pick out the best essay and send it off to Wade Cudeback—yes, here is something in return for your Magnetic Mountains and Reversing Falls and the marathon runner Paul Revere. The thought depressed him: Where did the seminarian tutors of St. Simeon's ever take him? Yet in his youth had he not often traversed those grounds, those battle-contested grounds of Yoruba kingdoms? From Ìsarà to Ilesa, at least four times a year—twice only as he grew older and became inured to a prolonged exile—passing through Saki, Iseyin, and the ancient city of Oyo, walking, cycling, entombed in a dust-filled rickety transport. Through the years of training, were the seminarians ever taught to look? Had his youth truly vanished through so much history without even knowing that one had to *look*!

Still, there was more than enough time now to make up for lost time. He had made his tentative beginning with his adventurous return to Iseyin, so different from his "unseeing" passages through that hilly town of weavers during his seminarian days. And the musical pageant planned to celebrate the centenary of the first Christian mission in Egbaland—that was indeed part of the process—what better way could one find to recall history? Travelling would unearth more material. Now the roads were better, one could even learn to drive. Maybe acquire a "jallopie" like Wade Cudeback. The teacher gave a derisive laugh—when? On his schoolteacher's salary? Such ambition! Best to limit such plans to what he could accomplish on his new Raleigh bicycle. And of course the railway. Ah yes, the railway. Muted echoes of his raucous first encounter with the railway circled his skull in the silent afternoon, punctuated by the motto he had adopted, before leaving home, as his guiding homily. Together with the railway song all children knew by heart, even those who had never seen the powerful monster, it began once again to play a contrapuntal rhythm to the turns of the carriage wheels—*He has no future . . . who fails to affect his present . . . who fails to affect his present . . . who fails to affect his present . . . Mo ti gun'ke, mo ti so . . . mo ti gun'ke mo ti so . . . who fails to affect his present . . . faka fiki faka fi . . . who fails to affect his future . . . oke ti alajapa ko le gun . . . mo ti gun . . . mo ti so . . . faka fiki faka fi . . . who fails to affect his present*—and he found that he was afraid. Have I climbed that hill? Is my pace like the tortoise of the song? Have I climbed? Would I slip? *Faka fiki faka fii . . .*

It had not made much sense at the time, but this first-ever departure, bound for enrollment at the seminary in Ilesa, simply had to be done by railway. It was both curiosity and adventure. The motor vehicle was already commonplace; one saw the lorries at least every other day, and the occasional sedan when an important visitor came into town. But the railway was mere legend to many like him in Ìsarà; it had chosen most cruelly to bypass all of Ijebu area, snake through Ifo and Abeokuta to Ibadan and the north. So to Abeokuta he half-trekked with his companion, Damian, and joined a passenger lorry in Owode—all for the lure of a ride on rails between Abeokuta, Ibadan, and Ede. There would be no choice after that but to tramp the distance between Ede and Iwo, mostly on footpaths, with his earthly possessions—including parting gifts—carried in turn by him and his not-much-older companion, who was also his guide and protector. More bush paths led to Oyo, but the path would sometimes broaden, revealing tracks of an intrepid lorry—passenger, goods, or timber. Between Oyo and Iseyin, motorisation was routine. Thereafter, it would be desultory, with Iseyin to Shaki most likely a measured dialogue with their feet. The intervening distance to Ilesa was also on foot, although his father had been assured that there were donkeys there for hire, and possibly bicycles and hammock bearers. They would both ride the hired bicycle to Ilesa; then Damian would stay overnight and return it to its place of hire the following day, leaving Yode alone in school.

Damian, the Edo boy, had somehow lost his way into Ìsarà and stayed on, hoping to learn the trade of printing by annexing himself to Josiah. His reasoning hinged on the obvious: Josiah was a Christian and a church elder. The Christians used books. Bought books. They even owned bookshops. Books were the result of printing. Proven: Sooner or later Josiah would lead him to the path of his printing trade. In the meantime, he farmed with him and looked after his house. Damian had a dark history, so Yode eyed him from time to time, wondering whether or not to reveal that he had somehow unearthed that secret. He was a little apprehensive of Damian, who spoke such a weirdly toned version of his Ìsarà dialect. He had left Benin, fleeing a taskmaster of an uncle, lived off motor parks, and eked out a living as one of the army of porters to be found at railway stations. The fare that brought him to Ìsarà had been saved, despite days of hunger, for such a final act of desperation. He had sought no destination, merely entered the lorry that rumbled towards its take-off as his own stomach signalled its pangs of privation and the limits of its endurance. The lorry stopped at Ìsarà; Damian disembarked and lay across the road.

Between them, the pact was sealed. The only question was how soon they could dodge the straggle of well-wishers who had escorted them to the boundary, nearly half the population of Ìsarà. They headed into a ring road—no more than a footpath—which circled Ìsarà, then joined up with the track that would take them into Egba-land, to Owode, and then the railway station at Lafenwa. And Akin-yode, as yet ignorant of the existence of Ashtabula and Montcalm's battlegrounds, sank into the exotic world of a railway carriage. The noise, the chaos of every station enraptured him, the railway bridges, the water pumps at which the railway stopped to "drink," the piercing whistle, which was almost drowned by the rhythmic, measured grind of wheels accelerating and decelerating downhill and uphill, the ceremonial approaches and departures from stations. The one-armed blue-red signals by the tracks snapped into new positions seemingly without human agency—until Damian, amused, pointed out the little concrete hut mounted high above the landscape, and the sweaty arms that pulled at levers. Later, he saw similar levers on ground level, among the coils of rail, manned by peak-capped signalsmen in stiff khaki jackets and shorts.

Damian's accounts had fallen short of this railway world of iron and steel and fat wooden slippers; nothing could match the flag in the hand of the station guard, his censorious eye sweeping up and down the platform, flag upraised, smartly dropped, followed by a nod of acknowledgment from the grimy, sweat-soaked engine driver, who leaned so casually, so confidently, so fully "in control" of this monster, in which they could actually stretch their legs and walk, unlike the cooped-up journeys in motor lorries. Everything was excessive! Shrieking children amid farm produce; the *akowe** clans, complete with Madam and children and portmanteaus, all probably on transfer; the coat and tie, the occasional trilby hat or bowler, the arrogant condescending glances at the spluttering, squalling mass of the "other" humanity. Nothing of Damian's description ever prepared him for the wooden benches with comfortable space between them and a wide passage the length and breadth of the carriages, right down the middle, quite unlike any of the passenger lorries he had ever entered; nothing prepared him for the stamped reels of tickets!—paid for through the little grille in the window of Lafenwa station—or for the sure-footed train guard, who seemed to defy the rolling and pitching of the train, touching the back of the benches only from time to time when the train gave an unusual lurch. Nothing prepared him for the rumble of the iron girders as the rolling wheels took on their timbre and augmented it, wrapping it round his head and filling up the carriage with sounds just short of prolonged thunder; and Damian had said nothing at all of the tunnel into which the train suddenly disappeared—it was a mere culvert over which a motor road did pass but it filled Yode with instant terror until in the dim light he saw Damian's mouth again open in mocking laughter, so he half-shut his eyes. The train clung to its sooty shroud even after it had emerged, close wrapped in the after-spew of its dark, pungent smoke, which had collected as the train gained entry beneath the culvert. That avalanche of grit forced backwards as the archway of the culvert received its first blast passed harmlessly through the carriage for most of the passengers, the practised ones, who knew that they must shut their eyes at that point. But it stuck to their hair and clothing, and some hastily covered up the food they were eating and their drinks, put their hands over the children's eyes, or forced the babies' heads into their laps. The monster steadily belched out its own entrails and was in turn swallowed by them. When the grit stung Yode's eyeball, he knew he had heeded Damian's warning too

* White-collar workers.

late—mind you, Damian had only warned him about the moments when the train went down a steep incline and the carriages caught up with the smoke before it dispersed. Then also when those brisk harmattan winds chose to blow in the wrong direction. But nothing at all about tunnels, however short. People went blind with the grit, Damian and his father's travelling friends who lived up north had explained countless times—that was why there were many blind beggars from the north; the grit from the train damaged their retinas. They travelled in open freight trains with their cattle or simply sneaked a ride, and that was the result—blindness. Yode had wanted to ask if the cattle went blind too, but he was much too awed by the power of these seasoned travellers from the exotic foreign territory of the railway line—Enugu, Makurdi, Kano, Oshogbo—and anyway, who gave children the right to ask questions in the presence of elders when a child was not even part of the discussion? And Damian had never been farther north than Ibadan. The grit stung him as it slid beneath the eyelid and Yode panicked, rubbing it hard.

"Don't!"

Damian forced his hand away and prised open the eyelid with thumb and forefinger. It stung like mad and he tried to close it but Damian's Edo fingers were stronger.

"Roll your eyeball to the right." He did and tears flowed freely while the stubborn grit stung him like a thousand wasps. "Now to the left."

Damian murmured curses on the elusive piece of grit, took off his fingers, thinking that it had somehow fallen out. Yode blinked hard once, then twice, and back came the pain again and he yelped. So Damian glued his fingers to the eyelids yet again, ordering, "Keep them as wide open as you can," and blew a wad of hot air across the eyeball. "Got it," he screamed in triumph. "It has swum right into the centre of the eye." He yanked out the tail of Yode's shirt, expertly dabbed the eye, and—instant relief—there it was. He held it out to Yode, who was alarmed at the sheer size of the charcoal piece, moistened by his tears. The relief was enormous; he leaned back in his seat and inhaled deeply the pungent smell of the smoke, which he quite liked. A faint suspicion that this odour might prove unhealthy if inhaled for long periods did not stop him from enjoying the tang of raw indigo dye. His mind went back to the sounds and sensations of the passage through the tunnel and across the bridges. It seemed no different from the *igbale** into which real humans disappeared, to reemerge as *alagemo.* † Slyly opening his eye, he inspected Damian. No, he did not think that he had turned into *alagemo* himself. The thought of *agemo* ‡ had merely aroused his urge to ask THE QUESTION. Even to phrase it in his mind seemed far too huge an undertaking—yet until it was asked, it hung between them like an ominous bat suspended from the rafters. Going to St. Simeon's seminary, leaving home for the first time and for such a prolonged period, was a rite of passage; he would not return the same child as he went. Had his father not called him and told him: You are going into a man's world. Remember that. You must make your world there, your friends, your future companions. As for the white man, remember he is very powerful, but he is only a man; so be like a man towards him, but a respectful man, because he is your teacher, and he is the one who rules your father's land. And then the farmer became confused and drove him out of the living room.

But one became a man in stages, not all at once. And a question like this . . . suppose it had to do with some shameful family secret, a silted-up well which was wisely kept covered up in the family compound? Tangled with weeds, its still, brackish water left stagnant for generation after generation? This would be no abandoned quarry-turned-playground into which a child could cast stones or drop a casual bucket. Not even one indulged as he was by his outlandish companion, who looked on Yode as one destined for great things in life and therefore entitled to be treated with some deference. At the time of the event, Yode had stored it away as an awesome thing whose real meaning he would demand as soon as he was old enough. After that, the only question that remained was: When would he be old enough? If leaving home for the first time—not merely leaving briefly but separating from home with one's entire belongings in a wooden box, nuzzling one's bare feet—if that was not being old enough, well, when would he be old enough? Suppose at this new abode a schoolfriend also attempted to kill himself, what should he do?

* Secret robing room for masquerades; subterranean house of the ancestral mask.
† Of the spirit-mask family.
‡ Same as *alagemo.*

If the worst came to the worst, Damian would simply never speak to him again. It was best to wait until the journey was nearly over, thus shortening the period of his silent punishment.

Damian would leave him to his fate in the seminary and return to his parents. Perhaps he would report him for broaching the forbidden subject. Still, there was nothing his father could do until the first holidays. Again Yode considered waiting until the very last station before Ede, then posing the question. They had taken Damian away; he came back with his head shaven, looking drugged. There was certain to be a long story behind it, not something to be rushed, otherwise what was the point? So he divided up the risks. Either Damian would tell him the terrible secret, giving him time to elaborate on any details—or the rest of the journey would be passed in spoken rebuke, or in silence. He hoped, in the latter case, that Damian would choose silence. At least he would have tried his best to find out why a youth, only two years above his own fourteen years, had tried to kill himself.

The train kept up its ponderous progress, bearing him away to a new grouping, putting an end to neighbourhood and sibling fights, family pressures, the iron fists of teachers, and the uncertain faith of both parents struggling against the silent pull of their abandoned deities. Yode already felt that he was acquiring a new status. He assessed Damian opposite him more critically and felt that it was only a matter of time before he became just as old. Perhaps THE QUESTION ought to wait until he was as old, with that faint swathe of darkness covering his upper lip. But then, Damian might return to his own hometown while he was away. He had, after all, come to Ìsarà by running away. There was this also, and it became Yode's primary concern—there was the question of one's Christian duty. Damian might try it again, finish off what he had begun, what everyone—his father, the Jagun, Pa Node—had been so appalled about. It would all be over. He would not even be home to be part of the disruption of routine, to eavesdrop on the stream of witnesses, accusers, counsellors, hushed gossip . . . All he would be left with was guilt, guilt for his failure to make Damian confide in him. He had to ask now, before this final separation from home, for a length of time that had already begun to weigh on him like a first intimation of eternity.

Mo ti gun'ke, mo ti so
Mo ti gun'ke mo ti so
Oke ti alajapa ko le gun
Mo ti gun, mo ti so
Faka fiki faka fii . . .

"What do you find so amusing?"

"This train. In fact, trains in general."

"And what is so amusing about trains? You would have preferred to go all the way by lorry?"

Yode did not bother to admit that it was the children's railway song which had suddenly drummed itself through his mind. More than likely his companion would only remark that a boy of his age should not even think of children's games, not when he was about to become a boarder in an *oyinbo** seminary. In any case, Yode wanted some time to think, to decide how he would phrase this all-consuming question.

A long blast from the train rescued him from the need to elaborate. This would mean they were approaching a level crossing, going round a sharp curve, approaching a station—or simply that the driver was feeling bored. From his window seat he leaned out cautiously— *NEVER LEAN OUT OF THE WINDOWS! A tree branch might sweep you out through the window or a telegraph pole brain you—* but he did not need to lean too far out as his bench was on the inside of the train's curved spine, a monstrous millipede it seemed at such moments. Yode began to count the coaches, a methodical instinct taking over, as if anticipating and preparing himself for the lessons ahead, but only expressing traits that had already been remarked at St. James's primary school, just on the outskirts of the market near the Odemo's palace. He squinted to reduce his eyeball surface, more respectful now of coal dust and smoke. Sinuous coaches wrapped themselves around the vegetation as if to deny their mechanical world. Yode had long decided that if there was a horned species of the snake, like the horned beetle, for instance, the railway train was surely modelled on it.

Olodo station, and the noise was overwhelming; it looked like

* White man.

market day. Hawkers swarmed over the train even as it pulled properly to a stop. The human traffic struggled in both directions—women laden with trays of trinkets, bundles of cloth strangled by ropes at midriff, but tidily, balanced freely on a young girl's head, textures and colours madly at variance with the staid wooden interior of the coaches. Hen coops and dangling guinea fowl, the squawks and spirals of feathers, occasional fights with beak and claws, quickly stifled, result of their own confusion and uncertain fate. The heady smell of palm wine, dirt-speckled froth in the broiling sun, vegetables by the basketful; a sudden bundle, tied at the stalks, would be thrust through the windows, forced into a complaisant hand, which weighed it thoughtfully, returned it as another, deemed fuller, fresher, or simply different, was thrust in the face of the hesitant buyer; the reek of raw eggs, some already smashed, yolk congealed or seeping through the base of the baskets; the boiled eggs, a choice offered between farm hens' and wild guinea fowls', the difference apparent in the speckles; fried *sawa-sawa* and the inevitable bowl of fried peppers; the halfpenny loaves of Shackleford, or "sugar bread," which would be sliced in half, the whitebait tucked in the slit, the peppery paste sealing off the midday snack. Headties and screaming faces, the racing feet of eager sellers, leaping from window to window, stair to stair, strapped-on babies bobbing up and down with loudly exhaled breaths, threatening to fall off, their hands dangling helplessly and lips flapping from the mother-bounces, yet miraculously secured. A huge basin was raised, covered with layers of sacking, the sacking was pulled aside, and a full blast of steam rivalling the railway engine's hit Yode in the face; beneath, re-heated lumps of yam or boiled corn on the cob. Farther away on the platform you could see the blackened half-barrels or basins on improvised hearths from which the mobile stock had been replenished, then covered in sacking to keep warm for the traveller. The curses and banter; anger one moment vanishes magically, re-emerges in laughter and teasing offers: I'll follow you home if you like, or you can take my daughter. You're sure you are not too young for her? The next basin of boiled yam floated past their window, sweeping along the route of the fruits, vegetables and peppers, *odunkun,* coco yam, *esuru,* and innumerable other species of the yam tuber, and Damian had had enough. If Yode chose to stare open-mouthed for flies to enter, he had better ideas for his jaws.

"Wouldn't you like some boiled yam?"

"Hm? Oh, yams. Yes, yes, in fact I think I am feeling quite hungry."

"I should think so. Just think when last we ate. And that was quite some walking distance, from the motor park to Lafenwa."

"*Abiamo . . .*"*

Swift motions as the woman stopped in mid-stride, set the bowl down, her baby tossed forward as if to fly over her head but stoutly secured by the shawl around her waist. She asked how many pieces, the sharp practised blade already slicing through a whole tuber, while Yode wondered if Damian meant him to pay also for his share, when his father had provided them both with money for the journey.

"Don't forget the salt, Iyawo." Damian, very sternly, man of the world in his own element, ignoring the woman's protests, her insistence that she had already sprinkled salt on the creamy interior of the yam. But Damian shook his head, unbending. "Salt, put extra salt on the leaf. Then we can sprinkle it on to our tastes." And to Yode, "Never let these women cheat you. You had better learn how to deal with them if you are going to do more of these travels." He shut up Yode, who protested that he was no novice at the market, by reminding him that this was not a market nor was it Ìsarà. This was THE WORLD. The railway denizens are different from the rest of humanity. "Mark my words and save yourself later grief." When the woman reached out her hand for payment, Damian further showed who was in charge. He pointed down the platform to where his hungry eyes had spied the seller of roast pork—something to go with the yam was needed. "Iyawo, if you don't mind, that pork-seller over there." The woman knew she had no choice; she cast an anxious look at faces poked through other windows, prospective customers, let out her best hawker's high-pitched yell: "*Iya! Gb'elede wa.*"† Yode succumbed immediately and took out the coins to pay her off, seeing her eagerness to be gone, her body rocking on the balls of her feet while a hand cupped itself around the bottom of the restless baby on her back. She half-turned in a practised manoeuvre, raising her left arm and jerking her buttocks, and the child half-slewed leftward, its head bobbing up beneath the raised armpit. She pasted a small sliver of yam between its lips and looked very pleased to have the money

---

* Nursing mother.
† Woman, bring the roasted pork.

waiting for her when she next turned round. And so it was the turn of the roast pork and the game of haggling began, moving from one tempting piece to the other.

"I'll be back in a moment," Damian said. "I'll leave the choice to you; I want to stretch my legs a little on the platform before I attack the yam."

Wrong, of course. Totally wrong. The lesson, repeated for at least a week by the ragtag preparatory committee, was: *NEVER GET OFF A TRAIN AT THE STATION!* He stared at Damian, who, affecting the utmost casualness, strolled down the carriage corridor, disappeared round the door, and re-emerged moments later among the teeming traders on the platform. Yode stared, was hesitating to cry out a caution, when the pork-seller seized back the portion still undergoing absent-minded weighing in his hand and made to go. "No, no, wait." He dug into his pocket and brought out the asking price, without haggling. So much for Damian's lesson, and he the cause of this carelessness.

Pushing his way through with his long arms, on short bandy legs, Damian was already at the entrance to the station building, but he did not remain within it, since Yode saw him shortly reappear behind the building, duck beneath an open window, thinking he was unobserved, then vanish altogether between what looked like a row of kiosks and prefabricated dwellings.

The terrified scream startled his neighbours in the carriage: "Demiyen!"

But Damian was already beyond hearing, his face, lightly cicatrixed on the forecheeks close to his nostrils, was wreathed in the contented smile of homecoming, home being anywhere that rendered due recognition and adult service in exchange for his penny. The apprentice farmer puffed out his chest, ready to transform himself among strangers into an experienced printer BY ROYAL APPOINTMENT to—well, why not?—the Odemo of Ìsarà. He soon found what he was seeking; his nose had led him unerringly. As he took his seat he studied his companions and prepared to improvise a superior status.

Within Akinyode's breast, a sudden descent of calm, and resignation. He was alone, cast on the wide, wild world, facing a new life by himself. As he slowly bit into his food he felt suitably old, filled with the certainty that he had seen Damian for the last time, that he had taken his leave as whimsically as he had appeared in Ìsarà, found lying in the red dust of Ìsarà road, just outside the makeshift motor park, just lying there, resigned to any fate that might overtake him. The night guards had come upon the stranger—the lorry arrived at dusk—and when they challenged him he merely stared at them, not even deigning to respond to their presence. A night marauder, no doubt, waiting for full darkness to link up with his gang, perhaps the advance scout who would sneak into a compound in full darkness, then open the doors to his waiting comrades skulking among crooked passages of the township. So they tied his hands together and blew their whistles. The other guards came and they discussed him. When dawn came they took him to Jagun, and he sent for his friend Josiah. The stranger's emaciated frame and hollowed cheeks, not to mention the manner of his appearance in the town, swiftly adjusted the drama-laden babbling of the night guards; and when a bowl of *eko* and a wrap of *moin-moin* were set before him, his ravenous assault on the meal confirmed the surmises of the two men. The guards were thanked for their vigilance, and Josiah assigned him to the Oba's household. As he picked up a few more words in the language of his hosts, Damian—which was the name he had bestowed upon himself when he first ran away from Benin—confided that his ambition was to learn a trade, and that printing was his choice. And could he go and work for that benign papa who had first suggested that he be fed after his apprehension and who, he learned, was a Christian? He confessed to being disturbed by the pagan carvings that surrounded the Oba's courtyard. They frightened him, he said, they gave him nightmares. The Oba's attendant to whom he spoke promised to pass on his wishes. Later, Damian heard raucous laughter from a corner of the courtyard where the attendant had gathered his cronies and was regaling them with the tale of this *kobokobo** beggar who had nightmares in the Oba's palace. They made no attempt to hide the fact that he was the butt of their ridicule, tried to rival one another for the funniest imitation of his accent. They did not stop even when they saw him watching; rather, they took their show towards him, tugged at his clothing, danced and staggered round, and collapsed on their backs with laughter.

Late afternoon of the same day, a hushed gathering in the audi-

* Alien; speaker of an incomprehensible language.

ence room of the Odemo, Jagun in attendance, and Josiah. There was a woman also, seated on the patterned oval matting, her legs drawn up sideways. A little girl stood by the door, somewhat frightened by the array of elders, and then the culprit was led in by two palace stalwarts. He cast a glance round the room, which he was entering for the first time, then dropped his gaze to a spot before his feet as he recognised the woman seated on the ground. A tap behind his right shoulder reminded him of the custom of his adopted place; he threw himself on the ground in prostration and remained there. Pa Josiah spoke.

"Do you know that woman, Demiyen?"

What did they want him to say? How did this woman find out that he lived here? What brought her along to disrupt his plans?

"Demiyen, we are asking you—look at that woman. Have you seen her before?"

Jagun was impatient. "Someone get me the *koboko*. We shall see if that does not open his mouth."

An attendant ran off while Josiah made one more attempt. "Did you leave the palace today? Did you go out to make a purchase from this woman?"

And Damian burst into huge, racking sobs. Nothing could be said or done, no amount of shaking could staunch it—threats, pleas, the raised *koboko* in the hand of Jagun, not even the intimidating thwack as he brought it down expertly on the floor, just missing Damian's prostrate back by a mere hairsbreadth. Frustrated, the Odemo gestured and his attendants half-dragged, half-carried the jellied form away, his sobs still echoing in their ears. Josiah turned to the woman: "Tell Kabiyesi what happened exactly."

The woman made obeisance to the Oba anew. "Kabiyesi, *k'i e pe*. It was surely the watchfulness of our ancestors that prevented what would have happened today, within the hallowed walls of our own father in this town. Usually I am alone in the stall, but today I took Ajike with me. That was how I was able to send someone to follow him and find out where he lives. Caustic soda! First Ajike offered him the soap when he said he wanted soda. She held out the tin of soap to him but he said, no, it was the caustic soda he wanted, the powder, not the ready-made soap. I was inside the stall and I overheard him. So I came out. I said to myself, Who is this *kobokobo* coming here to ask for caustic soda? I didn't know of any soap-maker in Ìsarà who was a *kobokobo*. I asked him where he came from but he wouldn't tell me. That was when I became suspicious. I had heard about one stranger who had been picked up by the nightguards, but I thought they had long sent him away to prison. So I asked him, What do you want with caustic soda? He was staring at me, no, not even staring at me but at something else in front of him. I said, Is this a lunatic? As if my mind knew what he was about to do, he started singing."

She was interrupted by exclamations round the room. Eyes widened in a mixture of wonder and anticipation, and it was the Odemo himself who asked, "Singing? Did you say singing?"

"In that *kobokai* language of his which no one could understand. People were passing by, stopping, then moving away. He went on singing for some time, without even looking at me. Then, I don't know, maybe the song was finished or he was tired. Anyway, he turned as if he was seeing me for the first time and asked me, 'Where is that soda?' So I repeated what I said before—'What do you want the soda for?' That was when he said, 'What is the matter with this woman? Do you have a law here against a man doing away with his life?' Kabiyesi, can you imagine how I felt? I shouted 'What?' but he went on as if he had not even heard me. He said, 'You are here to serve customers, not so? So just give me the powder and take your money. Or do you think you're the only market woman in this world?' *E gbani e l'aja!* Kabiyesi, my blood was running cold; I didn't know what to do. So, I think when he saw that he would not get what he wanted from my stall—I mean, my fathers, God forbid! In this town? That was when he started to walk away."

The length and breadth of the chamber expelled a long sigh; knowing looks flew from one grizzled head to another. Jagun snapped his finger around his head to ward off the intended evil, while the attendants snapped their thumbs against each other, murmuring *"To, to, to . . ."* Josiah contented himself with a silent prayer of thanksgiving, which he divided evenly between the presiding spirits of *osugbo** and Christ the Son of God, ensuring in his now-practised way that he gave precedence to neither. He had perfected this even-handed style of communion—but only in crisis, when he was not

---

* Meeting-house of a council of elders.

truly at ease with the direction he must choose. Church services were simpler, so were Christian prayer meetings, but there were too many ambiguities in the matter of life and death, a grayness of attribution which, despite his faith, still lingered. Still, he managed to conceal it from all new converts who came to him for counsel, but not from his son.

"Praise be, Ajike was with me. Tell me, what could I have done if she had not been there? I let the man go off till he was nearly hidden by the corner of the market; then I whispered to Ajike, 'Follow that man quickly, don't let him see you, just follow him from a distance and find out where he lives. Don't come back unless you have seen him to his home.' Node's girl is a sharp one, I can tell you, and thank God she takes after her father. Or what do you think I felt when she came back and said to me—my knees simply collapsed when she told me—she said she had followed him into Kabiyesi's courtyard! I shouted, 'Are you sure?' and she said to me, 'I know the Aafin, that is where the Odemo lives, not so?' I tell you, that child is simply too old for her years."

Mo ti gun'ke mo ti so, mo ti gun'ke mo ti so . . .

"Feeling homesick already?"

The train picked that moment to roll, and a familiar figure was pitched forwards against him. So quickly attuned had he become to the motions of the train that, busy also with his thoughts, he had missed all the ritual of station-leaving, had been oblivious to whistle, scampering feet, the last-minute hawking cries of the tradeswomen, had missed even Damian's "rascal leap" onto the moving train. His astonishment at his return was overwhelmed by a strong feeling of resentment, tinged only absentmindedly with relief. He had become fully reconciled to his abandonment and was feeling no further anxiety about the immediate future. Worse still, Damian's loss of balance had been somewhat excessive, really spectacular, and when he opened his mouth to speak, barely an inch from Yode's face, he let loose an introductory belch whose smell revealed just where he had been since his disappearance.

"You were drinking," he accused.

Damian made valiant efforts to regain his balance, then sank into his seat. "Only *burukutu,*" he admitted. "Very cheap at this station. They brew it right behind the station building, fresh-fresh from guinea corn. And you know, the woman remembered me. She remembered me! She was so happy to welcome me, she did not even take payment. I tell you, railway people . . ."

"You did not invite me to come." Akinyode found that he was very resentful.

Damian's eyes opened wide. "Ask you to come? You! Do you know where you are going? Let me tell you, you think they have *pito* there? Ho, let me tell you, my brother is in one of those places, there is one in Ughelli, not much different from the one you'll be attending, judging from what I hear. Let me tell you, Josiah's son, you must forget things like *burukutu*. Or *pito*. In that place, you will drink only BEVERAGES. Yes, beverages. Ovaltine, cocoa, tea, and coffee. Beverages. You think they have even palm wine there? Your father warned me, he said he would thrash me if I let you have anything on the way except bread and tinned sardines. O-oh, because I let you eat some yam and roast pork—by the way, where is . . . ?" Yode thrust the parcel at him. "Good. Well, I was only being nice, because we are old friends. But he has told me all about the school rules, you know, he talks of nothing but this seminary when we are alone on the farm. For instance, I know by heart the list of all the things you must bring with you—"

"I know everything, thank you," Yode snapped.

"O-oh. So you do. And you know you will not be allowed to speak that Ijebu language in there. And you can only keep milk and sugar in your cupboard. And BEVERAGES. No *gari*. No *ebiripo*. No *robo*, *aadun* . . ." He crammed the yam in his mouth, tearing at the pork and speaking with his mouth full.

Irritated, Akinyode tried to change the subject. "I did not see you coming in."

A look of infinite disappointment suffused Damian's face. "You did not . . . do you mean . . . ?"

"I did not." Akinyode was puzzled by this look akin to pain on his companion's face.

"But I waved at you," Damian accused. "I thought you were watching me."

"I saw you only just now."

"You mean you did not see me wait until the wheels had begun to roll and gather speed . . . ?"

"Well, you were inside by then, weren't you?"

"Of course not," Damian exploded. "I was on the platform. What is the point waving at you just to watch me climb onto a stationary train? I caught it in motion. That's the way we do it."

Akinyode was appalled. This was exactly what should not be done. On the list of rail-travel taboos was this very one, above even the leaning-out-of-windows prohibition. Those leg amputees on Beggars' Row in the cities, how do you think they got their legs cut off? Slipping under the train, of course, as they tried to trainhop after the train had moved. Showing off. Expensive *omo ita.** Rascality is one thing, but at the cost of a leg? And sometimes even loss of life?

"I suppose," said Akinyode slowly, "it would not have mattered to you anyway."

A flicker of suspicion passed over Damian's eyes; his tipsiness appeared to be suspended, if only for some moments. "What would not matter?"

Akinyode pressed on. "Whether you killed yourself or not."

Damian's eyes went vacant and Akinyode found he had nearly bitten his tongue. But it was now too late to draw back. "You tried to kill yourself. With caustic soda. I heard Baba and Chief Jagun discussing it. Didn't Jagun shave your head and make incisions on it?"

Involuntarily, Damian's hand shot up towards his head. But he stopped before it touched. He let the arm fall slowly, then dropped his head against the carriage wall. He let his eyelids shut slowly, uttering no sound. Until they reached Ibadan his young companion could not swear whether he was asleep or was merely pretending.

Akinyode's heels struck the box of possessions beneath the bench. It was stuffed also with gifts, some of them coming in at the last minute: a shirt, a pocket knife, a book—it was a text of Christian homilies—a disguised wallet which contained the most valued items—the threepenny and sixpenny pieces, the few shillings, all with the head of King Edward, the king of England, that nation whose history, albeit bowdlerised, they all knew by heart. The box contained a bed sheet, two embroidered pillowcases, a coverlet of local weave—Ilesa was quite chilly in the harmattan, the seminarian circular had warned them. His notebook of guiding precepts was

* Rascality.

already beside him on the bench. And of course Damian was right, there was the packet of sugar, tins of evaporated milk, sweetened cocoa, which he preferred to Ovaltine in any case, and—a decision which his father had left to him—a tiny jar containing "protection," made by the hand of Jagun himself. He was free to throw that in the bush before he entered the hallowed precincts of St. Simeon's Seminary, or to keep it with him. The choice was his. For the teacher-trainee, it was not too much of a dilemma; he had already resolved to hand it to Damian, hopeful that it would shield him from any more suicidal impulses.

It seemed to have worked. At least, Damian never again attempted suicide. And it was only appropriate that Damian should be the one to sit behind the steering wheel and launch Node's gleaming motor on its maiden voyage. First, he was no longer Damian. His transformation was so complete that no one even remembered the name he had brought into Ìsarà, one which he had shed as easily as he had first acquired it. Not that anyone ever called him Damian. Demiyen it was from the first rendition. De-mi-yen, his new townspeople assumed, was how he himself would have pronounced his name if only he spoke Ijebu. But Demiyen was no longer even that. Challenged to a fight by a truculent layabout on the playing fields of St. James's primary school one Saturday, he had replied to his aggressor's taunts with his own war cries and self-boosting in his native Edo tongue. Then, infected by the many sounds around him, some urging on the fight, some mocking the *kobokobo,* others attempting to break it up, he had, without even being aware of it, suddenly shed his Edo rallying cries and broken into the Ìsarà dialect. It was one word only, and the contrast with his earlier barrage in Edo was so startling that the crowd was momentarily transfixed. The taunt came out perfectly, urged by the flow of adrenaline—*"Wemuja!"** It became his sole response to the prolonged verbal prances of his opponent—*"Wemuja!"* And the crowd swung over to his side and urged him on with shouts of *"Wemuja!"* After the combatants had been separated—the contest being more or less even—he was carried shoulder-high and accompanied home with a rhythmic chant of

* You know nothing of a real fight.

"*We-mu-jaa, We-mu-jaa!*" Pa Josiah came out of his cottage to see the cause of the commotion, saw his farmhand floating over a sea of heads and arms, dancing up the steep incline. When they saw him standing with arms on his hips, legs set wide apart, and thunder in his eyes, they hurriedly set down their hero and vanished, leaving Damian to face the wrath of his master for his desecration of a peaceful afternoon. One sideways swipe as he tried to sneak around Josiah into the backyard sent him reeling in the dust. But he was beyond pain, still borne on the wave of his unplanned acceptance by his age-group in Ìsarà. Two weeks later, even Pa Josiah had begun to call him Wemuja.

Wemuja had changed in other ways. He had filled out; no extra inches to his height, only to his arms and his chest and his leg muscles, which seemed content to make up in girth what they lacked in length. His arms were disproportionately long. But it was the bandyness of the legs which astonished Akinyode. He simply had not known that his former companion's legs were that bowed. Yet this new appearance fitted him for the role of driver of the timber lorry. The short limbs sprouted from the same tangle of growth that produced the giant boles which weighed down the lorry and threatened to up-end the novel contraption as it strained against invisible leashes holding it to the foot of the hill. The lorry had taken on its first-ever load the night before, hewn down from Node's concession between Ìsarà and Sagamu, then driven into Ìsarà in the morning for its formal baptism. The reception group waited at the top of the hill, looking down on the lorry's approach. Wemuja's head would have been missed but for the broad-brimmed scoutmaster or ex-army hat he sported, pinned up on one side. And even this was barely visible over the steering wheel. He drove with his arms wrapped around the circumference, hugging the wheel. Drummers had appeared miraculously from passages which opened into the road along the gradient. Akinyode smiled; it was futile to try to keep such things from them. They joined the vehicle, hopped and pranced uphill with it, easily keeping pace with its slow speed. Node had been lifted outdoors and a smile of contentment struggled to alter the shape of his nearly immobile lips.

The proudest man however was Wemuja. He had long given up his ambition to be a printer, switching his allegiance, after that rail journey with Akinyode, to driving a railway engine. The route to that profession, he reasoned, lay in understudying the lorry drivers who plied the Ìsarà route, and he spent his meagre earnings from Josiah to pay for lessons over the years. Then he overheard the schoolteacher and his father discussing Node's plans to go into the timber business and even to purchase a lorry. His mind was made up; the entire course of his existence was mapped definitively that very moment. He, and no one else, would drive that lorry. He intensified his lessons, and soon even Pa Josiah could no longer deny that there was a driver in the extended family. Did not his own son advocate the timber trade as a first step to the printing of books? To his new friends, Wemuja boasted that he was not just a lorry driver but was in the book-production business. And if the schoolteacher was also around, he winked at him and said, "Mr. Teacher and I, we are in the same profession."

As Wemuja expertly parked the lorry on the tiny plateau above Node's compound and leapt down from the driver's cabin, Akinyode looked at his beaming, contented face with a hint of envy. Had he reached his Ashtabula? He had probably risen much earlier than the teacher had that morning, full of anticipation for the initial step. He would check all those mysterious gauges in the engine and fill the radiator with water. His assistant, Alanko, would secure the wooden blocks that would serve as wedges between the load and the platform of the lorry. Wemuja, he was certain, would himself test the tyre pressures, the hawser. A breakfast of *eba* certainly, a terrifying mound in which he would make a deep scoop to create space for the vegetable stew from a tin container, meat, and perhaps a bit of stockfish. Cool water from a jar chilled overnight in the dew, far from the Reversing Falls of Ashtabula or its underground streams, and certainly more refreshing.

A voice cut through his reverie. It was Jagun, commenting, "So it was Commer you decided upon after all."

Akinyode nodded. "It is more expensive but our Lagos people say it is the best."

"Very strong they say."

"Ve-ry. Much stronger than Ford, which was the one we thought of to begin with."

Wemuja intervened with definitive authority. "Ford is all right for passenger lorry, Baba, or Bedford. But for timber, you need engine like Commer." He turned, shouted an order to his mate to bring down the gourd of palm wine which they had collected on their way. Alanko was a contrast to his boss, weedy, tufts of hair patchily strewn around his skull as if he had been a porter at the railway station carrying baskets of eggs and bags of kola nuts on his bare head. Wemuja strolled to the side of the lorry to relieve him of the gourd; he looked as if he only had to vault on the back of the heavy log, wrap his bandy legs around it, and he would ride the entire lorry without any use of the engine, a veritable cowboy on a timber horse galloping to Ashtabula!

A strong hand gripped his shoulder. It was again Jagun, and he drew him away from the others, towards where his father was standing. "It is good that you came," he said, as they walked. "I would have sent Josiah to you but now that you are here . . ." He paused until they arrived where the elder Soditan was waiting. He grinned at his crony. "I have begun the *oro awo** with our Tisa." His father, he noticed, did not change expression. "Well, *omo* Josiah, the long and short of the matter is, our king is ailing. We have consulted Ifa, and it seems we have not long to search for a new king."

Akinyode looked from one to the other. Surely this had nothing to do with him. For another thing, it was a mild break in the unwritten etiquette. There was one relief for which he was always grateful during those unseasonal visits—a lack of demands, of impositions. This matter, however, sounded as if it might prove the father of all impositions. So he waited, apprehensive.

"I know what you must be thinking," Jagun continued. "This is not an affair of children. You are thinking that it has nothing to do with you, but you are wrong, Tisa. Times are changing. The white man is here and he pokes his nose into everything. So it is a good thing that we also have those who understand his way of thinking and can pass on to him our thoughts on matters which concern us. Because, you see, we already know whom we want for the next Odemo."

Akinyode spoke very slowly, unable any longer to prolong the silence that hung upon his answer. "Well, you must remember, I am only a teacher. I don't know about these matters. Those in Lagos—"

* The secret talk.

His father snorted. "Those in Lagos, yes, we know about those in Lagos. Of course we must get in touch with those in Lagos, and it is you who must do it. The matter concerns you more than those in Lagos."

Now he was truly alarmed. "Concerns me?" For a moment his thoughts went wild, his lean face jerking between the two men. Surely they did not mean . . .

His father read his thoughts precisely. "No. Do you think Jagun would be talking to you if he meant *that?* But it touches you. It touches the House of Lígùn. So get yourself and your friends together. Because we know all those who think it is their father's private throne, and they will bring the seat of government in Lagos into this matter."

Akinyode badly wanted time to think. "We still have some time. The king may survive another ten, even twenty, years."

The two older men looked at each other. The father made a dismissive gesture but Jagun laid a hand on his arm and laughed. "You sent him to the mission seminary, so don't complain." He turned to Akinyode. "Tisa, Ifa has had its say on the matter. Do you think we would speak on such a matter without consulting deeply into the heart of knowledge?"

The teacher sensed vaguely that he had just been administered a rebuke. He shrugged. "I suppose the same Ifa has approved the successor you have in mind?"

Jagun grinned his approval. "You are a quick pupil, Tisa. We will talk more about it on the way to Iya Agba."

"Yes, let's go now," Josiah urged. "Your grandmother has something to show you." His demeanour had changed and Akinyode looked at him with more apprehension, refusing at first to move.

"What is it?"

"I said she has something to show you. You think you will find out what it is by standing there?"

The little notebook of precepts, prefaced in capitals by that very first motto which had accompanied him on his enrollment journey to Ilesa, also contained excerpts from church sermons, proverbs, analects, jottings, moral observations, snippets of vital information such as overseas college and university addresses, page references to articles in journals which had engaged his professional and other interests. There were even a few verses, copied from Cudeback's letters or directly from books. The notebook remained his constant companion. As usual when he opened it, he let his eyes linger on that first page, where, over eighteen years before, he had inscribed the lines from Archdeacon Howell's farewell sermon: "He has no future who fails to affect his present." It was his last attendance at St. James's Church before his departure for Ilesa, and it had seemed to him that the preacher addressed his sermon to no one else, just to him alone. It stamped a special mandate on his departure, coated it in an aura of special designation which remained with him all through college and even through his career. He often assessed the activities of his friends, their plans, through these special lenses placed before his eyes by the unsuspecting prelate. Even Damian, the would-be printer turned farmer turned would-be railway worker, settling finally into the driver's seat of a timber lorry—even Damian's progress had been viewed through this singular perspective. Everything Damian had ever done, from his first act of running away from Benin to this one, becoming Node's driver—had not every act been guided by his resolve to "affect his present"? His feat of self-transformation from Damian to Wemuja had merely capped this firm resolve to direct his life.

And this it was that produced in him the greatest disquiet. Compared with Wemuja, was he truly in full control of his present? His friend Sipe stood in a class by himself, a being resolved to affect not just his own present but that of everyone within affecting orbit. So, Akinyode, he demanded of himself, did you even choose to be a teacher? Or did you just settle into it because that was what was expected? And now the affair of his grandmother . . .

He soon found the reference he sought and laid the notebook beside the pile of dated journals. They made up his Ìsarà library—two improvised Peak milk cartons which housed the precious source material for planning and decisions that required his utmost seclusion. The disputations might take place in Abeokuta, but it was to Ìsarà he came to sort matters out in his own mind, away from the uneven sessions of bantering and earnest debates and business schemings among The Circle. The visit to his grandmother had upset him, moved him in quite unexpected ways, rousing him to an accelerated sense of urgency, yet inducing a contrary state of enervation.

His father and Jagun had looked on, impassive, while the slight figure acted out what she called her final rites. "This is the way I wish to be buried." The two older men looked at each other and evinced no further interest; they had seen it all too often; it was what they brought him here to see. She now lay on her back, having sat up on their arrival. "This mat, now, say it is a bolt of white brocade, you know, the kind I still keep at the bottom of my box, though that is now somewhat yellowish with age . . . you will roll me up in the cloth, like this" . . . and she pulled up the mat on either side, covering her emaciated frame up to the chest. "And then you lift me up and put me in the coffin. Don't bother to put any dress on me, I just want to be wrapped up as I've just shown you. And let me tell you something else—"

Jagun interrupting, "Iya Ile Lígùn—"

"I haven't finished."

"Iya, your grandson merely came to tell you of the new house he's building for you."

"Then he can occupy it. And the other thing I was going to say. Don't you dare perform any Christian worship over me. You will dig the grave just outside there, in the courtyard—"

Josiah threw up his hands. "You see, she won't listen."

Jagun tried again. "You cannot stay here, so no one is burying you here. Since your husband left us, your in-laws have been asking to take back their brother's house."

"In the courtyard, you heard me."

Akinyode knelt by her side. "Iya Agba, why don't you simply come back to Abeokuta with me."

"What for? So you can bury me in that foreign land?"

"Then stay with your son," Jagun pleaded. "How often do you want him to beg you to go and live with him?"

"I am not living with another man's wives."

Josiah flung his arms to heaven. "You hear her? Another man's wives! This is me, your son Josiah. Josiah! Another man's wives, she says. And all this because I became a Christian. Have you seen any of my wives living under my roof?"

Akinyode rose and dusted his knees. "She has become used to living alone."

Josiah snorted. "She's stubborn. Stubborn as the very day she gave birth to me. Did she not insist she would go to the market even though I was already halfway out of her womb?"

Laughing, Jagun asked, "How do you know? You were hardly present."

"Well, I heard my baba say it often enough."

"Perhaps when the new house is ready," Akinyode suggested, "and we take her to see it . . ."

"Of course, of course," Josiah mocked. "As long as we're prepared to carry her. You will ask her to do her 'final rites' again, then seize her when she is rolled up in the mat. That's the only way you will get her out of here."

Iya Ile Lígùn, who they thought had fallen into one of her frequent slumbers, spoke up. "Who is talking about a mat? I said, the white brocade. What sort of death do you think I will die that you want to use a mat on me? Did you ever see me in the courtyard of *agemo?*"

Jagun began to herd them out. "Let's go, let's go. This one will grow ears from even beyond the grave."

Akinyode stared hard at the smoke-rimed rafters, thinking of this new imposition on his resources. No one had discussed it with him. It was assumed; of course Tisa would build the house for his aged grandmother. If he did not, who else would? There it was. Those *iyekan* of his late grandfather were claiming back their family house. There was hardly any point even contesting this in the Customary courts. Both Jagun and his father knew where the rights lay and had decided on the only remedy: a new cottage—and, since it would be built by the "foreign" son, a cottage with corrugated iron sheets and a cement finish, not the familiar mud-plastered two-room affair, its floor blackened with *eleboto.** Yet even that "simple affair" cost money. As for the elders in this matter, it went beyond putting a roof over his grandmother's head. Was he not a grown man with his own family? At the moment, visits to Ìsarà meant that he stayed with his father, while his family took over his mother's house. Now he would have a house of his own, two or three rooms to begin with, expanding as resources came to hand. They had it all worked out. Akinyode

* Dung plaster.

knew that Jagun would call on him the following morning, take him out to "show you something." His cunning hand would describe a circle over an untended piece of land. "There it is, Tisa, it is yours to do as you wish. Your father saved it for you. God will provide the 'strength' to complete it for your children."

He tried hard to project himself through the next ten, no, even five, years. Would Aké have become a distant, even resented, interlude? His hand groped for the lever of the kerosene lamp and turned down the wick. Now flickering on his retina was Sipe's handwriting, the vistas he conjured up so lavishly with all his madcap projects, even as Sipe remained stubbornly bound to prosaic earth. How much longer do I console myself with merely fleshing out those alien worlds evoked by exotic names, the smells, the textures and sounds? He conceded that Sipe and he—indeed all ex-Ilés—burned with the desire to affect their present, in some form or other. There was no "other" in Sipe's own motions of change; those motions led in one direction only—"to be free of the drudgery of salaried work, to become a man of independent means." And his passionate harangues, shifting from rebuke to mockery to challenges to boastfulness: "You can all stay put and continue to wonder what kind of ferns will grow in the gardens of Laniero or what ornamental trees line the avenues near Alessandro of Milano. Just leave the rest to the Resolute Rooster. He will help you get at the contents of those warehouses!"

Was Sipe right?

At thirty-two, married, with two infant children . . . The housing was free but there were those basics—clothes, food, social demands, soon it would be time for books and school uniforms. Surely it was not too early to give due weight to these thoughts. He thought of Morola in Aké, probably fast asleep by now, or else adjusting the baby's wrapper for the twentieth time that evening. That one had come hard on the heels of the first, only fifteen months in between. Even his father had cautioned him against a repeat: Three years at least, that is how we brought you into the world. Do you want her milk to dry up on her? Go sour? And you call yourself a teacher—is that how the missionaries go about it? Chastened, he resolved to pay greater heed to those intervals in the future. And of course there was the problem of her health; his father had strong ideas about that and was already "taking steps." He would pursue it to the exclusion of all else, perhaps even follow him back to Abeokuta on his return journey. He would not entrust such sensitive matters to a mere messenger. That was the other thing—whatever he had done, and whatever there still was to do, it all meant money.

It was still a long way to the New Year but it was not too early to begin stock-taking. The New Year Resolution—a quasi-religious chore—could wait, although he already had a fair idea what that would be. The last resolution, now winding down with the year, had succeeded even by his stringent standards—there was no self-reproach on that score. He had saved well above the goal he set himself, and this was quite apart from his monthly contribution to the Syndicate. But that contribution was routine. If the Great Adventure was to be realised, however, yes, Sipe undoubtedly had the right approach. Again he uncovered in himself a sneaking admiration for the Tempter—the man had no doubts whatsoever. And he moved! Even as he presented a new idea to the ex-Ilés, he had already tried out variations of it in practical terms. The greatest irony was that often it was he, Akinyode, who opened a path to him, quite unwittingly. The teacher would be struck by a news item, an essay in a journal, a letter to the editor, and would quote it to the young entrepreneur in the normal course of a discussion, little thinking of the commercial aspects of the tract. That, however, was precisely what Sipe did see. Gradually, even he began to acquire the habit. Soon he was actually suggesting business ideas to Sipe and trying out a few of his own. The trouble with Sipe was that he could not remain satisfied with half measures, with part-time interest or the casual investment "on the side." He wanted his entire circle to abandon their jobs, transfer to Lagos, which was the land of the "bold and the daring," and take the plunge into—for him—the certainty of success.

No, not yet, though God knows, that Mephistopheles had already taken over a portion of his mind. He reviewed his own attempted ventures of the year, always keeping in the forefront the difference between his friend and himself: His ventures were not an end in themselves but a means to a medley of ends, all under constant review. Certainly a higher degree, studied for and awarded overseas. Return at least a bachelor of arts. Or law. A bachelor of law, just like his father-in-law. Divinity was also a possible beginning—B.D. And afterwards? Perhaps become an official of the teachers' union. Or principal of a secondary school . . . contribute a book on methods of education, something special, unique, some new scheme for the development of childhood intelligence, a study from which the white education inspectors who visited their schools might even benefit, might acknowledge as something novel in the history of educational systems. Why, he could even return to teach in his alma mater, the training seminary in obscure Ilesa, so often confused with the bigger Ilesha between Ife and Oshogbo. Well, was that not part of the mission of the ex-Ilés, "to put our own Ilesa on the map, to rescue from obscurity this cradle of our intellect and maternal bosom of our professional family." At least, so exhorted the Right Reverend Beeston.

I enjoy teaching, he said softly into the night, repeating it with emphasis. True, a few over-pious articles in *The Nigerian Teacher* tended to put one off the profession for ever; Soditan was content to admit that he simply found teaching cogenial. And he enjoyed being one of the family, a new family begun at the teacher training seminary, one which increased all the time through numerous encounters with odd and scintillating minds. Wade Cudeback, that far-flung member of the family, trundling through Ashtabula in his jalopy—were such encounters not part of the rewards of his profession? And the others on home ground: stodgy textbook fanatics, stereotype characters, brilliant eccentrics, and earthy individualists. That Eyo Ita, for instance, his first-ever meeting with an intellectual from the Delta Region, a supremely self-confident man, patronising in his approach to white officialdom. He could not think of a more capable choice for the magazine of the Nigeria Union of Teachers. The erudite Miss A. Taylor—why he did not know, but he never thought of her name without the initial. Easily the sensation of the union's last conference, having barely returned from England, where she had bagged a master's each in the arts and the sciences. And she threw her energies straight into the union, the light of battle in her eyes— education, education for the entire protectorate! Was this perhaps what he looked forward to, the inspiration of the vision of his own return to the country after the Great Adventure, after the "return of the Argonaut with the Golden Fleece"? If one could pick out a turning point in one's life at such a young age, that, Akinyode felt, would be it—the annual conference which brought such giants together. And the drama! A bullish Daodu taking on the headmaster from Awka, who had come wrapped up in a single-minded mission from his people. "Two orthographies for the Igbo language? Do tell us, we here in the union, tell us what sets the Igbo language apart from Hausa, Yoruba, Itsekiri, Idoma, etc., etc. This union calls for the standardisation of Igbo orthography in conformity with what exists for the languages I have just listed. Right, speak to us in both Igbo orthographies and let us hear the difference!" Then the confused though stubborn response of the poor headmaster as he strove to fulfill the mandate imposed on him by his electors. For a while, the Reverend I. O. was content to let him splutter; then he sprang up to deliver the *coup de grâce*. "Your position, let me suggest to you, is not really that of holding out for two orthographies, but of arguing for the retention of the one which you prefer. In short, everything you have said, sir, points to a partisanship, not to a conviction on the need for two orthographies. May I suggest therefore that we are on the same side? You accept the position of the union, am I right? That obstacle overcome, we can proceed to speak with one voice, letting all Babel loose when the choice comes to which orthography should be adopted." And the assembly proceeded to their resolution, calling on the government director of education to move at once on the issue and regularise the situation.

Daodu also swinging the union fully behind him on the matter of local composers. Daodu loved to talk, of course, but even more re-markable, he knew how to listen! And he could never resist the urge to relive the victories. "Ha"—rubbing his hands together as he stopped afterwards for tea in Soditan's home—"that seals it." He visibly preened himself. " 'On the Banks of Allan Waters' must now compete with '*E se rere o.*' That's all we ask, let all melodies contend! Pity you didn't meet the union's patron, Adeniyi-Jones, afterwards, but I have warned him I shall be bringing you. It is important that he meets the rising stars of our educational firmament. And I'll be interested to know what you think of him. We must keep up our assessment of these older mentors or they will fall asleep. Yes, tell me, at least you heard his address, what did you think of it?"

All in all, yes, he found himself in agreement with the white-haired patron—the school as the "factory of humanity," in which "teachers are the artisans." The young teacher wished he had stopped there, not gone on to propose to that gathering of "artisans" that the competent teacher "be like a candle which lights others, while consuming itself." Now that was what he, Head Teacher Akinyode Soditan, Jebusite of the clan of Ile Lígùn, Ìsarà, Remo, had no intention of being. Nor did he observe anything in the expressions of his listening colleagues which suggested that they also intended to "consume themselves." Certainly nothing in the demeanour of the dapper "Triple E," Mr. E. E. Effiong—an Efik to boot, which conferred on him the right to advertise himself as "Quadruple E" if he thus chose—nothing in that gnomish face suggested any desire towards such self-immolation in the name of his profession. His face was weathered stone throughout the patron's flight into hyperbole. Effiong was the geography teacher in Abeokuta Grammar School and was rumoured to be on his way to becoming the first African member of the Royal Geographical Society. Nor did the Asaba representative, Mr. Onyah, seem any more enamoured of the Jonesian doctrine—but then, he was a special case, and encounters with him were reputed to be guarded. The Colonial Office had its eyes on him, it was rumoured, because of his radical, even subversive, ideas. He had declared that the Nigerian teacher's first duty was to replace the "educated mind"—which he declared was the same thing as a "colonial mind"—with a "cultivated mind." For fifteen minutes the intense personality had lectured the assembly on this all-important difference, leaving his colleagues more baffled than ever, and mostly at a loss to see why the Colonial Office was afraid of him. Daodu was among the exceptions; he invited him to join his staff any time he chose.

It was nearly a year since that conference, but the euphoria had yet to wear off. Was he not the same obscure head teacher who had launched the battle against the age-test for admission into primary schools? Daodu and Miss A. Taylor had added their determined voices, and together they had carried the day. The union had been duly impressed. In a country where birth certificates were a rarity, young Soditan had argued, how do you assess the age of an aspiring pupil? The head teacher's "success" was blown up out of all proportion in Ìsarà. It provoked a rash of messages that he come home immediately and be welcomed as a worthy envoy of Ìsarà. The elderly ones, his father's closest friends, also wanted him back, but only to undergo various rites for protection. Enemies, enemies . . . your son is rubbing shoulders with the high and mighty, so bring him home, Josiah, bring him home and have him prepared for that wicked world. Do not leave him naked among strangers!

And those who were not strangers? Those who were anything but strangers? Each day brought a new relation, the dependent of a casual acquaintance or colleague, each with his own need, her own dependency. Go to Josiah's son, he's there. He will know what to do, and if he cannot do it, he knows who to summon to your aid. You can stay with him for a while until you find a place of your own. This was a phenomenon he could not fully fathom. Unlike Sipe, he pursued a quiet life. A taste in well-cut clothes, yes, that was common to all the young men in and outside his circle; beyond that, no outward expression of opulence. He had purchased a brand-new Raleigh bicycle, on which he sometimes partly rode the forty miles to Ìsarà. This again was nothing. He threw no parties, celebrated anniversaries only with his closest friends. So where had it all begun? How did the invasion begin, where would it end? He could understand if he was like Sipe, who possessed the talent of making the mere prospect of a shilling shimmer in the eyes of others like a hundred pounds already in his palm. Yet whenever he visited Sipe, he found no hangers-on, no distant relations arrived in the middle of the night with baggage and dependents. Was there some secret amulet which Sipe buried in his front porch to deflect all intending guests? He wished he could find the secret. He knew he had better find the secret before the old year ended, that dangerous period when people made plans and involved others like him, who were always the last to know!

The Great Adventure—yes, that was also a solution. Away in one of those overseas colleges, he dared any of his tormentors to turn up on his doorstep. But that required the means, the wherewithal. It seemed one only journeyed back to the beginning—to Sipe Efuape and his enterprising genius, bursting to fulfill itself and enrich himself and his selected friends.

Impulsively he turned up the wick again, sat up, and began to rummage through his library, turning the well-worn pages, thumbed and flagged and underlined in red and black. The night was clearly one that would not quickly yield to sleep, so he set the kerosene lamp on the window ledge. Rumours of war. One in every five of those journals, dog-eared, sometimes even termite-nibbled, hinted at the inevitability of war—it was the other intrusive element, very unsettling. How could one even plan beneath the threat of a global war? Would they become a prize to be fought over? In whose hands would the protectorate end? For now he merely sought out a context for his business options, flicking the pages till he found what he was looking for—that "statistical talisman," thus mocked Sipe, "which you have hung around your neck for an entire decade to ward off every straightforward business decision!"

It contained the phrase that appealed so much to his instincts for security in certitudes, not Sipe's breezy lunges towards all speculations that merely hinted at profit. There it was, the key expression to every speculation. It stood out starkly, bold and challenging—"mathematical exactitude." Now that was the key. Only this made sense. If one could plan with mathematical exactitude, then all business enterprises became rational endeavours, no different from a salaried job, which yielded a return precisely on a specified day of every month. He had first encountered it in an old copy of *The Elders Review,* under an expression which neither he nor anyone else in The Circle even knew existed: "Reflections on the World Depression." Really! Was Ìsarà depressed at that time? Not that he or any native of Ìsarà knew of. Was the Northern or Southern Protectorate part of this Depression? But the real bone of wild contention had to do with the fascinating claim of mathematical exactitudes in farming activities. For the teacher, only some form of security in such expectations could protect one against failure, or indeed against Sipe's propensities for speculative ventures. Surely this was one way which was truly guaranteed to "affect the present"? *We are about to complete an entire year of general worldwide depression. The "dark day" was that of October 24, 1929, which made the world cycle of trade stagnation complete, for it was on that day, after vain attempts had been made to put off the impending gray, that American industry found itself face-to-face with a crisis. . . .* How many times did he have to wave this warning in Sipe's face—don't keep tying our prospects to these world industrial seesaws! See what happened to "the world" in 1929! Bombarded with signs and predictions of global war, he had resurrected that ancient "talisman" to contest Sipe's plans. But Sipe was unmoved. The way he planned their future, the downfall of those world giants would even guarantee a "killing" for their own business schemes. "One world's Depression is another world's buoyancy—did our world here even know of that Depression?" The logic failed to persuade the teacher, or indeed any member of their Syndicate. He skipped rapidly through. . . . Yes, there was also Mussolini's reference to that Hauptmann fellow, whose books he had then ordered but never received: *We have only to recall the poem of Gerhart Hauptmann, the great German dramatist, who pictures the poor hand-weaver trying to compete with the crushing loom.* Well, if he did travel overseas, he would certainly track down Mr. Hauptmann, the unknown writer who had provoked his revisit to Iseyin. Wade Cudeback too could claim some of the credit, but it was that Hauptmann reference that took his thoughts straight back to Iseyin. As for the villain Mussolini, he must have a humane side to him after all if he could be moved by a poet's depiction of the "poor weaver." Were they any poorer than the weavers at Iseyin, he wondered anew? He experienced an overwhelming urge to find the poem, again relishing his excursion to Iseyin, so different from those school journeys through the town when he had not yet learned to *look.* Were there other crucial aspects of local industry which St. Simeon's had trained them to ignore? The passage he sought was on the next page, heavily underlined in red and black: *This year we celebrate the twenty-fifth anniversary of the foundation of the International Institute of Agriculture by His Majesty King Victor Emmanuel III of Italy on the initiative of the late David Lubin, economist and merchant, of San Francisco. This institute collects daily, even hourly, from all parts of the world, by telegraph and radio, governmental information from official sources on the crop conditions of the various countries. After their tabulations, the experts can state with mathematical exactitude what the world supply of wheat will be in any current year.*

Of all the debates ever embarked upon by the ex-Ilés, this had proved one of the most intense, certainly the most prolonged. The implications were taken personally; after all, there was hardly one of them who did not have an ongoing farming occupation within the family. If wheat, why not maize? Groundnuts? Cocoa? Even Osibo, whose fastidiousness made him look down on farm work, was drawn into partisan positions. This was too vast, too hyperbolic a claim.

Drug production, yes. Iron and steel ingots, maybe—all it required was to assess the potential of new mines, anticipate the exhaustion rate of ongoing ones. But farming? Farming was a hazard at best, a slave of the vagaries of rain and sunshine, locusts, kwela bird, foot-and-mouth disease, the black-pod blight, and fungoid parasites. Yet here was this European supranationalist claiming that all the variables could be anticipated! Even Onafowokan, who taught algebra and geometry at Igbore, felt that this was not merely an impossible claim; it was sacrilegious. No wonder there befell America the plague of the Great Depression, from which—note—the African peoples were not only spared, but of which they remained blissfully unaware! If that was not a divine punishment, then the Seven Plagues of Egypt were not divinely inflicted. Both Mussolini and that man Lubin were saying, in effect, that there was no God. Harvest was a season, a God-ordained season, not a mathematical piece of exactitude!

To Akinyode, however, there were crucial down-to-earth considerations tied up with Lubin's institute. He still hesitated over a commitment to a small cocoa farm which his father had then been negotiating on his behalf. So he waved the letter from his go-between, Oderinde, at the others and demanded a hearing. "Argue all you want," he urged. "What I would like us to do is find some means of profiting from Lubin's institute. Why don't we simply agree that Benito Mussolini should have said mathematical *approximation* instead of exactitude? Right? Approximation. Of course even the mere gathering of accurate statistics from all over the world is formidable enough. And our society definitely believes in God—or gods. That means we also believe in what we call an act of God—which is the same as reverses of human expectations. Right? After all, Job is there as a warning; so are those fat and lean years following each other and playing havoc with Mr. Pharaoh's granaries! So none of us will ever claim that farming is an exact science—I mean, who can actually predict the harvest in any given year?"

The Circle mulled this over; it seemed a reasonable compromise. And they prided themselves in always giving even the devil his due. So one after the other, with a last-ditch resistance here and there, they took off their hats to the late David Lubin and conceded their envy of the International Institute of Agriculture. Ogunba accepted the task of writing a letter on their behalf to "Akede Eko." It would demand that the colonial government set up a branch of that institute in Lagos, which would cater to the protectorate farmers in an approximate way, not infringing on the whims of the gods with any provocative assumptions. But even an approximating centre was needed at home. What was the sense of going to Italy or San Francisco in order to find out—even by telegraph—the quantity of maize, cocoa, cassava, or timber Ìsarà would produce the following year?

For Efuape, the entire exercise was a waste of time. Another timid, drudgery-enamoured venture! Did it make sense to run a postage-stamp-sized farm which had to be overseen in one's absence anyway? He pooh-poohed Oderinde's scouting mission, snatching the letter from Soditan's hands and reading it aloud. Did Soditan think that Lubin's institute had time for dwarf ventures like this "microscopic patch of land in the tropic jungle"? Mussolini was far too busy to be bothered with the like of Yode's piffling amateur cocoa plantation. And the passionate but fragmented syntax of Oderinde only added ammunition to his artillery as he shot it down in jeers! *For such a flourish and fructful cocoa farm to be going for a mere fifteen pounds is nothing short of a Christmas miracle from God.* In that letter Oderinde had also threatened that if the teacher did not come to see the farm, latest in three weeks time, *I will come in personal to see you because, as for this matter, if the mountain has not coming to Mohammed, Mohammed will then go to the mountain.* "Well, my dear pupil teacher, does this Mohammed plan to bring the cocoa farm along with him? It will fit into the pocket of his *agbada* without difficulty, I'm sure!" All mathematical exactitudes and approximations vanished in the uproarious laughter.

Unmoved, Akinyode continued to nurse that prospect. Cocoa was constantly in the news. And it held, he admitted, a deep childhood attraction—rows of cocoa trees with their luscious pods were embedded in his earliest concepts of earth as green and golden spaces. The gold was wealth, there was no denying that. The richest farmers he knew had cocoa farms. And there was the authority of his friend Opeilu, a produce inspector, who would sometimes bemoan his job, which was to weigh and grade the riches of others in the shape of cocoa seeds. The proposed farm was at Ifo, some thirty miles away to the south. Transport service to Lagos was reasonable, and from Aké, Ifo lay midway on the route to Lagos. That was definitely part of the attraction. But cocoa?

Again he resorted to his information bank, selecting one journal from the more recent pile, which lay segregated on a shelf above his bedpost, directly behind his head. Along the way to the sought-out page, war intervened yet again, rearing its head through warnings by the League of Nations over the matter of Eritrea. But why, why? the head teacher demanded. And that proposal—arbitration—what did this mean? Mussolini lived in Italy, Haile Selassie in Abyssinia. What was there to "arbitrate" when only one could be an intruder in the other's territory? Ogunba was right, the drums of war were already being sounded, only the dancers still hesitated. Akinyode proceeded to the essay signed "A Produce Broker." Its message was simple but negative: The best days were over for the cocoa industry in the Gold Coast. Soditan's dilemma was how to balance this with the strong demurrer entered by the editors of the journal themselves. Now that was the nub of the matter. In between the two, the adventurous cocoa grower must himself take a position, launch forth towards his fortune or withdraw his horns, as Sipe would say, "like a frightened snail whose antennae had felt the sheerest touch of adverse reality." *In printing this article, it is probably desirable that we should make it clear that we do not agree with the writer.* Probably? What else is the job of editors but to assert their own opinion on such crucial issues? Akinyode could never overcome the irritation he felt at this editorial coyness. The editors were British, which probably accounted for it—they had this tendency towards apologetic, even tentative, language in straightforward matters. A disagreement meant a second opinion, and journals are meant to record opinions. He succeeded in overlooking this quirk for now and continued: *The main reason for the suggestion appears to be one of doubt as to the ability of the Gold Coast farmers to increase their efficiency. This is a challenge to which, we hope and believe, the Gold Coast farmers will reply.* Challenge, yes, but—and there the teacher entered his . . . not so much disagreement as qualification—everything still depended on demand, as any market woman would impress on you. This was where David Lubin played such a dominant role in all his speculations, but only, alas, in a wishful way. If, if, if! If only he could find out, with or with as near "mathematical exactitude" as possible, how much cocoa was being produced in the world at any given time, then indeed he could take a decision on Oderinde's find. But to enter the competitive world of cocoa just like that—well, maybe Sipe would. Certainly not him. That was one sure way of ending up an involuntary producer of fermented cocoa wine. And how many people outside Ijebu really drank that stuff?

Well, if not cocoa, what then? Cotton? Not unless he wanted to live in the far-off north. He tried to think of some of his townsmen who lived in the cotton belt—Kano, Sokoto, Katsina. Famade, perhaps, his tailoring friend? He was well placed to make enquiries for him. Or Oye, the ex-serviceman—he would jump to attention on receiving a request from his old mentor. The problem was finding out the situation of world supply and demand. And there was timber, but seriously now, like Node, not with any more romantic thoughts of books and backyard paper mills à la Ashtabula. Yes, timber was gradually proving itself. The colonial government burrowed deeper and deeper into the interior like soldier ants, opening up virgin areas. New brands of heavy-duty lorries appeared on the roads, laden with mahogany, afara, teak, iroko . . . He revelled for some moments in a picture of himself riding, Wemuja-style, on the back of a giant log, an endless log which began in his own concession in Ìsarà, was felled with a thunderous splash all the way across the creeks of Epe, on a waterfront where the flying sprays would reach Efuape's house and shatter his complacency—yes, Mr. Rooster, here I come, you didn't think I had it in me, did you?—then smashing against the other side of the Atlantic and bouncing down the Reversing Falls, where his friend Wade Cudeback's contemplation would be rudely broken by this sight beyond the marvels of his Magnetic Mountain. What would the man say as his pen pal coolly stepped off the back of that if-all-the-trees-were-one-tree monstrosity from the heart of Ìsarà's forests, as yet unpenetrated by man or machine? What would be his greeting? Mr.—no—Prince Soditan, I presume? Merchant prince, of course . . .

The teacher pulled himself up abruptly, alarmed at himself. Akinyode, what is going on in your head? Has Sipe finally taken over your mind? This is worse than daydreaming, this is madness! Where, for a start, do you obtain the capital? Even a second-hand motor lorry is beyond the savings of a lifetime for a pupil teacher with a wife and two infant children and an extended family that acknowledges no limit! What do you do for capital?

And what of the looming war? If there is war and your meagre capital has taken flight to some commercial centre of a beleaguered nation, that is it! Fii-oom, good-bye! Even if it is not cash, you use up your savings or take a loan to obtain the timber, float it down the Niger or Ogun River and onto the high seas. You sit down to await cash on delivery. War begins. Sea routes blocked by Adolf Hitler. End of life savings. This again was a key difference. Sipe saw the war as OPPORTUNITY! *You read only the negative articles, Yode, only the negative ones. Don't you know a war brings about demands, creates its own needs? An entire industry springs up to support the madness of war. Rubber, for instance. Have you thought of rubber? This is the time to acquire a rubber plantation or two. Forget your David Lubin—war needs food, cash crops, iron and steel, even the gum arabica which you so Jebusitically boil in your backyard, you will be amazed how it will shoot up to astronomical heights both in demand and prices. Soap! Have you forgotten the article you showed me in* The Nigerian Teacher *on the soap-making industry? Ask yourself, why does a teachers' journal bother its head with soap-making? The British who edit that journal are looking for cheap supplies. They want to turn you all into cheap labour, earning a pittance, for their war needs. But if we go into it in a businesslike manner, manage a factory which guarantees a regular supply, not depend on the whims and leisure caprices of a bunch of exhausted teachers . . . I don't say it has to be soap; in fact I hate soap factories—have you ever visited one? The fumes are poison, they cling to your clothes. You feel you need a wash as soon as you are out of there. But we don't even have to manufacture soap; we become the middlemen and leave all those journals like* The Nigerian Teacher *to encourage the home amateurs, then buy from them and deal directly with the big companies—UAC and Lever Brothers and others. The sky is the limit, so why keep looking over your shoulders at the approaching war? Look at the silver lining for a change . . . In fact, it is no silver lining but a rich seam, waiting to be mined by the fearless . . .*

Admit it now, Soditan murmured to himself as his eyelids finally began to droop and he turned the lampwick down for the last time that night, it was not . . . no, he intended to be scrupulously fair to himself . . . it was only partly the travelogues of Cudeback and his chance encounter with the Mussolini-Hauptmann dialogue which spurred his bicycle excursion to Iseyin. Animating him also was the son of Efuape, Sipe, the merchant adventurer to whose commercial urgings he had sought a more modest counter. If Sipe could venture all the way to Italy to trade in worsted wool, albeit by mail, he would see what Iseyin, a home of weavers nearer to hand, could provide. No one had expected the soft-living, Lagos-besotted Sipe to accept the challenge thrown at him, but the Resolute Rooster surprised them all, accepting both the challenge and risks of the journey. Alas for the son of Efuape! A few days to setting-out, he developed a stubborn boil, as he put it, *right within that parting in the lump of flesh which God, the true inventor of bicycles, had shaped to fit athwart the saddle of the bicycle.*

Akinyode rode and strolled alone through the dusty streets of Saki, glimpsing, through gloomy mud interiors, busy looms festooned in coloured threads, flashing shuttles and pedals packing the steady-spun lines from spindles into the famous Saki fabric on upright frames. *As I pushed my bicycle slowly through the main street of weavers, having dismounted the better to savour the smell of dyes and bask in the industry of our ancient craft, I felt like a two-legged spider strolling through arcades of multicoloured webs.* How Wade Cudeback would respond on receiving this first-ever adventurous challenge to his own thrilling correspondence, Akinyode had yet to find out. But a copy of the letter to his cousin "Saaki" Akinsanya had already elicited a most envious response, uncharacteristically effusive. It was further reinforced by a threat that the schoolteacher's next exploration would not take place without him. Sipe, on his part, could not decide if it was the receipt of the letter from his would-be travelling companion which had *made my boil boil over with such disappointment that it erupted, to my great embarrassment, as I was at that moment reading your missive aloud to a group of visitors who had come to sympathise with my predicament.* Or was it, he proposed, the fact that among his audience was their friend Dr. Otolorin, for he had called *not simply to sympathise, but with a wicked scalpel ready to lance the troublesome boil, and had only paused to listen to the contents of your mettlesome epistle.* The boil, Sipe confessed, began to loosen its stubborn consistency on the appearance of Otolorin's scalpel and proceeded *on its own volition, to do that which I had so fervently prayed for these past four weeks. Such is the power of fear, my dear Yode, and the terror which even a human boil has of a doctor's knife.*

But it was nostalgia, unquestionably, which took him beyond the planned limits of the trip. From Iseyin he found that his bicycle wheels turned inexorably towards Ilesa. The motor road was not fully opened and the frequency of lorries meant that he could pay for space for both himself and his bicycle, which rode tightly strapped against the side of the lorry. For several long minutes after he had cycled from Ilesa's improvised motor park to the seminary, Akinyode stood before the gates of St. Simeon's, uncertain whether or not he really wanted to pass through. For the first time he became uncertain of his attachment. Was it all imagined? Was it yet again an emotion which he felt he *ought* to experience? The compound was silent, which he expected, as it was vacation time. He paused and listened, half-expecting to hear the drone of the Reverend Beeston's motorcycle as it raced dangerously round the gate pillars—a favourite act of his. What would he say to him? How would he judge the progress his pupil had made since he quit these grounds for the last time and took on Beeston's role for other trainee teachers in Aké? And the rest of the staff? Was Dr. Mackintosh, the music teacher, still on active service?

Akinyode pushed his bicycle through the gates, headed for the open field behind the principal's office, where Dr. Mackintosh had undergone his sad experience of cultural defeat. "A knowledge of classical music is indispensable to the cultivated mind," he preached, as he embarked on suiting some action to his words. The experiment had begun modestly enough; a few students were singled out, young Soditan at the fore of those who had shown some musical aptitude. Every Sunday morning—that is, those Sunday mornings when Dr. Mackintosh succeeded in rousing himself from a Saturday-night stupor induced by visits to a notorious corner of Ilesa township—he would lure his victims into his living room, serve out cups of tea, and crank up his rusty gramophone. He prefaced his choice of records with a brief lecture, shut his eyes, raised his forehead to the ceiling, and proceeded to intone the range of emotions which he expected his pupils to undergo as the strings of violins or massed choral voices suffused his living room. His eyes were invariably shut as the record played, his head nodding gently to the imaginary baton of the conductor—this was when his pupils attacked the saucerful of short-bread biscuits, the main attraction of the Sunday-morning sessions for the majority.

Akinyode wheeled his bicycle thoughtfully across the lawn, the neglected grass tickling his ankles. Any moment, it seemed, Dr. Mackintosh would appear, clutching an armful of Bakelite discs and humming a Bach fugue, totally oblivious of his surroundings. He would probably look at him with reproach, as it was he, Akinyode, who had most disappointed him when he took his music experiments out onto that very lawn to embrace the entire colony of seminarians. *Et tu, Soditan?*

And poor Akinyode had felt so sad for the good-natured Mackintosh; the guilt made him wince afresh each time he heard his music drifting through St. Simeon's fields from his bungalow. The buildup towards the advertised concert! The trayloads of sandwiches, buns and cakes, teas and lemonades, prepared by the teachers' wives. Chairs and benches dragged from schoolrooms and the chapel. Special guests from the rival training school, St. Andrew's in Oyo, all come for the event of the term, a treat from Mackintosh's collection of classical records. The chairs on the front row for teachers, the benches to the rear for pupils. And Mackintosh had also invited the touring inspector of education to participate in the experiment of imparting classical music appreciation to young Africans and weaning them from their crude though vigorous music. To this end he now took his place among the students, his physical presence echoing his living-room commentaries and narrations on the motion of the music, its colours and textures, caressing the scenery it evoked, not too remote from what they all knew, and of course there had been photos of Scottish hills and dales in Dr. Mackintosh's living room . . .

"Imagine a river flowing . . . the wind gently swaying the willows . . . sunlight glinting on pebbles as a trout threads a silvery path through the ripples . . ."

The benches hardened against some sixty-odd buttocks. Slowly, Akinyode became aware that the night was filled with menace. He prayed hard, staring across the lawn at the wooden chapel with its wide low-slung windows, a tar-coated structure that never failed to remind him of the police barracks at Ibadan past which he trudged on his journey to the seminary. He then turned his concentration on the pale, animated profile whose ghostly arms furtively sliced through and enfolded the night air as he conjured up nostalgic images of homeland. The music washed over attentive heads. Akinyode gritted his teeth, tensed his muscles, and prayed.

The night had been specially chosen—full moon. There was also a working light provided by a hurricane lamp placed near the phonograph itself, next to a large *araba* tree. The tree cast scattered shadows over the assembly. A light breeze fanned their faces and the grass felt cool on their bare feet. From time to time a bat squeaked across their heads, arousing a genuine interest for the duration of its passage. An assistant had been detailed to change the records and re-crank the gramophone while Mackintosh introduced the next item on the musical fare.

"And now think of mountain peaks, and snow falling gently through fir trees. Then, this next movement, you will imagine a storm which has been brewing in the distance. It now approaches, sweeps through the mountain gorges. The scattered fleeces of white clouds are framed against an inky-dark heaven—behind it all is the frown of an angry God. When the cymbals clash . . ."

And the black heads dropped, one after the other, sank onto their chests, oblivious now to Mackintosh's unspoken programme notes. The local clouds then shifted from the face of the moon and revealed the pride of Dr. Mackintosh slumped in various postures, heads on adjoining shoulders, on their own laps, sprawled over benches. Some had taken advantage of their well-to-the-rear positions and given up the struggle completely. They abandoned their benches altogether and spread out comfortably on the cushioning grass. A few snores actually punctuated the second movement of Schubert's Third. Not one, and this was what broke the heart of Dr. Mackintosh, not one Simeonite was left awake that night, not even one, he murmured over and over again as the music stopped and he gazed, horror-stricken, at the philistinic motley.

But it was the presence of Akinyode Soditan, seated right next to him yet oblivious to the world, which broke his heart. He had shown the greatest promise, and Dr. Mackintosh had remarked him to his colleagues. Soditan's eyes were wide open, fixed solidly on the *araba* tree, the last in the line of objects which he had commandeered that night to save him from the waves of sleep that threatened his sorely tried eyelids. At first Mackintosh had permitted himself to grasp at this small crumb of consolation as he rose and surveyed the field of prostrate bodies. Turning to his favourite pupil, he ordered: "Soditan, wake up these savages!"

But Yode remained in his ramrod position, eyes staring but unseeing, and Mackintosh knew that the very worst had indeed happened. He touched him on the shoulder, and young Soditan keeled over, then began to scramble up in fright, not knowing where he was. The Scot let out a heartrending sigh, as one who felt that he had indeed drained his cup of gall to the bitter dregs.

Et tu, Soditan?

II

EFUAPE

Misty dawn in the riverine town of Epe. A young tax inspector put finishing touches to his battle strategy and nodded with satisfaction. Sipe, son of Efuape, had long identified the main obstacle to his grand design—the solution was to disarm that individual, and the rest of the ex-Ilés would follow his lead. It was time to abandon piecemeal, tentative action. Crumbs! Yes, that was it, crumbs! It was all that had so far fallen in their hands while others made off with the body of the feast. Did the Arimojes of this world possess two heads? No. Just one, like them, like every other human being. If anything, if one went by what each head contained, that *ara oke** probably had even less than one—was the man not completely illiterate? Yet it had not prevented him from becoming a millionaire—or so it was rumoured. Rumour or not, no one disputed that his feet were on the highest rungs of the ladder of wealth. His houses were vast palaces; the number of motor lorries that bore the sign ARIMOJE TRANSPORT SERVICES—even in that rudimentary stage of the motor vehicle in West Africa—was the envious talk of the country. Not bad, not bad at all for an illiterate. Perhaps that was the trouble with himself and The Circle—they were crippled by too much literacy.

Certainly Akinyode was. He, Sipe, had far more sense of the world. Since his abrupt departure from the teacher training seminary, so many years ago that the pain of it had utterly vanished, his reading horizons had been confined to mail-order catalogues. His favourite was Lennards, from whose glossy pages he conjured shimmering vistas of an opulent future. The magic wand took various shapes— patent leather or tanned leather shoes, ties, ready-made suits, windcheaters, felt hats, watches, fountain pens and assorted stationery, handbags, vanity cases and toilet accessories. When he dipped into

* Country bumpkin.

journals of the kind that had seduced the mind of his friend Akinyode Soditan, it was only to seek out the advertisement pages, those foreign companies forever seeking raw materials or agents to dispose of their own products. And of course the shipping notices—that was crucial to his reputation: Whatever Sipe promised by a certain date would be delivered on that very date, or earlier. His Christmas cards and New Year calendars, for instance, complete with envelopes, arrived at least a month even before the orders of the C.M.S. Bookshops. Sipe canvassed for his orders—which expanded all the time—mainly from the young professionals, a few businessmen also, but mostly office clerks, teachers, and college students. His clientele was flung across the country, from Lagos to Port Harcourt and Kano, so he was careful to commence his contacts very early, order, clear, and mail those seasonal cards and gifts to their destination in time to avoid the postal rush at end of year.

But these were small, dilettante beginnings; now it was time to move on and win more territory, challenge the Lebanese and Indian traders who monopolised the cloth trade. Go to Ereko, Idumagbo, Ebute Metta, and Isale Eko—whose rosy faces did one see smirking in the shadowy interior of shops, shelves bursting with rolls and rolls of chiffon, voile, gabardine, worsted wool, and every kind of apparel and their accessories? It was these Middle Easterners, keeping a sharp eye on their local shop assistants as they measured out the cloths to local customers. The jewellery shops also belonged to them. Everything well-turned-out ladies or gentlemen of refinement required to hold up their own in society, the Lebanese and the Indians reaped the profit thereof. Well, it was time for the Jebusite to match the Levantine in enterprise, and this was his message to those vacillating seminarians.

Akinyode was the problem. No sooner did Sipe succeed in firing their imagination with a BOLD NEW PLAN, than the schoolteacher would embark on some diversion for extending the debate—at the end of which, the will to act in concert would peter out. Always he brought up something or other he had just read, in the same journals—the irony of it!—on which Sipe depended for his business aspirations. For the teacher, even the abdication of King Edward of England had only prompted a whole new series of considerations. Suppose it led to civil war in England? Would their investments be guaranteed protection? From then on, it was an entire afternoon spent discussing the English War of the Roses while Sipe fumed silently. Oh, he also took part in reconstructing and arguing details of that war, but at least he had the grace to be angry with himself afterwards. For the rest of The Circle, however, it was a Sunday afternoon spent most profitably. Profitably! Did these friends of his understand the meaning of profit? And so a meeting which he had expressly summoned to look into the logistics of locating abattoirs to supply tons of dried bones to a firm in Birmingham was frittered away with purely speculative manoeuvres of some incomprehensible battles fought by figures encased in iron and steel across some remote English plains! Who cared whether there were intriguing parallels between those battles and the Kiriji or Ijaiye wars of Yorubaland? What was it to him if the famed Dahomean "Amazons" could have taught the House of York or Lancaster a lesson or two in military tactics? They did not even touch aspects that truly concerned them in those Supplies Wanted columns of the journals which had provoked the meeting! What, for instance, was the nature of the products for which the bones were needed? Was it perhaps something they could themselves manufacture on their own? Bones were required for *something*—what was that something?

And the Belgian bonds—Hypothek and Creditbank—Efuape had primed his friends' expectations and they were all ready to fill out the application forms. Investments guaranteed, on good authority, to quadruple in value within two years. But trust the teacher to run into a reference to an ancient indictment by a British knight who had uncovered unspeakable cruelties by the Belgians in the Congo! So, up came the moral issues. Arguments that swung backwards and forwards and ended in nothing! How do we know for certain, Sipe had insisted? The European powers were rival territory-grabbers—could anyone deny that? Roger Casement was an Englishman—could they be certain that this campaign was not simply anti-Belgian propaganda? And in any case the man was long dead, hanged for a traitor. Whoever heard of civilised people cutting off ears and hands for failure to fulfill the supply quota of cassava and rubber and whatever else? Did they think that those Belgians had never read the fable of the goose that laid the golden egg? Self-interest made such action illogical! It was far too improbable. Did the British cut off anyone's ear in their West African colonies and protectorates? Well, he had bested Yode in that argument—at least the teacher failed to produce a convincing counter. But his triumph was short-lived, it proved no more than a Pyrrhic victory. The Circle resolved that the teacher write to England for further details—which of course took care of the closing date for making that most enticing investment. Yode, Sipe ruefully concluded, was a cunning procrastinator!

This time, he would take the wind out of his sails, take them all by surprise. He would insist no more that they all abandon their jobs—his new plans now permitted them to wear their chains of slavery, so beloved of them, poor timid souls! No more insistence on the immediate hire of imposing premises with a blazing signboard which would announce the entry of EX-ILÉS ENTERPRISES into one of the main commercial streets of Lagos. No, they would not even hire a store. No overhead. There would be no risky investments. The key to this new operation was so simple: Employ a full-time agent who would operate from his own home. In case of an emergency—let us say, the arrival of a large order which could not be immediately distributed—Sipe's living room would be converted to a temporary warehouse. The essence was a rapid turnover: advance orders from clientele—arrival of goods—immediate distribution, but this time on a nonstop basis. Their employee would act both as clearing and forwarding agent. Then watch the progress for a year. The first line of business was already decided by him—clothing, and Italian clothing at that. He had made the contacts, his suppliers were ready—only the capital was missing, and a fair proportion of that was already guaranteed. Sipe felt he had earned the right to give himself full marks for his new strategy and the groundwork that surely guaranteed its success. Yes, success, that eloquent conqueror of misgivings, would, without further urging from him, make even Yode "cast his chalk of slavery at the blackboard and take his place among the adventurous heroes of our time." He flicked through the thin file of letters from his prospective partners in Italy, his already buoyant spirits further uplifted by the names that rang in seemingly familiar accents to his Remo ears. Morigi? *Ha, mee r'igi, ere r'emi ri.* Benito? *B'eni to se, be ra mi se.* Milano? *Emi Sipe re mi lano.* * One more year as a wage slave. If the others could bear it, so could he. But only one

---

* Do I see a tree? No, I see no trees, only profit. Beni to? As one who can do it, so does one proceed. Milano? Indeed it is I, Sipe, who blazes the path.

more year; after that, the local government council in Epe would have to find itself a new tax inspector.

There remained only one unresolved question: what to do with the Spirit of Layeni! Impulsively he called out, "Mrs. E."

"I am nearly ready." And his wife peeked out through an opening in the curtain that separated the living room from her bedroom, hair halfway piled up above her head, smelling lightly of the effects of the hot iron. Sipe glanced up, was startled yet again by her beauty and saddened equally by her continuing childlessness. He caught his breath, lost his nerve, and muttered a reminder of the departure time of their ferry. The advice he had suddenly thought of seeking from his spouse was swept aside as he gazed upon her loveliness and chafed at the luck that married its desired fulfillment. And he reasoned also that to bring her into the orbit of the Spirit of Layeni, even through knowledge of his plans, might jeopardise the remedies she undertook for her cure. One never knew what might happen in these matters. Invocation of such spirits could destroy those very planes on which her cure depended. So Mrs. E. withdrew her head and returned to her toilette. He shook his head at the lopsidedness of Fate. Time, Sipe, give it more time. . . . He took out the Lennards catalogue and marked a shimmering frock, which he would order now for her next birthday. His spirits rose again and he decided it was time to clip the pink carnation on the wide lapel of his gray worsted suit . . .

They had set out for Otuyemi's wedding early enough, taking no chances, but the day which had dawned over such rosy vistas now seemed resolved to end in total disaster. Worst of all was his feeling of incongruity in the stranded company in which he found himself; a three-button suit of worsted wool set Sipe apart from the other passengers who huddled in the shade of the broken-down lorry. Their loud to mumbled variations on the themes of anxiety and resignation had long ceased to divert him; the letters he had begun to compose in his mind to the bridegroom to explain his absence, and of course to the ex-Ilés recounting the day's misadventures, lay suspended in midphrase. On the dirt road between Ijebu-Ode and Iperu at midday, trapped in his brand-new catalogue-order suit complete with a silk-lined waistcoat, the once proud ensemble now sadly shrouded by the dust of voyage that had seeped steadily through floorboards and loosely welded joints—it was difficult at this moment to find those witty turns of phrase with which he delighted to challenge his friends. The wilful vehicle had, naturally, chosen the most arid sector of the road for its final rebellion, far from the lush forest and vast stretches of cocoa and kola-nut plantations through which they had earlier driven with such confidence. Now there was only scrub and hot November wind. When he took out the breast-pocket handkerchief which he had folded into a fleur-de-lys that morning, after applying its regulation drops of Yardley's Olde English Lavender, he was not surprised to find a handful of dust fly out from its folds. No, it was decidedly straining the mind to attempt to order his experiences in that inclement hour.

Still, the time had to be occupied somehow, and so it came about that, without actually setting out to do so, Sipe began to "bring his books up to date." It was an exercise which came with the training for his abandoned profession, and one which he undertook with moderate frequency, far less often than, for instance, the schoolteacher. This resumption only made him more dejected. His card, even before he reeled off his myriad undertakings for detailed assessment, read, "Poor. Below expectations." He pronounced the verdict only just audibly. Yet such was the heartfelt gloom his voice conveyed that his fellow travellers thought that the judgment had been passed on the efforts of the sweaty, grease-stained driver and his mate, who still wrestled chunks of engine parts from beneath the vehicle, clambered through the bonnet, and re-emerged through a hole in the floorboard of the driver's cabin—all to no avail. The passengers were inclined to agree with him but found the remark rather unhelpful. A motor vehicle was still largely a mystery, and breakdowns were simply part of its God-given character. In any case, as they looked him up and down, they could not help wondering what he was doing in a passenger lorry at all, even if he had occupied the "first-class" compartment, that is, the front cabin, separated from the driver by a token wood partition. His appearance placed him firmly among the occupants of those few cars which had passed them along the road.

Sipe's self-recriminations knew no bounds, taking on himself the blame for his predicament—even including the breakdown of the vehicle. There was nothing he could have done about the ferry that had broken down in Lagos the previous day, yet he felt that he ought to have anticipated this and made alternative arrangements. He had gone to the pier in all confidence, Mrs. E., as he fondly called his beautiful wife, dressed with matching elegance beside him. On such mornings Sipe experienced what he called pure happiness, a sense of soulful enlargement as he relished the frank stares of admiration from the townspeople of Epe. The direct route between Epe and Ijebu-Ode was cut. The ferry would have taken them to Ikorodu, where a Morris Minor car and a Ford pickup had been chartered to take the guests, their finery untarnished, to the society wedding. The pier itself had contributed an additional sense of achievement—"the beginnings of bigger things to come"—as he stood on the new-laid planks, the supports still smelling of tar. Within mere weeks of his transfer to Epe from Lagos, he had persuaded the District Officer of the urgent need to replace the shaky embarkation pier. His argument was sound: The Resident would soon visit, inaugurating the new local governments—which really meant a few lucky ones—carved out from the former Ijebu-Ode administrative territory. A new pier, duly publicised by the Epe Descendants Union resident in Lagos, would place Epe at the top of the list of towns to be so honoured. It was the last sensation of pleasure Sipe would obtain that day. The ferry, which so reliably plied between Lagos, Epe, and Ikorodu every other day, had had its propellers twisted into a shapeless hulk by a drifting log the previous night and had barely limped into Lagos. At Ikorodu the motorcars waited for the pair as long as was reasonable, then departed with the other guests. Dejected, Sipe escorted his wife back to their home. They had both decided to make the best of a bad job—Mrs. E. would stay home while Sipe, unencumbered, undertook the epic journey on behalf of both.

Sipe prided himself on his resourcefulness. Within an hour he had obtained a canoe with outboard motor—road transportation from Epe was now out of the question. He would go first to Lagos and hope that there would be a lorry or pickup travelling towards Ijebu-Ode. Sipe disembarked at Ebute-Ero, where he not only found a lorry but obtained the seat in the front cabin, easily displacing a produce inspector who was still hesitating over the extra fare. They made good speed and his spirits began to rise. And then the engine coughed once, twice, a few times more, began to hiccup with increasing violence, and finally shuddered to a halt. The passengers all disembarked and waited. Sipe at first stood at the rear, ready to flag down any passing vehicle. The afternoon grew longer. Not a lorry passed them, and the few cars were full. A motorcyclist did stop and Sipe was momentarily tempted to buy a ride to Iperu on the pillion. Another look at the rider soon changed his mind, however—whatever little gloss remained on his suit would be fully extinguished by the dust before they had gone half a mile. And the lorry engine did begin at the time to give some hints of resuscitation, raising hopes in the breasts of the passengers. The sun glowered down as the minutes dragged by. The younger ones of the travellers had long taken refuge beneath the lorry itself; others sought varying degrees of relief within or beside it. Incredibly, a nursing mother had constructed quite a passable shelter with the aid of her headtie and wrapper and the meagre shade cast by a scrub that the early harmattan drought had somehow overlooked. It was her resourcefulness indeed that had first triggered off the urge to share the day's reverses with Akinyode. *My dear Yode,* he began, *never let it be gainsaid—necessity is indeed the mother of invention, and I did make her acquaintance today, in the most unlikely of places. And a mother, let me hasten to add, is the master of necessity.* It was a good opening, he thought. The teacher, overwhelmed by that opening salvo, would first put the letter aside, mix himself some ginger or lemon juice, and sink back in his armchair to relish the rest of his narrative.

Long after that letter had been abandoned, Sipe observed a most unusual increase in the traffic. It was decidedly out of place. The roads between Ijebu townships and Lagos constituted his familiar beat, and he had never, in the years since he saw his first motorcar, never seen such a frequency of motor traffic outside Lagos. At first he had been merely annoyed to find that they were all going in the wrong direction, that is, away from his own destination. And then he paid attention to the passengers—such as could be discerned through the dust—and saw that the men were variants of his own sleekly outfitted figure. Evidently another wedding. It took a while for Sipe to recognise in their exhausted, not anticipatory, bearing that they were not going to another wedding; they were coming from one! And then, as he identified a couple whose clothes he had himself helped to procure for the occasion, the crushing truth descended on him—they were all coming from *the* wedding. It was all over. The church ceremony, the photographic session, the reception. In another hour or two the bride would be ceremonially extracted from her parents' home while the bridegroom, waiting in his own home with impatience, would undergo the customary badinage.

Sipe felt thoroughly ill-used; how on earth would he explain his absence to Otuyemi? And who, at such short notice, had Otuyemi found to propose the toast of the bridegroom? For a moment he took consolation in the fact that he had not, after all, defaulted as best man, then corrected himself. If he had been the best man, he would have slept in Iperu the previous day, overseeing all the arrangements. His posting to Epe had, however, derailed that proposal, and Otuyemi had been quite understanding. But to fail in the end even to turn up and liven up the occasion with one of his memorable speeches, sparkling with wit and skeetering just on the edge of the naughty, that gall he found bitter and excessive. As he watched the passing motorcars trailing one another at careful intervals to avoid the cloud raised by the preceding vehicle, he added a comment to his abandoned letter: *I felt, my dear Yode, like one of the foolish virgins in that biblical parable.*

Homeward bound—Sipe finally crossed the road to the other side and caught a market lorry on its way back to Ikorodu—he took out two sheets of paper from his inner breast pocket. One contained what looked like a shopping list, the other a series of questions and answers. At the bottom of the sheet was a question, in capitals and in his own handwriting, which summed up his dilemma: DO I PROCEED OR NOT?

The teacher training seminary at Ilesa was now little more than a recollected idyll of youthful comradeship, though Sipe still enjoyed answering to a famous name bestowed on him at that institution. The question he now addressed to himself was: Do I still deserve this title? Have I demonstrated, in recent times, that control of any situation in which I happen to be, anywhere, anytime? Or have I permitted myself to be tossed here and there, drifting like that foolish log that messed up the propellers of the Epe–Lagos–Ikorodu ferry? Where is the young Efuape who threw the Right Reverend Beeston into such spiritual turmoil with the fast and furious ideas that he presented to that worthy gentleman, mainly ideas for the enhanced status of the products of St. Simeon's? How disturbed that college principal had been when he had confronted him with the news that students of St. Simeon's would no longer refer to themselves as Simeans, nor would they accept in future to be addressed as such!

Akinyode, ever the browser in exotic texts, had stumbled on the word "simian." Until then, its existence was unknown to any student in the seminary. It did not even exist in their prescribed *Elementary English Dictionary*, and they had to wait until night, when a volunteer squad, led by Efuape, broke into the staff library and borrowed the much bigger *Oxford Dictionary*. There it was, horror of horrors! Then followed the question: Had the white teachers known this all along? Had they furtively enjoyed a racial joke at the students' expense all these years? It was not like Sipe to await the resolution of such questions or to give his tutors the benefit of the doubt. He marched straight to the principal's office and announced to him a decision that had not yet been taken. That was the young Efuape, the man of resolution, whose favourite phrase was: "If we must do it, let us do it with instant flash and flair." Was it now that same Sipe who could not even organise the elements to get him on time to a wedding which—the cruellest part of it all—he had almost single-handedly planned, even to the courtship of the bride, which he undertook on behalf of the irresolute Otuyemi? Could such a weakling conjure up the Spirit of Layeni?

Reverend Beeston's revenge, which came not long after, had been painful at the time. There was first that gentleman's suspicion of this brash young man who answered to the nickname Resolute Rooster, to which the shameless youth, stepping jauntily across the lawns or classroom corridors, would—depending on his mood—respond, "Thaz me—Cock of the Walk!" The principal had overheard this ritual exchange more than once and pondered long on the moral health of such an individual. There was something suggestive about the appellation, so he summoned his student to his office one day and questioned him closely—his background, his leisure occupations, his future ambitions, his favourite reading. Sipe supplied nothing but candid replies, which, however, sounded incomplete to the principal. Something had to be wrong about this confident youth who even managed to look uniquely dandified in the drab Anglican-ethic uniform, which was designed to abolish individuality. He resolved to keep a close watch on Efuape for the rest of his career.

That period proved to be mercifully short, from the principal's point of view. Of his class, Efuape ranked among the top three students; only he, Akinyode, and Egunjobi shared the top position on any consistent basis. Among that circle of friends, however, Otuyemi was a poor performer, and Sipe thought nothing of helping him with his homework. From homework to class tests to examination was a progression that developed without much thought. Efuape was trapped passing his friend his answer sheets to copy. Hauled before the gleeful principal, Sipe stared silently at the pictures of former principals of St. Simeon's hanging above the head of the incumbent, his gift of gab sent on abrupt vacation. Reverend Beeston was vindicated. This lapse was proof of what he had always suspected—any youth who answered to the name Resolute Rooster had to have something innately evil in him. To that worthy priest's eternal frustration, however, the movement of the answer paper had been detected only on its homeward journey, that is, as Sipe tried to retrieve it, sliding it inwards with his toes, out of view, he thought, of the invigilator. He refused to confess where it had been. The three students sitting to the left, right, and rear of him were questioned at length, threatened with the eternal perdition of their souls if they shielded the culprit—all to no avail. They had been truly hunched over their answer papers as regulation demanded. Otuyemi agonised over his own position, set off more than once to confess his part in the escapade, but was waylaid by Efuape and finally silenced by his eloquent sermon. Two heads might be better than one, he argued, but certainly not on the guillotine. Otuyemi had never heard of the guillotine but it gained his attention. Moreover, Efuape drummed it into his head that he was leaving St. Simeon's to fulfill his destiny, which was to play John the Baptist to their financial Saviour in whatever form he might appear and launch them on his dreamboat headed for the perilous seas of Enterprise, and since Fate had laid its finger on him to be their Sindbad the Sailor, to take them on the Golden Road to Samarkand and revolutionise their lives in the manner of the merchant princes of antiquity, and no revolution was ever complete without its martyrs—preferably on the guillotine—he, Sipe, son of Efuape, willingly laid his head on the scaffold and would rise like a phoenix from the ashes of defeat to return through the portals in a gleaming motorcar and blow dust in the face of the Reverend Beeston, who would never boast of his own motorcar in all his life, you just wait and see, and you, Otuyemi, must therefore remain and bear witness to history fulfilling itself and be content to be recruited into the army that would lay siege to the fabulous kingdoms of wealth—just join up as soon as you struggle through your certificate here, and you can even come to me for extra lessons during your holidays. The catalogue of bloody precedents from myth, history, and hearsay bludgeoned Otuyemi into submission, to Efuape's immense relief.

He packed his bags, departed from the hallowed gates of St. Simeon's, "a fallen angel, a fashion-wise Adam, banished through the gates of our earthly paradise," preached Reverend Beeston the following Sunday. But young Efuape did not return home to Ìsarà. He went straight to Lagos and began to look for work. When his colleagues returned home on their next holidays, the Rooster was firmly established as a clerk in the tax office at Yaba, his charm and confidence having captivated the European chief inspector of taxes. It was a coup without parallel in the history of the young products of St. Simeon's. Without a proper certificate to speak of, with no testimonial save one written by yet another friend of his own age and social status—but composed by Sipe himself—the young man landed a white-collar job at no less a salary than twenty-four pounds per annum, with paid annual leave, promotion and advancement scales, and a pension at the end. It was higher pay and brighter prospects than the normal St. Simeon's graduate could expect. Akinyode and Otuyemi organised the party of the year for Sipe, who had once again lived up to the name of Resolute Rooster, turning such a serious reverse to maximum advantage.

As the wind whipped his face and the dust filtered in through every permissive cranny of the homebound vehicle, Sipe admitted to himself that he had never known himself so irresolute. Naturally, he never intended, not even for a moment, to make a living out of the career of a civil servant. His present job was only a base for future operations. Scheme after scheme had passed through his mind with a rapidity that was only checked by one simple issue: capital. A working capital and a minimum guarantee of success. In the process of seeking the former he had stumbled on the forbidden path that would lead most rapidly towards the latter. They had all heard of such things. Even at St. Simeon's there were fellow students who resorted to stranger methods to achieve the desired examination results: special black powder, rubbed in the centre of the head while secret incantations were muttered; answer papers touched with a special talisman from the Orient; furtive visits to the cemetery at night, leaving behind pouches of bones and earth, over which were pronounced a magic formula from the Sixth and Seventh Books of Moses. A brilliant scholar in his own right, Efuape had scoffed at such credulity. Now his foot was poised over that dread terrain, and his erstwhile scepticism was receiving knocks from the beckoning hand of lucrative advancement.

A "Benefit Fund" was the earliest child of his fertile brain. "We band together, put aside a percentage of our salaries regularly, place it in a post-office savings account or a bank fixed deposit. It accumulates a steady interest. In an emergency or in case of a venture to be approved by all members, any of us can withdraw a portion of that sum." To Ogunba fell the task of drawing up a constitution. Referred to Sipe for further vetting, it returned unaltered, except for the name itself. "Benefit Fund Club" had progressed to "Cooperative Society." From "Cooperative Society" it was one short step to an "Investment Syndicate," with outlines of an unmistakable business company pencilled into the margin. Only a few minor changes, Sipe insisted, only some minor tidying up, replacing the fuzzy edges with a more dynamic outlook, shifting from a Boy Scout mentality to that of a full-grown combatant. Finally there was no holding the young tycoon.

"Let us give up this *esusu* mentality," he harangued them at the next meeting of the "board of directors," which consisted of all six contributors to the now-eclipsed Benefit Fund. "Do we or do we not want our independence? Then why these half-measures, my comrades of St. Simeon's? Here we are, young, energetic, the hope and backbone of a burgeoning colonial territory. The future spreads itself before us like a feast for the brave, so why do we hesitate to throw off the shackles of salaried existence? Our pioneers await us. They have trodden the path of thorns and climbed the rocky prospects. From these heights they reach out to take us by the hand and aid our ascent. One after the other they abandoned their white-collar jobs—postal clerks, sanitary inspectors, council officers, miserable accountants, hospital orderlies, petty surveyors—name it, you will find their vacated places, some of which you and I now occupy with shaming complacency . . ." And Sipe reeled off the names of the "young heroes," none of them quite as successful as the illiterate Arimoje, but all now meeting their erstwhile employers on equal terms, including the white ones. His oratory was heady stuff, the ex-Ilés admitted, but their prudence remained unshaken. They would go with him as far as the Benefit Fund, but the word "Syndicate" proved its own downfall—it sounded too businesslike, they complained.

In frustration Sipe had turned to an outsider. Onayemi was a childhood acquaintance with whom he had attended primary school. Onayemi dropped out early, went to work as a house servant in a District Officer's residence in Ikare, moved on to Lagos, where he served as salesman to John Holt for a year. He then started business for himself, supplying kola nuts and palm kernels to a branch of Lever Brothers. Onayemi, now a moderately successful businessman, was ready to invest in Sipe's projects. And the proof of his seriousness was his insistence on a certain "mystic service" which had ensured the success of his own enterprise. Without it, Onayemi would never think of embarking on a new venture, nor even expand an existing one. This "service" involved the invocation of the spirit of an unseen guardian—in his case, the ancestor Layeni.

The head teacher, despite some misgivings, had entrusted to him the sum of twenty-five pounds, "to be invested as you wish" or treated as a loan to be returned without interest. Despite this boost, Sipe still required Onayemi's promised contribution—and his business experience. And this partner would not stir until the spirit had been evoked: "Don't you see," he patiently explained, "if we go ahead without invoking this spirit, we may lose the entire capital." To Sipe's still-practical mind, this was the most twisted form of commercial reasoning he had ever encountered. Yet everyone he spoke to—guardedly, always feigning a disinterested curiosity—everyone assured him that there was no wealthy man or woman who ever attained success without some such procedure. Sometimes it was worse, some really hideous ritual that required the use of parts of the human body. Invoking a spirit was cleaner. Although more dangerous, it threatened no more than the actual participants. The medium was the most exposed; he required special fortification, which more than justified the demand of a rather high proportion of the capital, never a straightforward, fixed sum. And of course the rewards were guaranteed to come in direct proportion to that first investment, which would in turn affect, proportionately, all subsequent ventures. This, Sipe's quick mind deduced, was to discourage the kind of escape route that had suggested itself to him—to lower the initial outlay to next to nothing, then increase it after the spirit had given his blessing and could be shrewdly abandoned. Cunning, calculating spirits, he thought. Or perhaps one should say mediums.

Next was the thought of what would be Akinyode's reaction. True, the teacher had left the direction of the enterprise to him. As for the choice of making his contribution an outright loan, Sipe had rejected that completely; the profits must be shared equally. His mind did not conceive of losses. But Akinyode would balk at what might appear to him as some kind of satanic rites. Should he simply go ahead and list the medium's fee as a legitimate expense—which indeed it was? Like a promotion exercise? Onayemi's medium as public relations officer to the spirit world? The concept was not all that ludicrous; a medium, after all, is an intermediary. The spirits need cajoling, a little bullying, elements of seduction—yes, it was no different from a public relations exercise. But suppose the spirit was invoked and it advised against the project altogether, how would he then explain the loss of a third of Akinyode's capital? Also, when the next venture began, would they again . . . NO! On that point at least, Sipe was quite resolved. If Onayemi was so much in thrall to Layeni, he would simply have to take what was left of his capital and quit the Syndicate. The spirit could have one bite, no more. Yet even regarding that first and only bite, the Resolute Rooster found himself most uncharacteristically irresolute.

Efuape re-read the contents of the paper. Onayemi had prepared the conjuring brief, based on his prior experiences in this kind of affair. A date had been computed as a propitious night—two earlier appointments had been shelved, again because of Sipe's vacillation. To help him resolve his doubts, his business partner then prepared a list of preliminary questions, which he had taken to the medium in Odogbolu. He had written them down, then taken down the medium's responses. Sipe's daring did not extend to the spirit world; at no time did he plan to be present at the "service." So he settled for this method of communicating "by double proxy," a twice-removed correspondence with the spirit world. No one could now accuse him justly of consorting with "dark powers," if indeed the more sinister spirits were involved. Efuape reviewed the questions and answers for the twentieth time, finding yet another reason to be sorry that he had missed the wedding. That was the occasion he would have seized to probe Akinyode's reactions indirectly, merely showing him the questionnaire and the answers, then asking casually if he thought that such a procedure could be considered satanic in any way. It would have been the best way to approach it. Now he would simply have to take his own decision. It was not possible to travel to see his friend before the new date, and Onayemi had warned that the medium could not guarantee another propitious night in the immediate future. The sheet was carefully dated September 19, and the hour entered—between five and six P.M. Even the subject of the interview with the medium was stated and underlined.

Invocation of the Spirit of Layeni. On the Questions of the Proposed Mystic Services by T. S. Onayemi

Questions presented to the medium:

1. Is it wholly profitable if this (Name of Business) is done and should there be no course of shortening one's life?
2. What of sacrifice of commission to be duly offered every month?

Across the second item Sipe had drawn a thick line. Onayemi had mentioned nothing about sacrificing any commission on the business to any spirit. When he tackled him on this, his would-be partner explained that it did not refer to their venture since this was not commission-based. Patiently, he outlined the differences.

He, Onayemi, had started out as a salesman for John Holt and had had to sacrifice his commission every month to the medium for the first year. He had included the question specifically to assure them both that this claim did not apply to this new venture. But what, asked Sipe, had he lived on during that period? What did he earn, in effect? Onayemi explained mysteriously that being a salesman was a many-sided affair—beyond that, he would not elaborate. The regular commission was mere bonus, a pittance, and the Spirit of Layeni was more than welcome to it. Firmly, Sipe shook his head as he leapt over that section. Pittance or no pittance, under no circumstances would any spirit extort a full year's commission from him. Onayemi was a good businessman when dealing with mortals but he had yet to learn how to drive a hard bargain with guardian spirits. He moved to the next item:

3. Is there any rule which can cause any ineffect on its part?
4. What do you aware of the ingredient whether they are strong enough to be compounded or not?

Sipe could not resist an indulgent smile. It proved something—he was not quite certain what—but a large proportion of successful businessmen were either illiterate or semiliterate. He turned to the second sheet of paper, which contained the answers to the first. It was headed:

Paper II. *Reply or Rejoinder of the Spirit to Questions as Numbered in Paper I.*

What a punctilious civil servant this Onayemi would have made! Obviously wasted in the private sector, but no doubt he kept good books in his business. Sipe already knew the answers by heart but went through them again:

Question 1. No least course to regret the experiment.
Question 2. Inconstancy of this will issue serious fruits.

And in brackets, Onayemi had added: *Time—New Moon—Sacrifice.* That of course did not concern their own enterprise, and Sipe emitted a sigh of sympathy as he pictured poor Onayemi expending his commission on goat, yams, palm oil, or whatever, dutifully carrying them to the medium as *saara* every full moon. Or did the medium insist on hard cash? Of course he would, come to think of it.

Question 3. Provided a clean room is dedicated to it and avoid two persons to salute the spirit.

This, Onayemi had again explained, referred to the suppliants. They could all be present at the service or they could select a representative. In the former case, only one person could salute the spirit when it made itself manifest. Sipe snorted—thank you for nothing. He had already made up his mind not to be anywhere near the "service" chamber. It was Onayemi's familiar, so let him go as their representative. The details did not interest him in the least; he had no curiosity to meet the guardian spirit of commercial enterprise, or indeed any being from another world, in any shape or form. Even foreigners did not interest him; the white skin was as close as he wanted to get to the world of ghosts. So let Onayemi bring in the results and take care of the procedure. Paper II continued:

> Question 4. Powerful. But the "Ruling Spirit" has to append his own personal prescription to compound with it for its benefit (spirit).

That "prescription," which Onayemi had evidently obtained as a result of further consultations with the medium, was then listed in a footnote:

1. Living Partridge (or dead)
2. Living Lilly (Compulsory)
3. White young pigeon
   Turn to powder some days before the experiment. Carefully wrapped with white cloth with virgin earth from the graveyard and throw into deep water citing or calling:

Thereafter followed a curious symbol, which evidently only the medium, and perhaps Onayemi, would be able to decipher, cite, or call. Sipe merely labelled it CURIOUS SIGN—in capital letters. The page was then certified with what again struck Sipe as a most inappropriate punctiliousness, considering the shady world into which they were about to venture: "Cited by me, T.S. Onayemi." The signature that followed was as polished and impressive as any he had ever encountered in the seminary, and that included his friend Akinyode's masterpiece, or indeed any that graced the myriad items of official correspondence that came his way during his years in the civil service. It seemed to have been cultivated as a conscious redress for a deficiency in what Osibo, the pharmacist dispenser, would often refer to as "the graces of the literate."

For the first time in his life, Sipe dozed off in a moving vehicle. Unable to resolve his dilemma, the entrepreneurial mind took refuge in a troubled sleep which was peopled by white colonial officers sitting in judgment over their prize tax officer. Why, they wanted to know, had he kept white pigeons in the office filing cabinet? He assured them that Onayemi could explain everything as soon as he returned from Odogbolu. In the meantime, if they cared to read his deposition they would understand that nothing had been done without formal authority of the chief medium, who had been personally ordained at the Anglican seminary, of which he was a faithful adherent. He was asked to produce the said deposition, and while he went to his desk, a prophet from the Cherubim and Seraphim Church of the Assembly of God danced in to a riot of tambourines and announced that he had come to bear witness and give testimony according to the Lord. Sipe, he swore, was a perjurer who stood in mortal danger of his soul. His wife was the true faithful, a member of his flock, whom he had tried to cure of barrenness, the poor unhappy woman. Sipe, to give that devil his due, unbeliever though he is, had indeed brought her to him, though again his sins must be pushed in his face, he paid only sporadic visits to the church. Frantically Sipe searched for his deposition to give the lie to the prophet, but when he opened a drawer he found only stacks and stacks of that CURIOUS SIGN whose recitation was to accompany the sprinkling of the white powder from the (compulsory) lily. The next drawer contained the partridge (dead), while the white young pigeon, which he last saw on the desk labelled Exhibit I, flew out of the third drawer, circled the room, and landed on the ceiling fan. Desperate, Sipe took out the sheets of CURIOUS SIGN—yes, he read it in capital letters—and distributed them to his judges. And what is this? they all screamed! Is this a joke? The prophet had evaporated at the mere appearance of the CURIOUS SIGN. Smugly, Sipe rounded on them. Right, he said, now we know who the Antichrist is—you saw him turn tail, didn't you? By their tails—and cloven hooves—we shall know them. He stopped laughing when he saw his judges merely stare stonily at him. Don't you understand, he screamed! This is ancient Hebrew—the original language of the Bible. No true Christian would dream of conjuring up spirits in any other tongue. The inspiration had come from—he did not know where. It had to be divine. He felt supremely confident. I assure you there is nothing satanic about it; on the contrary it is one of the oldest rites known to the CHOSEN PEOPLE—he said that too with capitals. They continued to stare, faces frozen hard, including the one in the middle, whose flared nostrils now betrayed the features of Reverend Beeston hiding behind the mask of the District Officer, wreathed round and round in garden creepers and flowers. Sipe watched him narrowly; now that he was being unmasked and deflowered he felt surer of himself. Beeston, he was certain, knew no Hebrew—Greek maybe, but no Hebrew. *Eloi eloi lama sabachthani!* It worked. His persecutors came to life once more; the chairman announced that the panel would shift the sitting to Odogbolu, where they would interrogate the medium in person. So Sipe informed them that the ferry had broken down. Of course they could send word to the Resident—he had a personal yacht and might be willing to oblige. As for the roads, that Epe-to-Lagos so-called road was one long stretch of marsh. Even in harmattan, he warned them, it was constantly waterlogged—again that touched a nerve. Don't tell me about waterlogged roads, screamed Reverend Beeston, leaping up, mask and petals completely peeling off his face. What do you know of the pioneering spirit? We opened up this godforsaken hole, and by God, if we have to close it up again just to get to the bottom of this business, we will. Let's go, gentlemen. I know this uppity native. I deal with his type every day. Onward—Christian—Simeans!

And Sipe felt himself seized by white arms that undulated the length and breadth of the hall, turned into long sea serpents, and this seemed out of place. Everyone knew that the sirens known as Mammy Wata existed only in the Delta creeks, and Epe was a long way from there. Unless of course the log that fouled up the propellers of the Lagos-bound ferry was no log at all but the salt-encrusted seaweed plaits of the Mammy Wata's hair or her swishing tail caught in the boat's propellers as she dived deep down in Epe creeks to clamber among the logs of timber floating down the Niger from the torrid interior—not that he ever intended to deal in timber, far too clumsy, and the lorries broke down so often before they even reached the waterways, which were more disguise than blessing. Leave that to Node, paralysed Node, to whom timber and tuber were one! You think you know it all, he screamed, you think you know it all, you have it all worked out, but how wrong you are! So the sinuous arms bounced him up and down, saying, No, we don't, but we know all about you. Nothing is beyond you. You have tried usury, otherwise known as money-lending, speculated in land, which always shifts under your feet, and not content with forging and fermenting local brew, called medicine, for foolish syndicates, you now consult astrologers. Oh yes, we know all about your visit to local herbalists, pretending that you want a cure for your childless wife but taking notes in notebooks, filling pages with those remedies for hernia, piles, *igbona*, fevers, *lakuregbe, sobia,* common dysentery, ringworm, oh yes, we know all about them. Call yourself a Christian and you have not learned to bear your yoke with humility and wait for God's time which is the best as every simple child could tell you. Beauty is all in the eye but a child is a man's wealth, and where is yours, you cheap inspector of taxes, where is your offspring, the product of your loins, and you with seven years of marriage to the local beauty envied by all but succumbing to your dashing roostery figure of a man. The arms shrank to normal and dropped him so suddenly, like rebellious waves, that his stomach leapt upwards to his throat and he complained to the leering Beeston: Look, forcing your ordination on me will not pay your dividends. I am the one and only Mephisto-Rooster, son of Efuape, so watch it or you won't even know what hit your simian face, you albino ape. Don't think we didn't know you had been laughing up your sleeve these many years, but we found you out, didn't we? Issuing us only bowdlerised dictionaries while you kept the one with the secret of the tongue and clamped the Sixth and Seventh Books of Moses under your bed so we could not learn the secret. I can do without you, Beeston, I tell you I can do without your type. Beeston's face was really ugly, hibiscus red as the face of Mephistopheles bearing off the damned soul of Mr. Faust, poor curious soul ruined by too much reading, which of course the teacher would defend, popping up beside the District Officer with his sad censorious demeanour—No, no, no, you must not say that, Rooster, too much reading never made Jack a dull boy. On the contrary, a little learning is a dangerous thing, drink deep, etcetera, don't you agree? Sipe's face fell. Oh no, don't tell me you are on their side. No, no, no, no, the teacher assured him, and we'll have dinner in a moment, you must be hungry. Sipe's stomach lurched painfully as fez caps on the police-shaven skulls butted him in the stomach for insulting the Resident. Another seized him beneath the armpits and the Right Reverend Beeston leapt up, crouched on the table, and revealed what he had always known—there it was, a long curved tail ending in a quivering arrowhead. So the Resident screamed, Blind him, blind him, he has seen what should not be seen. Out! Out! Drag him out! His two-tone tan leather Saxone shoes were ripped to pieces, dragged against the floor, caught between the wooden beams of the courtroom floor. They lifted him bodily, threw him into the waiting lorry, and the engine roared to life, roared and roared and suddenly all went quiet.

"Genturuman . . . genturuman. *Akowe.*" The driver shook him with amused patience. "Akowe, you no go get down? We done reach Ikorodu."

When Sipe eventually reached home, long past midnight, he did succeed in taking off his jacket by himself. It was Mrs. E., however, who took off his waistcoat and unlaced his Saxone shoes. There was nothing she could do but leave him to sleep in his worsted wool trousers, which, however, lived up to the catalogue guarantee and did not become rumpled or lose their crease by the following morning. One of his last thoughts as he crashed into bed was yet another footnote to his abandoned letter: *PPS. If ever I come face to face again with your beloved principal Reverend Beeston with his favourite theme—Sweet are the uses of adversity . . .* And suddenly he stopped, a beatific smile spreading all over his face. Layeni or no Layeni—he was certain now, more than ever, which line of business would engage their fullest attention. Those cars that passed him on the road, filled with the wedding guests—what made them all look so much alike? Indeed, come to think of it, was it not that same punishing worsted wool outfit he himself had been wearing under that scorching sun? That damnable Reverend Beeston—he appeared resolved to haunt his existence after all, but he had to give the devil his due—even Beeston's banalities appeared to have some ring of truth. Did missionaries make good businessmen, he wondered, just before he fell asleep.

III

LÍGÙN

Mariam shifted the bolt of mat in the corner of the room listlessly, without even looking down into the vacated space. To her husband, Josiah, the lone witness of her futile search, it was clear that she had no further interest in the result of her motions or, at least, no further expectations, and Josiah lost his temper.

"That makes some twenty times you have lifted that mat. Just what are you searching for?"

In a helpless tone which matched her gestures Mariam murmured, "I have told you, the cabin biscuit tin. The one with flower print."

His irritation rose even higher. "I know it's the tin. What is inside the tin?"

"But you know. The usual knickknacks . . ." and her voice trailed off into the practised murmur, which disappeared upwards into the bared roof. For by now she had climbed onto a stool; her indigo-dyed fingers raked the top of a wall and the junction of rafters but failed to make contact with any likely object. So she came down again and returned to a large basket which she had already gone through, and emptied its contents on the dung-plastered floor, polished black as her own skin. She began to separate the contents of the basket, carefully, shaking out the pieces of cloth. When she felt the back of her neck burning from Josiah's fierce gaze, she conceded, "And a little money."

Unappeased, Josiah snorted. "A little money. How much?"

Mariam's hand paused midway into its next probe, her spine snapping straight abruptly. "Oh yes, the lamp stand in the bedroom. Maybe . . ."

This time, Josiah screamed. "You searched it last night. I watched you. You dug in every crack of the wall and nearly tore out the bamboo beams! And if it is that same biscuit tin you've had since I foolishly married you, I cannot see any hole within the wall which is large enough to take it!"

Mariam gestured helplessly. "I can't think where else to look."

Squatting on the bamboo bench, on the edge nearest the door, Josiah looked out and nodded a grumpy greeting to an early passerby. He had said nothing when the frantic search began the night before, roused from his sleep by her movements, squinting at her. When he next woke up in the morning, the search turned out to have merely taken a pause for the night. He could not even recall her lying down during the night, only that when he opened his eyes in the faint glimmer of a yet distant dawn, he had glimpsed her through the doorway, crouched—he grinned—like an evil bird, as her puffed-up cheeks blew alive the breakfast fire. But then she would break off, look around her in response to a new idea, or leap up in the middle of stirring the corn-pap or lifting some firewood, dash to the newly thought-of hiding place, and proceed to violate its peace.

From his recumbent position he continued to watch her for a while, then got up, ignoring her entirely as he walked past into the courtyard, picked up a calabash of water, and flushed the last of the drowsiness from his face. After all, it was her cottage. If she chose to break it apart, that was her affair. Until her movements became unbearable and he wished he had not picked the previous night to be so liberal with the palm wine. His legs had felt heavy afterwards and he had succumbed to the invitation of the mat. Josiah liked his morning peace: a seat by the door, or a position by the window with his elbows on the broad lintel, chewing-stick idly traversing a set of teeth which gleamed from time to time in greetings to a passing acquaintance. Not like this morning, with flying arms dipping into and scratching at innocent hollows and receptacles.

Josiah sought consolation, reached into the depths of the pouch of his *agbada* and mentally dared her, as she glanced past him, to approach and look for her missing object in that vast pocket. He took out his snuffbox, slowly opened the lid, keeping a bemused eye on his distracted companion. Happily, she returned to her cooking. Years of practice nested the shallow tin snugly in his palm while short powerful fingers of the same left hand secured the cover. He pinched a few grains—it was too early in the day for a large dose—and flattened them into paste on the centre of his tongue. As he closed the tin carefully, his mood appeared to improve and he leaned back to enjoy himself. His sneeze came on cue and he felt better still.

"There is one place you haven't looked."

Mariam fell cleanly into the trap. She spun round. "Where? Where?"

Josiah stabbed the empty air through the doorway. His fingers pointed unwaveringly in the direction of the pit-latrine: "There!"

Mariam cursed herself, then cursed the man under her breath. Aloud, she merely complained. "Don't you think it's too early in the morning for that kind of play?" Unable to think of a fresh place to search for the moment, she turned to pay some attention to the frothing pot on the fire.

Josiah nodded in solemn agreement. "So it is. And now answer the question you have been dodging like a five-year-old: How much is this missing money that is driving you mad?"

"It is not even my money," she wailed.

"Oh God, protect me from this woman! Mariam! I said, how much money have you lost? I know it is not your money. I know it is not your money because you would not be dancing around like a scalded cat over your own money. I know it is not your money because if it had been your money you would have asked me straight out: Did you borrow the money I left here? I know it not your money because you do not keep your own money in that ancient biscuit tin. If you kept money in that tin it could only be because you did not want to confuse it with your own money. I know where you keep your own money, woman! So, for the last time . . ."

Mariam slowly stirred the *ogi,* a mere reflex action, born of daily preparations, but her mind was far away. "How will I tell them? This is not *oju lasan.* * Nobody entered this house. Nobody even knew the money was kept with me . . ."

Josiah opened his mouth to speak, closed it, and got up. He quietly gathered up his farm implements—he had stopped there the previous evening on his way from the farm—threw his work clothes in a heap into a basket, and left the home of his senior wife without his breakfast.

Mariam remained by the fire, stirring the porridge, her mind far away from her surroundings. The bottom began to congeal, and finally the smell of burning brought her back to earth. She shrugged,

* In the normal course of nature.

pulled out some of the wood to reduce the heat. She did not mind the acrid taste; indeed, that burnt layer, browned and hardened dough like flat sour cake, was a delicacy in which she indulged from time to time. But for the business of the missing money, the monthly contribution of *esusu* by her women's self-help group, she would be peeling off that layer right now, scooping it out through the frothing pap, and setting it aside for herself. But this mystery . . .

The sum was staggering. Even if it had not been a strictly women's affair, one of those secrets kept from everyone, including—indeed, especially—husbands, the sum was too huge to reveal as casually as Josiah had demanded. It could affect the chance of getting it back. Mariam felt only a slight twinge of conscience for thinking in such direction, Christian believer though she was. But these things did happen. Converting to the faith did not stop them happening. And she knew that one of the first questions the *onisegun* would ask might be: "Have you told anyone?" Well, she had in a way, but she had not really "told" Josiah. She had been careful not to mention the amount, or its source. It was fortunate that the money was not men's business, any more than its disappearance was the work of a sneak thief rather than someone's "doing." Her mind had already run through a list of those who might wish such a loss on her and work hard to bring it about. And then Tenten . . . could he have something to do with it? There were far too many reasons why she had to be careful. How often had she seen the *onisegun* shake his head regretfully, muttering, "What a pity. What a pity. It makes things very difficult. If only you had not mentioned it aloud. If only you had kept it within. Now, you see, you have dispersed it with the mouth. That is going to make it more difficult, very difficult. What the human mouth scatters . . . well, I don't have to tell you." Mariam grew more hopeful. At least she had not "scattered" the missing money. Wherever it was, it would stay intact. She would seek help from those who knew about these things.

The timing troubled her. Was it by chance that the money chose to vanish just when the matter of Tenten hung over her head? Far too many of these related events, as if some force had determined to put her to the test. Like Job. Tenten's death had shaken her. He was her only brother, which made her now the closest surviving kin. There were relations in Sagamu; she would send word to them. Ajike would take the message, a trustworthy girl from Node's compound, quite grown-up for her age.

Then her mind turned to her son the schoolteacher. He would laugh at her, of course; he did not understand these things. Well, he did know of them. He was raised in full knowledge of the dangers of the world and the many ways to avoid them. One could not succeed all the time, of course—the missing tin was one example. Tenten's few possessions of any value were also in the tin, and the heirloom jointly owned by them. Still, everything had a remedy of its own. It was only a question of knowing where to look. Nothing ever happened by chance; money painstakingly put aside by one's own female group—all petty traders, weavers, food-sellers and so on—such money did not simply fly through the roof. There were always those for whom such schemes spelled envy, those outside the self-help scheme and with no will—or means—to start one of their own, and even well-off ones, whose comfort would be destroyed at the mere sight of the success of others. That was why the members swore to keep it a secret, even from their children. One never knew. It wasn't only that a child might innocently blurt out the secret. Some children were actually born that way, unwitting instruments of the evil in others. Mariam said a silent prayer of gratitude that her womb had never brought forth such a monster.

The thought of the son, doing so well in his teaching profession, cheered her up immensely. She was even happier to recall that the period of training was definitely over. Ilesa had been much too far away. Now he was nearer home, settled into married life, two children already, and doing very well at work. Only the continuing illness of his wife cast a shadow over their happiness, some stomach ailment which kept coming back. Still, if they stubbornly refused to try local remedies, what could she do? Josiah kept trying. Perhaps she ought to write him a letter. In any case there were many things to discuss: the cocoa farm; his plans for his junior brother—too bad, all the reports suggested that that one was not doing well, not doing well at all. Neither at his profession, nor in the evening school arranged for him, since he was too old to be admitted into a regular school. Oh yes, and there was the matter of the palm oil—now that had been pending much too long, nearly three years and it still wasn't over, not for her husband anyway. Gifts should not provoke contention, least of all gifts on the occasion of a newborn child. The sooner that was laid to rest, the better. She would get the son to speak to his father on that matter. And a new year was approaching.

She got up then, set down the porridge pot, and flicked the ladle to get rid of drips. She cleaned the ladle further with her forefinger, and her tongue pronounced it pleasantly burnt. Just as well Josiah had left without eating—he hated burnt *ogi* and found her taste perverse. A final glance around the room just to make sure there was no cranny she had overlooked, and she picked up her sponge and soap and headed for the mud-walled space which served as bathroom. She entered, pushed the sheet of corrugated iron in position to serve as a screen. In a moment, the soothing feel of the night-chilled water had begun to improve her outlook on a new day.

Fatuka, her favourite letter-writer, grumbled at being dragged out of bed, but Mariam was unmoved. That was the only warp she knew of in Fatuka as an efficient working man. It was sad to see a grown man still lolling about in his wrapper, chewing-stick in mouth, when half the world was already at work and some farmers were even sheltering from the sun's ferocity after a hard morning's labour. It made no difference that Fatuka's duties required that clients come to see him in his own house, where the verandah served as office. He should conduct himself like any of the clerks in the Treasury office, don a shirt and pair of trousers, and be dutifully at his desk awaiting clients. Instead, Fatuka merely interrupted some mundane chore such as warming up some food, buying breakfast from the passing hawker, or washing his clothes; the worst part of it was the casualness with which he asked his clients to wait while he completed such unclerical chores. On this particular morning, Fatuka had barely dragged himself awake.

"But you wrote your son only last week," he grumbled.

"What is it to you?" she countered.

"He sends you too much money, that's your problem, Mariam. If he didn't, you wouldn't have so much to waste on letter-writers."

She pretended to get ready to leave. "Well, if you want me to waste it on someone else . . ."

"No one else will take you." He laughed. "They are all afraid of Teacher. If they make a spelling mistake or commit what he calls a grammatical error, they know they'll be in for it when he comes home."

"And you are not afraid, I suppose."

"Not me. I write in Yoruba, not like those others who want to show off their English. And I'll tell you something, the day even your son decides to challenge my Yoruba, I will show him who has stayed home in the home village and who only comes back three or four times a year to taste *ebiripo*."

By now Fatuka had gathered up his pen, inkwell, and writing pad, adjusted the fold of his wrapper, and planted himself in front of his desk. *"Ise ya.* Shall I tell you what you wrote about the last time?" She knew he was teasing her, referring to an exchange in the distant past.

He dipped the nib in the inkwell and hung it over the pad. Mariam's gaze traversed the distance between her and her son, and her voice sounded almost disembodied. "Ile Lígùn . . ."

Fatuka dropped his hand. "How often do I have to tell you. Look!" And he thrust the pad in her face. "Don't you see this corner is already covered with writing? And on the opposite side, do you see that? *Omo mi owon.** As the clerk will tell you in any government office, I have opened a file for you. This is your special writing pad, for you and for you only. To save time, I have written your address on the top of every sheet. Look, look." He flicked through all the sheets. "See? There are only three people in this village who have their own writing pads with me. Fadeke Alaso, and you know what a busy trader she is. And that stubborn mule Node."

Mariam nodded sympathetically. "God take pity on him."

Fatuka shrugged. "Did he take pity on himself? A stubborn fool, that's what he was. His son went to do business with the Saro, sent one letter, one letter only, and then not another word."

"It must be twelve years now."

"Fifteen years. Fifteen! But he kept writing to him, wasting his life savings."

"Why did you write for him, then? Why did you not stop?"

Again Fatuka shrugged. "You know how it is. At first, it seems only right. You also hope the son will return. I mean, we all grew up with Ba'tunde. By the time you are sure he is never coming back, it is too late to persuade the old man. You know how abusive he can be. Each time I wrote his letter I told him my thoughts. Once he even threat-

* My dear son.

ened me with his walking stick. Well, it is all over now. Poor Tenten
was the one who could tell us what he tried to say, and now he is
gone."

Fatuka had begun to scribble beneath the address. "So now, the
date is in. So is *'Omo mi owon.'* Let's get on with your letter."

Mariam tried to compose her thoughts again, shifting her gaze this
time onto the pen and pad, but seeing neither. Her mind, by habit,
was preceding the letter to its destination.

"Omo mi owon," Fatuka repeated impatiently, but he knew very
well that she could not begin to speak to a son whom she had not yet
conjured into her immediate presence, within sight and hearing. At
last she was ready.

*"My dear son, I send you many greetings, and especially for the
care you are taking of your junior brother. I am told he is ill with*
sobia, *but that the worm has begun to emerge. I am glad of that.
Remember that just as Iya Jeje is, that is, your own child, so should
Foluso be to you. Grown as he is, he is only a child. He does not know
better, so don't worry about the other troubles I know he is causing
you."* She sighed with relief. That thorny problem was neatly taken
care of. She could now proceed to weightier matters.

*"I am informed that the boy has lost a bit of weight. Tell Iyawo
not to let that worry her. Now, know your father has been using the
matter of the palm oil sent to you and your wife to abuse me. Your
father says it was a kerosene tin and I keep telling him that it was
only a keg. Your father was not at home that day, so how would he
know? I was the one who received it. I don't know who told him it
was a kerosene tin. Olorunise has not been back home since he went
on transfer, so he could not have said such a thing to him. Who then
is claiming it was a tin? The keg is here; I still use it to keep cooking
oil. I show it to him but he does not want to listen. So anytime we
quarrel he brings it up. He says, 'That is how you took half the oil
sent to your own son.' After two years! He is a strange man, your
father.*

*Anyway, enough about that. I forgot to add—*sobia *sometimes
brings a fever with it, so tell Foluso to take some of that* agbo *we
made you for Iya Jeje. He should not wait for fever to begin."*

Mariam fell silent, thinking rapidly and hesitating. She had to ask
for help, and she needed to let her son know why. Was a letter not

the same as scattering the matter with her mouth? Fatuka's case was more easily resolved; he was only a medium. And unlike what she sometimes heard about other letter-writers, he was *opa awo** itself when it came to keeping his clients' secrets. That was indeed what he had teased her about when he asked if he should remind her of the subject of her last letter to her son. On that occasion she had forgotten whether or not she had passed on some news, so she enquired—naturally, she thought—of the only person who could tell her, the letter-writer. The pompousness with which he had rebuked her! Like the bishop who sometimes came to deliver the sermon. Or even like one of those clerical officers at the Treasury announcing penalties for lateness in paying market rates! "Iya Foluso! You engage me to write your letters, not to memorialise the content of your personal affairs. When I have completed that assignation"—and he made a sound like one expelling air, then with his hands consigned the air into a deeper void—"that is the end of the contraction of business matter for me. I am not just an ordinary letter-writer. I am a coffeedetial secketries." Since Mariam could not read, she had missed the proclamation which affirmed his claim to all of Ìsarà in blazing colours on a board outside his window:

ADEbabs FATUKA—LETTER-WRIter aND COFFEEDetial SECKetries.
ALL ePIStolARY and DocUMental MATTERS UNderTAking.

But she knew that the sign-writer was her brother, the late Tenten, on whose recommendation she had first approached him.

That exchange had already put her mind at rest; this medium could not be regarded as a scattering agent. As for the letter itself, by the time it reached her son, she would have seen the *onisegun*. No harm could be done by letting her son know at this stage.

"My son, there is some trouble I must now tell you about. I have lost a large amount of money. It has given me great concern as I have never lost anything like this before. It is the esusu *money from my women's group, and as you know, I have always been the keeper if the person whose turn it is does not want to take it yet. There were*

---

* The staff of secrecy.

also some heirlooms and other small items in the tin, you know it, that tin with flower decoration which I have had before you were even born. And it has disappeared without trace. Anyway, I am looking into it with all the remedies I can muster, but first, I need some help from you in the matter of Tenten's burial because I have no one else to turn to, and the missing money has added to all my troubles."

She felt better. A sense of loneliness reduced meant even that her problems were nearly solved. She placed the modest fee on the table. It was time to turn her mind to other matters that Tenten's death had provoked. She watched Fatuka continue writing for a while and knew that he was sending her greetings to the teacher's wife and to both the children. From her file Fatuka retrieved a ready-stamped and addressed envelope, sealed the letter with a ritual finality, and handed it to her. She rose, adjusted her shawl, and bade the letter-writer good day.

Fatuka let her walk the length of the pathway, then made the usual bet with himself: Would she head straight for the postbox or would she first look for a chance traveller to Abeokuta? As he watched her turn first into the tailor's shop to make enquiries, he sighed. Nine years her letter-writer, and he had yet to persuade her to accept a plain envelope, keeping the stamp apart in case the letter found a personal courier—which was quite often the case. Her son no longer bothered. Whenever he found Mariam's letter awaiting him on his desk, he would first check the stamp. He soon became adept at easing off the ones that came unused.

The girl, Ajike, returned long after dark, just as an anxious Mariam was preparing to set out again for Node's household in order to consult with Ajike's mother. Now she stared at the dust-covered waif, her mind reluctant to accept the result of her mission to Sagamu, where the remnant clan of Fadebo was still to be found. The girl had brought back nothing but the tidy bones of rejection. No evasions, no excuses, no vague promises, not even those meagre strands of meat a woman could lodge between her teeth and pick upon to string out hope. Her relations had not even tried to get rid of her awkward messenger with a lie whose bitter truth would be only too apparent at the receiving end: "Go ahead, tell her we may even get there before you. I have to wait for So-and-So to return from a journey to Kontagora; she keeps the family purse and will know what to do" ... and so on. No, these broken branches of my family tree, she thought matter-of-factly, they have simply tossed back the bundle in my lap. But she would not give up immediately.

"You are sure it was Carpenter you saw?"

The girl remained firm. "Mama, I know Carpenter very well."

"And he said . . . ? What exactly did you hear him say? Try and remember the words he spoke. How did he put the message—try and remember, Ajike."

The girl repeated everything. "Brother Carpenter was in his workshop when I arrived. I greeted him and I gave him your greetings just as you told me. Then I delivered your message about Tenten. Before that he responded very well and asked about everyone at home. But when I gave him your message he raised his voice at me. He said, 'Well, what does she want me to do? The only farms we go to are the *akuro* beside the streams and those are miles away. The soil is burnt here; people travel far to get anything to sell in the market. They will be away for days.'"

The girl stopped but Mariam egged her on. "En-hen?"

"So I asked, 'What shall I tell Mama Foluso?' It was then he said, 'Are you blind, or do you see any customers in my shop? Tell her when you get back how many customers you saw ordering tables or beds or buying furniture. Not even coffins. Nobody seems to be dying in Sagamu, whatever they choose to do in Ìsarà.' Then he picked up his *buba,* put it on, and went away, leaving me in the workshop. I waited a long time for him to return. When I began to fear that I would miss the last lorry home, I left for the motor park."

"That was when you saw him again, *abi?*"

"Yes. He was sitting in the beer shop, drinking with some men. And the last lorry had left, so I had to take bicycle transport, then walk the rest of the way."

Mariam nodded. A well-brought-up girl, she thought appreciatively, could be relied upon to deliver a message faithfully. She knew that everything had happened exactly as Ajike had described it. Her mind shifted beyond her through the open door and she asked aloud, of no one in particular, "So who will bury Tenten?"

The girl began to shift from one leg to the other. The evening harmattan chill was setting in and she had clearly sweated from the long walk, mostly uphill. When she sneezed, Mariam remembered that Ajike ought to be returned quickly to her home. She undid the knot in the corner of her wrapper and brought out two *onini*, which she handed to her.

"You did very well, Ajike. Take this. And greet your mother for me. I'm on my way to thank her myself."

The girl curtseyed quickly and left, Mariam shouting a parting admonition after her to take her damp clothes off as soon as she arrived home. Ajike liked this elderly woman who lived by herself and sold all sorts of *wosi-wosi*. Often she would take it on herself to pause by her window and ask if she had any errands to run. She knew of her son, too, the next thing to an *oyinbo*, who taught in Abeokuta, perhaps the source of those rare items which she displayed on a rough table outside her window. Why didn't she own a real shop, Ajike wondered, skipping across the broken gutters on her way home.

Left alone, Mariam continued to stare through the door. She got up at last, went to the corner where she had stacked her merchandise for the night, and picked up the tin that contained the previous day's sales. It rang with the hopelessness of its meagre contents, the exact sum of which she knew already. That did not prevent her from taking off its lid, staring at the few coins, then replacing the tin in its place in a corner of the laden tray. As her eyes encountered the dung-plastered floor, she slapped the back of one hand into the cup of the other repeatedly and asked again, louder than before, "So who will bury Tenten?"

Carpenter was the head of her cluster of blood relations in Sagamu, yet he had dismissed her plight so offhandedly. Not even a promise to summon a family meeting. That said it all. Her new family in Ìsarà had done its part; she could ask no more of them. As soon as they learned of Tenten's death, Node's household had levied two shillings from each adult towards *egunsale*. * She knew only too well how little was the profit they made from their petty trading, even at festive seasons—harvest, New Year, and the Muslim festivals. Two shillings was a big hole in their savings, there was no doubt about that, even

* Pre-funeral rites.

for someone like Tenten, who had looked after Node since that unlucky farmer became paralysed. It was Tenten who brought about this intimacy with Node's household, turning himself into Node's arms, legs, tongue, and even mind since Node became totally disabled. Even so, she was touched by the promptness of their aid.

The women had brought the money as soon as they heard. She received them in that same room and watched as they solemnly piled the shillings on a mat at her feet—twenty-two shillings in all. Node had sent nothing, but she understood. With Tenten gone, who else was there that could read his thoughts, follow the faint tremor of his lips, and understand their message? Only she, Mariam. It was only when the shillings, the dark brown colour of *robo*—her mind sought out the strangest irrelevancies—only when the shillings began to pile up did she shed tears for Tenten, as if the loss of her only brother had finally come to her at the sight of this aid towards *egunsale*.

This was her new family, quite different from the Christian fellowship with whose members she did the monthly *esusu*. These were mostly wives from Node's compound, and his sisters also from their married homes. With them she undertook the forty-mile round-trip trek doing the markets between Ìsarà and Abeokuta, where they camped in her son's compound. Even before Node's illness, trade had pulled them together, being such close neighbours. Then Tenten pulled them closer still. His sign-writing venture had attracted only two patrons—the results showed very clearly that he was neither gifted nor more than barely literate. The palm-wine shack was the other patron, after Fatuka. Tenten had begun by working on her husband's farm but found his nature too cantankerous, so he moved in with Node and became his right-hand man on his farm. This was the new family she had found after her own disappeared to Sagamu and abandoned her to her marriage with Josiah. Raising her face to the women as they grouped around her in her living room, she had not felt bereaved. They said little, and that was mostly to do with the message they would take to *osugbo*. The eldest wife of Node undertook that errand—Tenten was ready for burial. And not just the burial for a nobody. None of the rites that were his due should be skimped. Tenten had people of his own.

And then the shocks began. First, *osugbo* declared that Tenten was not their death. It was not possible! Mariam could not believe her ears. Not *osugbo's* death? What did they mean? That Tenten was not one of them? Since her own conversion, she had striven to bring her brother also into the Christian fold but had finally accepted failure. That was when she saw how Tenten had taken charge of Node in his helpless state—not even a mother hen looked after her chicks the way her brother looked after Node. He had been avoided, abandoned by others who called themselves his friends—and they were Christians. So Mariam ceased to pester Tenten, left him to his pursuits, which, from what she saw, did not appear to be short on "charity" or "love thine neighbour," any more than the activities of those of her own Christian faith. And perhaps it was from that new outlook also that she found she had begun to listen for the drums of *osugbo*, as if she sought to understand the message of their ponderous throb.

She shocked her church group finally, in the schoolroom where they held their Bible class. The catechist was expounding a Bible passage when he stopped, pointed a trembling finger through the window at a stern-faced, silent procession clad in indigo wrappers and patterned shawls, heading for the *osugbo* house near the *aafin.* *

"Your Christian mission," he exhorted his flock, "remains unfinished as long as such pagan sights as these defile your gaze in Ijebuland. Your faith is sham unless you bring them into the fold of our Lord Jesus Christ."

"Why?" Mariam demanded before she could stop herself. "They do no harm."

It was the longest silence ever, and Mariam found herself the centre of unaccustomed turmoil in the Bible class. Catechist Aderounmu, transferred to Ìsarà barely three months before, began to wonder if he had not been thrown, unprotected, into the very tower of Babel. He would have been totally devastated if he had heard what Mariam, at first a little cowed by her outburst, then somewhat recovered, muttered under her breath: "After all, Yode's father is also a Christian. Yet he says that the church bells only sound in the ear, while the drums of *osugbo* resound in the pit of one's stomach."

After this, however, her momentary rebelliousness dissipated of itself and she began to murmur explanations. She apologised. It was all clearly the voice of the devil which spoke through her. The class

* Palace.

was relieved and reassured. And when she added, truthfully, that it was the unchristianly conduct of some of their own Christian fellowship that had troubled her, the catechist was convinced that it had indeed been no more than a momentary aberration. Mariam bowed her head to receive his admonition and agreed to pay a fine of threepence.

So now, this same *osugbo* dared deny that Tenten was their death! Whose death was her brother's, then, and who would bury him? The church?

In a sudden burst of energy, Mariam took up her headtie, turned it into a sash around her waist, and went bareheaded into the night.

Node, three-quarters paralysed, spent most of his nights and days in a specially woven cane-and-wicker chair. Josiah's son had sent it, the handiwork of his pupils. Its design had been inspired by an illustrated article in *In Leisure Hours* which advocated the use of local materials for "sensible, cheap, and durable native furniture." The article did not lie. The reclining chair had become glossy with unbroken occupation while Node's body converted itself to its curvature. Node's son Ba'tunde then had it copied by a local artisan, shipped the copy to Freetown in Sierra Leone, where a prospective business partner was setting up a factory for the manufacture of "durable furniture made in native styles but with European elegance." Ba'tunde wrote one letter, then washed his hands of the nuisance of a paralysed father. But first he broke into the cripple's secret cache—Node believed neither in banks nor in the post office savings scheme—and made off with nearly the entire life-savings of the helpless father. Node became even more dependent on his wives—and on Tenten, his principal farmhand. He took it all, like his paralysis, with an unnatural calm, which was not shared by the rest of the household.

His paralysis especially. This was undoubtedly the work of an enemy within. Only Node, whose mind evidently had also been affected by his stroke, could even think that it was a failure of his body all of its own. He had, moreover, the example of his father before him; he had also succumbed to the same affliction. To cap it all, he was one of the convertites who religiously believed in the good Lord's "Vengeance is mine." Not so his wives, whom, despite his conversion, he had refused to disperse. His youngest, however, was the one acknowledged in the church register. And the others, supported by neighbours and relations, all knew that she was the agent through whom his enemy had worked this evil. And they knew, even more confidently, who this enemy was.

Tenten, and quite early too, broke through the carapace that first encased Node's mind. His stubborn patience earned him the language that was forced through the patriarch's twisted lips, and he learned also how to speak to him in turn. Thus Tenten it was who let Node know, barely in time, that the "agent" had been identified, and that justice had been plotted against her, his youngest wife, Binutu. The other wives and his relations had met and consulted. The result was unambiguous—the hand was the hand of Alarade, his closest friend; and the agent was Saanu's mother. So Binutu was dragged forth and faced with her accusers. Yes, she admitted it, she had indeed slept with Alarade; Saanu was not even Node's child, but her lover's. Their affair had begun a long time before, since she began to trade in Lagos, staying, as was right, in the household of the best friend of her husband. But to act as agent to harm her husband? No! She demanded any test they could think of—the truth would reveal her innocence. They locked her up, confined her to a room while they debated her sentence.

The news travelled quickly to Binutu's relations in Ode. They came to Ìsarà in the dead of night and set up camp, facing the home of Node. Their demand was simple: They wanted Binutu given back to them, with her child, both safe and sound. Node's side replied that this was a crime committed against a son of Ìsarà; Ìsarà and Ìsarà alone would decide what to do. The accusers let it be known that Jagun, against whose word as mouthpiece of Ifa no one dared voice a doubt, had himself confirmed their findings. What did Ode mean? How dared they interfere? The town seethed with rumours. Node's compound became a war camp under siege.

Node raced against time, and it was lucky that he had Tenten as ally. What passed between them both no one knew for certain. But Tenten went back and forth between Node and the house of *osugbo*. Finally, five days after it all began, he returned with the spokesman of *osugbo* himself in tow. The case was not unusual, he declared. Quite simple. The earlier consultations were indeed accurate: Binutu was the agent, no question at all about that. But why had no one thought of also consulting the same Ifa to find out whether or not she had been, as was common, an unwitting agent? "You all rushed off with half the message; you failed to probe further, to find out whether or not she had brought the thing of her own will, with her own knowledge, or whether Alarade had used her without her knowledge! Has none of you ever heard of *magun*, for instance, which a man can place on his wife? He does this without her knowledge, to protect her chastity and punish the intruder on his private land. Do you think that *magun* is an only child? How stupidly you have all behaved!" The priest chastised them thoroughly, made them so crestfallen that even the matter of Binutu's infidelity was somehow forgotten. Well, not entirely forgotten, simply accepted as one of those sins that prove fortunate in the end. For Node was now incapable of producing more children, so who could fail to see the hand of Fate in a wife's infidelity which had resulted in a child!

And thus peace returned to Node's corner of Ìsarà. *Osugbo* fined Binutu two fowl, a bolt of white cloth, and a keg of palm oil, which her relations gladly paid before they departed for home. In addition she had to go through cleansing for the evil that had been placed upon her. She made *ekuru* and served it through the town. Messengers were sent to inform Alarade in Lagos that his present abode would have to become his permanent home unless he was prepared to undo the heinous injury he had so treacherously inflicted on a trusting friend. The child, Saanu, belonged of course to the man whose roof still sheltered Binutu as wife. And there the matter ended.

Mariam replayed the drama through her mind as she trudged through a black night, pockmarked by oil lamps and slashed by weak wedges of hurricane-lamp light through open doors and windows. Node would have the answer to this riddle, of that she was certain. Even without Tenten, he would know just what to do. Like her brother, Mariam had also acquired an ease of communication with Node; the only difference was that while Tenten had appeared to read his mind, she had to place her ear against his lips, then somehow make sense of the belchlike spurts that issued through near-immobile lips. When Tenten was compelled to stay on the farm for days at a time, Node's household would often turn to her for help when Node's wishes became impossible for them to understand. Yet Tenten,

Tenten who moved back and forth between *osugbo* and Node's household during the crisis of Node's paralysis, that same Tenten it was whose death, they claimed, was not *osugbo*'s. So who would bury him? Her mind flew to many possible answers. Had Tenten, for instance, died still "owing" them? There were stories, never really resolved. If it was not *osugbo*, there was always some other cult, stubbornly awaiting the closing of the balance sheet before they would even permit relations near the corpse. They took over the body, even the house, if he owned it. And that was that. A new initiate could promise many things—it all depended what he craved: wealth, recognition, children . . . even longevity. Everything had a price and that price did not exclude even the life of an innocent. Every preacher knew a hundred such stories, each one with its own bloodcurdling details. The listeners had long learned to accept the frequent change of details for each dire event—after all, was there ever smoke without fire? The details were considered trivial. Mariam regretted now that she had not stayed closer to her brother; maybe she would have gleaned something to help her understand why he was now untouchable to the *osugbo* after his death.

When she placed her ear close to the lopsided opening between Node's lips after posing the question for a third time, she was astonished at the simplicity of the answer which she deciphered from those jumbled sounds.

"Didn't you know? *Osugbo* cannot bury Tenten. He is an albino. The rites for an albino's death are forbidden to them."

Mariam exploded angrily. "But why did they not simply say so?"

She understood the contortion of face to mean that she should again place her ear close to his lips. "Who did you send?" he asked.

"Iya Ajike."

A throaty chuckle came through Node's lips. "You mean you sent one of you? Hm. See how foolish you women are? You expect *osugbo* to tell you what they can or cannot do? Of course all they will tell you is: He is not our death. If they tell you they cannot perform the death rites, the next thing you will want to know is why."

"Well, why not?" Mariam insisted.

"You see? Now go to the *ogboni**—I mean, let Josiah go. Either

---

* An ancient conclave of elders.

Tenten is their death, or they will tell you who must receive him as theirs. They will do what is needed."

Mariam sighed and took her leave, then headed for Josiah's home. From a distance she could see a glimmer of light issuing from the cottage and she breathed a sigh of relief. Josiah played many roles in Ìsarà's affairs, not all of which she understood, only that it often meant long hours into the night, meeting at the home of a chief, in the palace, or in *iledi* itself. Josiah had forsworn *osugbo* after his baptism, but that did not prevent his taking his seat at their meeting place when the affairs of Ìsarà brought the elders together in the courtyard of *osugbo*. She breathed a silent prayer to God that Josiah would cease altogether from accompanying them into the inner recesses. There, she knew, was where the danger lay. Then there was the matter of the other wife. Mariam shrugged. At least she did not have to seek him there tonight. Josiah took everything the wrong way these days. Something, she did not know what, had been eating him of late, making him more grumpy than usual. Their marriage had never been easy but lately it had grown tempestuous. Every little thing resulted in a quarrel.

Josiah sat on a raffia bench, squinting in the light of an oil lamp into a book held close to his face. His spectacles were the consequence of his adventure into the reading world, and the sight stopped Mariam in her tracks. She had not known that Josiah had begun to read. Clearly the efforts of her son whenever he came home on holidays had begun to yield results. Half-bitten pieces of kola nut lay strewn on the bench beside him, a certain sign that whatever Josiah was doing caused him great effort. But it was the sight of her husband hunched over a C. M. S. hymnal companion, looking for all the world like an owl with those spectacles, that brought some light relief into Mariam's mood. She stood, stared, and a chuckle escaped her, which she promptly stifled.

Josiah had heard, however, and looked up angrily. Mariam then knocked unnecessarily on the side of the doorway. "Can I come in?"

"What did you find to laugh at? Did an *opidan** precede you here to keep you amused?"

Mariam refused to rise to the bait. She entered fully into the room

* A magic-performing masquerade.

and came straight to the point. "Baba Yode, only you can talk to the *ogboni* over the matter of Tenten."

"I no longer enter *osugbo,*" Josiah lied, and turned back to his book.

"You don't have to. Jagun is your friend and you visit him at home. He can speak to them for me."

Josiah shook his head. "I am a Christian. I even hold a title in the church. Just think how it would sound when it is found out that I took my in-law to *ogboni* for burial."

"And what of me? Am I not a Christian too? I am his only sister. Am I now to abandon his corpse?"

"Hn-hn, you see the difference. You are his blood relation. Everybody will understand. In my own case—"

"Did you not marry me? What does that make Tenten to you?"

"*Iyekan,* not *ibatan.* The burial of Tenten is a blood matter. I can have no hand in it."

Something was not quite right. Mariam recognised the stubborn streak, but accompanying it was a plain irrationality which could not survive any form of scrutiny. She thought of calling on Babarinde, the neighbouring goldsmith, to intervene in the discussion, so certain was she that Josiah was not making sense. How could he refuse to act as simple intermediary between his wife and the elders of *osugbo*? She had no living relations in Ìsarà, no uncles, not even a distant cousin. So who was she supposed to turn to when such a matter came up? Yes, that would be the best course. Let a man take her part in this matter. As she turned to go, however, another thought struck her. Perhaps there was a simpler reason for Josiah's stubbornness. And for his recent moods, come to think of it. Feigning innocence, she said, "All right. I shall find someone else to be the father of the family. So will you give me your *egunsale* now, or shall I let the women come and collect it tomorrow?"

Mariam knew she had hit home when he flung the hymn book aside and leapt up angrily. "Do you understand nothing of what I am telling you? *Egunsale* is what they are going to use to make all the *etutu* and other things which you know are forbidden to me. And you still want me to put money into something like that? Just take yourself away, woman. If you want to bury Tenten in my backyard, I shall dig the grave myself. We will say a prayer over him. But *ogboni*? I did not lead him to *iledi* when he was alive. So I am not taking his body there, now that he is dead. Now get back to your house and leave me in peace." He turned his back on her and stormed off into his inner room, flinging back at her a reminder not to leave the door ajar "to your sister witches."

So Mariam knew that her guess was correct; Josiah was stone broke. "I will have to write to your son," she said.

Nodding vigorously, he turned round. "You should have done that to start with instead of trying to make me do something unchristianly. Write and tell him to send you money for *egunsale*. He is far removed from it all. I doubt if he even knows what *egunsale* is, so he won't be committing a sin."

"All right," Mariam agreed. "I shall write him another letter. Do you want me to ask that he send something for you too?"

The barb went home and Josiah reacted as she expected, furiously. "Did I tell you I needed money? And even if I did, who are you to help me ask for money from my own son? Just go about your business, woman, and let me be." He stormed into his bedroom, pulling down the matting which served as curtain. Then he stood behind it and watched Mariam's knowing grin, grinding his teeth in frustration since he could not do what he really wished, which was to rush out, grab her by the neck, and fling her out of doors. How would he face the parish priest if she chose to make a report of such a simple matter between husband and wife? His mind reached out then to his son the schoolteacher. He was not only married to one wife; he actually shared the same roof with her. Did he ever undergo such trying moments, Josiah asked himself? And how did he cope? He, Josiah, could at least seek consolation in the home of his second wife. Come to think of it . . . Josiah went round the house and picked up his farming tools. He would leave for work the following morning from the house of Desinwa, his second wife.

Two elderly men emerged from the shadows before her cottage when she returned. They bore a staff which she recognised—it belonged to the *olifan*—and she wondered why she had not thought of them. They greeted her as the wife of Josiah, mother of Akinyode and Foluso, and the one born after the man once known as Tenten. Then they asked her if she had missed anything.

Strange, she found that their presence did not surprise her at all. If anything, she felt she had anticipated some such visit, and when she told them about the missing tin, she was not astonished by what happened next. The shorter man flipped his shoulder shawl aside and beneath it was the missing tin. He held it out to her, its flowered patterns still discernible though its once-bright colours were now faded to a pale brown, monochrome with age.

"Is this what you missed?"

She nodded.

Holding out the box to her, the man continued. "We have removed only what is not yours. Look inside the tin. If you wish to dispute what has been taken, now is the time to tell us."

Mariam found that her hands trembled somewhat as she took the box and prised open the lid. She did not bother to undo the knot in the piece of cloth in which the *esusu* account was tied; even the shape confirmed that no one had tampered with it. But the family heirlooms were gone, and so was a small packet that contained an *iyun* bracelet and a copper ring which Tenten had long ago given her for safekeeping. She looked in turn at the two impassive faces, which, in the dim glow from surrounding cottages, looked like dark skulls on which the white, tight-fitting caps appeared to float. The evening had turned chilly, as with most harmattan evenings, and she shivered.

"No," she said softly. "Everything is here which is mine."

This time the other man spoke. "We cannot bury Tenten but he is our death. We have sent for those who will bury him. Send the *egunsale* to us at *iledi* and all the rites will be performed. Later, someone will take you to where he has been buried."

He hit the ground with his staff once, then turned away. Soon there were only the two slouched shadows receding into the night.

IV

TISA

T he head teacher was a firm believer in cause and effect, so when a sigh emerged from the depths of his disputed soul and the slouched form of the Genie of the Bottle followed, he assigned credit where credit was due: His sigh had indeed produced the apparition. *Aje ku l'ana, omo ku l'oni; tani ko s'aimo pe aje lo p'omo naa je?** Come to think of it, was the Genie himself not a kind of *aje?* The teacher savoured the thought, stored it away with a smile for future airing among his fellow ex-Ilés. And he did not imply the Genie's physical appearance but the genus: Genie. And no puns intended, he frowned at his invisible audience. The Genie's presence at that moment provided its own answer to the question: Which side of the disputed territory would such a blatantly biased intrusion reinforce? The urge to escape from his desk for the rest of the day, and not simply for a dinner break, now gained the upper hand.

Earlier, his chances had been even, though desperate. Alone in his makeshift study, that is, the famed corner of his front living room into which Soditan sometimes gave the appearance of having been stamped from adolescence, he had battled against the ambush of the dying year, his mind near-jammed by the log of accumulated chores. From time to time he would taunt himself, audibly, not simply muttering aloud. The teacher did not believe in wasting breath, and when a crisis stirred his spirit into protest—or admonition—he would address himself directly, volume trimmed to the solitary audience, punctuation supplied by his habit of sucking in air with his tongue from behind the ridge of the upper teeth. Such deliberate monologues also served to rehearse his voice in preparation for reading the Sunday lesson. It was now Saturday afternoon, quite late. If his work

---

* The witch cried last night and the child died at dawn; who dare claim it was not the witch that murdered the child?

had gone according to plan, he would by now be in the emptied schoolroom, moulding his voice around the selected passage, noting sections for stress and perfecting different tones for a variety of subtle inflections. Unlike some other lay readers, the teacher did not believe in bravura renditions, or indeed any form of vocal ostentation.

For some moments, he pretended that the Genie was not there. The battle was already lost, he acknowledged, but at least he would spend a little time frustrating his intruder. It was futile to deny that the rout had begun much earlier. The mean blow beneath the belt—slightly above, to be precise; the teacher was well tutored in the human anatomy and did not encourage imprecision—that blow had been sneaked in under a feint of aromas which came from the direction of the kitchen. His acute sense of smell had already identified the advance guard of crayfish and peppers simmering in palm oil. Accurately, he anticipated the composition of the next wave of assault; his nostrils twitched and his stomach sounded a gentle drumroll. The crayfish stew's simmer merged with an agglutination of black-eyed beans, which had been left to consolidate their potency all afternoon, studded through and through with chunks of lean smoked pork and *odunkun.* The aroma cut through his study with impudent ease, clinging to the ceiling mat, investing the front room so thoroughly that the teacher could no longer pick up a file or a school report without absorbing the dense fumes through his fingertips. And so he sighed, and the Genie appeared, soundlessly, as was his wont, raking the inner recesses of the teacher's modest home with his steel-rimmed pebble glasses, his gaze coming finally to rest on the hallowed corner, benevolently, a wide beam slashed across his normally lethargic face.

Graciously, the teacher conceded that the Genie's presence was quite superfluous; his will to continue his work was already fully subverted. To his caller, however, he said, not looking up from his desk, "You are not here. I merely sighed and you appeared. All I have to do is sigh again and you will vanish."

But it was not a sigh that escaped from the teacher but a repeat of the long, low rumble from his stomach. The visitor looked startled, glanced questioningly, then with understanding, in the direction of the kitchen. Still, he made a mental note of the event, for it was most unusual. The teacher, he knew, was a being of such precise habits that his stomach should not rumble like that of mere mortals. His eating schedule, like his work, was planned to the last detail. One made way for the other on the designated minute, permitting no encroachments from exigencies. The Genie's nose, a much celebrated landmark even beyond the city limits, described a half-arc in the air. A massive outcrop which engaged in games with his spectacles, its upward jerk was timed to arrest the downslide of that contraption. One could see that it was a much-practised manoeuvre. His ears were just as impressive, broad coco-yam-shaped leaves, as fibrous-looking and almost as large. He had a skin of pure anthracite, contrasting so remarkably with that—unusual for an African—aquiline nose. His gaunt, tall frame enabled him to reach any shelf in his pharmacy without the aid of a ladder, packing case, or stool. And now his shuttlecock of an Adam's apple worked in sympathy with his own surrender to the message that had pervaded the sanctuary of his friend. Unlike the teacher, however, he felt only contentment and undisguised anticipation.

"I take it then," he smiled, "that Madam is home, and that you shall, in a short order of things, cease from thy labours?"

The teacher ignored him, so he let himself into the room, reaching effortlessly down to manipulate the latch at the very bottom of the lower half of the twin door. Inside the room, he stood over the teacher's table, his head brushing the low ceiling. Still the teacher refused to look up; he knew full well what the Genie's next utterance would be. It was not long in coming:

"Me-e-e-e-to-di-ko!"

For the pharmacist, the teacher's tyrannising stacks of files, school registers, circulars and memoranda, account books, inkwells, and rubber stamps and pads constantly presented an organising sleight-of-hand. It was evidence, he would remark, of a meticulous industry, an exceptional gift of those rare individuals with tidy instincts. He was not alone in his opinion. The teacher's desk, whether at home or in school, was a tableau of inanimate queuing. The pharmacist had no inhibition over restating the obvious, and no visit to the teacher's home was ever begun until he had performed the ritual of professing some variant of his admiration. This time, he spiked his eulogy with an equally familiar barb:

"No one can take it away from you, my dear Yode. I have said it before and will forever say it: Your desk, even at its busiest, manipulates the eye to perceive an order of the same quality as that conveyed by your noble garden to the cultivated eye." His eyes twinkled with mischief. "The difference, I suggest, is that while one is redolent with Nature's lavenders, the other only smells of gum arabica. Please . . ."

He raised his hand to stop the teacher's expected reaction. "An illustration only, my dear Yode, nothing but a comparison. I said nothing of the spirit of frugality, of Ijebuism, the fact that blood must out, and so on and so forth—no. I merely compared two different states of order, and their accompanying odours. Talking of which . . ."

He sniffed, ostentatiously this time, and jerked his head in the direction of the kitchen, then turned to flick with his long finger at the pile of papers immediately in front of the teacher.

"Naturally you will wish to work until Madam announces that the table is laid and dinner is on the table. I have, on the other hand, closed shop for the day and have sauntered here for an evening's leisure. As a considerate person, I shall leave you to continue your labours in tranquility." He dived down suddenly and picked up a journal from a pile in the basket. "Is this the latest? I suspect, regrettably, that I have fallen behind in my subscription. I have not received the last two or three issues."

"Find out for yourself," the teacher retorted. "As for dinner, I shall ask my wife to boil you some gum arabica."

"Of course, of course," the Genie said soothingly. "I have no doubt that in her practised hands even gum arabica will prove more than palatable."

He sat in the armchair and eased out his legs to their fullest length. The teacher cast a glance towards the windowsill on which the contentious jar of yellow viscous fluid with brown and black impurities sat conspicuously. He was quite unrepentant over his preference for this local product, which he made from the secretions of rain trees lining the broader paths of the parsonage. The fact that the school could obtain heavily discounted supplies of imported jars, with brushes, from the missionary bookshop did not deter him. At every handwork lesson, he supervised the pupils also in making their own gum and improvising brushes. The heavier glue for carpentry work was boiled from compressed slabs of resin, imported; that much he had had to concede. Their own product lacked the strength needed to hold the wooden joints together. But gum for paperwork, papier-mâché models for geography lessons, or indeed lampshades or fibre projects? No—he preferred to spend the school money on more worthwhile items.

Knowing that he had at most another half hour to work gave a renewed spurt to his flagging energies, and he bent over his desk, shutting out the presence of his visitor. In that half-hour reprieve he attempted to deserve some of that reputation which earned him the nickname corrupted from "Methodical."

First he tackled the draft balance sheets of the school accounts. That was a chore he hated, not so much from the nature of it but because he dreaded to make a mistake. He could leave it to the school secretary; in fact, until two years before he had always left it to that employee, whose task it really was, contenting himself with merely vetting his arithmetic. Two years ago, however . . . he shuddered over the memory of the downfall of that diligent servant of the diocese, who proved to have been more diligent in his own cause.

Next it was the turn of the class registers. The pharmacist was right; they were stacked in a distinguished pile, each edge so precisely matched with the next that they could be taken for a single thick ledger. It was his duty to close the registers for the year with a diagonal line across the space below the last entry, write his comments within the right of the two triangles thus created, and seal it off with his signature. The signature was another source of marvelling; across the lined page it looked like an ornamented cluster of music notes, appropriately perhaps, since music, like gardening, was one of his passions. The comments entered—they had of course been carefully drafted in advance, and reviewed at least half a dozen times in the past week—he replaced the registers in their previous position, cleanly stacked as before.

On their return journey, his hands bypassed the Christmas cards. They would wait till the following day, which, being Sunday, did not admit of the work he was then doing. The signing of Christmas cards, with insertions of special sentiments where appropriate, was a chore which could not be considered unseemly on God's ordered day of rest. He moved on to the file of letters to parents, which were arranged in different categories. Some were straightforward replies to normal parental enquiries—these were the easiest. Stern warnings to fee-defaulting parents followed; he signed them rapidly, first skimming through to ensure that their messages were exactly as persuasive, or stern and uncompromising, as he wanted them to be.

The musical flourish of his signature beneath the next group of letters would provide no music to the ears of their recipients. These were terminal, the result of teachers' meetings, earlier warnings, and even summons to the affected parents—a pupil caught cheating at examinations, stealing, incurable unhygienic habits "which endanger the health of others." One or two cases of premature sexuality. The chronic dunces, "whose places would be better occupied by others with proven aptitudes." In some cases, recommendation that the rejected pupil would be "best apprenticed to a trade where his scholastic abilities would never be tested." Even as he signed these letters, he prepared his plans for evading the descent of relations, guardians, and go-betweens. Would there ever come a day, he wondered, when they would understand? Such decisions were part and parcel of the business of teaching. Each classroom had its numerical limit, and there were always new pupils queuing to enter all classes at different times of the year. Parents came on transfer from other stations. Sometimes a school would be closed down—usually in a remote station—for lack of teachers. The bright ones among them had to be given preference; it was only just.

Now take young Odebambi. He leaned back in his chair, holding up the letter for a final scrutiny. An obviously talented pupil, but only in subjects that held his interest. The strange thing was that those subjects took turns, so that, in the end, he demonstrated not merely potential but brilliance in nearly all his subjects—history, geography, grammar, arithmetic, and so on. Even handwork. But would he do it all at once? Not Odebambi. Cajoling, field punishment, extra hours after school, floggings—nothing worked. Do not spare the cane, I beg you, the father would implore. You are his parent here; flog him for me until he learns some sense. Well, no one could accuse Soditan of shirking his obligations in that respect. He applied the rod and also applied, one after the other, all the "tried and tested" methods outlined in Reverend Hackson's *Manual for Teachers.* The term's examinations took place and Odebambi scored the highest marks in his current one or two favourite subjects, failed dismally in others; in short, an overall Fail. This was his second year in Primary III. Very rarely did the school permit a third chance in the same class, and Odebambi would perhaps have qualified to be such an exception.

He had one handicap, however, and it was one which the boy could not overcome. His father was a first cousin to the head teacher. It was just too bad, Soditan sighed. He returned to his position over the desk, dipped the ebony-handled pen into its inkwell, and slowly signed the death warrant. Below the signature he wrote, "Sorry, coz., there is really nothing more I can do."

Soditan's mood lightened almost immediately after, as he turned his attention to the loose music sheets lined up beside the registers, a flicker of amusement even passing over his face. He had now to select the songs both for the music hour during the next year and also for the school march—but it was not this which brought about his amusement. His forearm flexed involuntarily as he remembered the pupils' impertinent variation on that year's marching song. Well, boys will be boys. He tried not to be a hypocrite, recalling his own schooldays, but—discipline is discipline. Surprisingly, the first hint of the mischief had come from Adeturan, the Primary II teacher, who was held in awe because he suffered from the sleeping sickness. His bouts were so acute that sometimes, when he began to write out a sentence on the blackboard, his students watched the sentence disintegrate into a nonsense squiggle and trail off the edge of the board, leaving Adeturan struggling to recover his balance. Adeturan had his good points, however. He wielded a willing cane. And it was his normally comatose hearing that first detected the extra syllables inserted in the refrain, so that instead of:

> Boys wanted, boys wanted
> Boys of muscle, brain, and power
> Fit to cope with anything
> These are wanted every hour.
> Boys wanted, boys wanted . . .

the young, lusty voices belted out:

> Boys, won ntedi, tedi
> Boys, won ntedi, tedi . . .

The crime was established, but the rest was not so easy. The miscreants were practised ventriloquists, and when the teachers walked close to the ranks of marchers, the insertions disappeared in their immediate vicinity but continued farther down the line. Both sides pretended that nothing untoward was happening. The officiating teacher called out orders, drilled them into formation for the march into the assembly hall, and acted as if the parade were word-perfect.

The pupils escaped detection for a while. Their downfall came because they could not resist amplifying the new text with some physical action. It was the same Adeturan, whose determination so much overcame his sleeping bouts, who finally uncovered the clue. There was a telltale variation in the movements of the felons. If one looked closely, a few trunks here and there tilted forward—only a fraction of an angle—on the final accented and legitimate beat, then augmented that tilt by an additional jerk forward on the unauthorised "tedi." A few compulsive dancers went further; they did a swivel at the end, with a somewhat suggestive wiggle of the buttocks, especially as they marched up the flight of steps leading into the schoolroom for morning assembly. So the head teacher stationed Mr. Aeturan on the inside of the entrance, and as each "tedi" dancer passed through those portals, Adeturan neatly jerked him aside and waved him on into the far corner of the schoolroom. The others, completely masked by the front marchers on the upper steps, had no suspicion of the fate of their comrades. One after another, they were apprehended and herded together to await their fate. The bag— Soditan smiled with satisfaction—was twenty-three, three of them girls.

The head teacher was not without a sense of humour. He stood them at attention in his small office, then ordered "About turn!" They formed a quadrangle, facing the office walls, which now appeared to be lined by quivering khaki statuettes. Next the order was given for them to mark time to a brisk "Boys won ntedi." On the "tedi, tedi" they had to te'di to the full, touching their toes. As they had their faces to the wall and dared not turn round, they had no way of knowing whose turn it would be to receive two strokes on the two accented beats as the head teacher—assisted by Adeturan, who could be relied upon to stay wide awake at such official duties—wheeled briskly round the proffered buttocks, laying on solid strokes. It was difficult to keep accurate count among twenty-three buttocks, so some received more and others less than the intended half dozen. But there was nothing abnormal about that; collective punishment made no pretence at even-handedness—that much he had learned to accept in his own pupilage.

Akinyode finally made his choice for the new year. One was "Just Before the Battle, Mother" and the other a local air by Kilanko. The latter brought back the sense of triumph he had experienced during the hard-fought battle to introduce "native" compositions into the school curriculum. What seemed obvious to him had not been so obvious to the schools board and those who gave directions from Lagos. Happily he had received vigorous support of Daodu, the formidable Reverend I. O. Ransome-Kuti, who had lately become the secretary-general of the National Union of Teachers. His booming presence had routed the conservatives, and Mr. Kilanko himself was led in, to loud applause, to perform his music before the Teachers' Congress. The missionaries, he reflected, had been far more accommodating about the innovation, but the director for education had not even wanted to hear of it.

Akinyode became pensive. Yes, there were these tiny triumphs, but were they enough? Fulfillment, he enquired—silently, because there was a listener in the room besides himself—fulfillment, what does it mean? He glanced swiftly round his modest dwelling—did these walls completely circumscribe his future? Was Sipe right, Sipe, who read only timidity in his elected profession? And his young wife—perhaps she should not have had the second child so soon . . . those incessant stomach pains—was she really content with being the wife of a pupil teacher, even a head teacher highly thought-of at such a young age? There were much older teachers who had not been considered worthy of his level of responsibility. He recalled again the shock that had accompanied his letter of appointment. And his father had been cautious: They will try to kill you, he warned. If they can, they will harm you. So you must come home first and let us prepare the necessary protection. Protestations were unavailing, but then he . . . Do I really believe? And afterwards, did I not walk feeling safer, return the stares of those older men with confidence? Have I ever since been afraid to shake hands with them, not even caring what kind of dye-blackened rings they wore on their fingers? It was not the envious ones who could impair his future, no, but what of that future itself—what prospects did it hold for one in a primary school?

Abruptly he put aside the music sheets, lifted out of planned sequence a file marked PERSONAL and leaned back in his chair once again, holding up some sheets of lined notepaper clipped together. The handwriting on them had an attractive vigour, a marked contrast to the soft elegance of that of the teacher.

"What," he demanded of the Genie, "what shall I do about Sipe?"

"Oh. Mephistopheles?"

The ex-Ilés had attended a performance of *Faust* at the Roman Catholic seminary. Such treats were rare, and the ex-Ilés, as was their habit, made of it an "occasion." The dandified group struck the rest of the audience dumb with admiration. They barely recognised their neighbourhood pharmacist; the head teacher, with Ogunba and two others of his staff; Opeilu, the produce inspector (on casual leave from Adio for the occasion); Sotikare, the town clerk; and Akinsanya, the trade unionist, who had joined them from Lagos to grace this rare treat of European opera. The credit for their stunning entrance and presence in that hall belonged almost exclusively to their "outfitter" and social organiser, Sipe, the master schemer and adventurer. After the night's musical induction into the world of high-risk dare, high stakes, and damnation, Sipe, by common consent, was stripped of his erstwhile name, Resolute Rooster, and conferred with that of the archetypal Tempter. As usual, Sipe wore the new name like a carnation, playing variations on it as the mood seized him. This letter in the teacher's hand, for instance, had been signed, Resolutely yours, Mephisto-Rooster.

"Has it occurred to you," Akinyode continued, "dispenser of foreign potions that you are, that this Sipe is actually the most conservative, homebound, parochial country-boy Jebusite of the lot of us, and yet he always introduces these alien, seductive vistas into everybody's life."

"Just business," remarked the Genie.

"That is the point. To him they are nothing but prospective trading partners. He sees no difference between, let us say, a Belgian firm and an Italian."

"Well, is there?"

"Maybe not. But if I had to choose between a Gunter Henklehacker—or whatever the name is of that machine-spare-parts factory he proposed last year—and these Italian firms, I would definitely choose the Italians."

"You, Yode, are a romantic."

"That's what he says. And he says that's why I shall die a teacher, and as poor as a church mouse. He says it in one breath, then tries to save me from myself in the next mail. But wait, listen to the names—Signore Porta Agostino Beila & Co., Messrs. Instituto Ameriale Laniero X Italiano, via Alesandro Manzoni, Milano. Montanari Caro, Esq., 12 via Morigi . . ." He paused suddenly, then began to chuckle. The Genie watched his host's laughter become uncontrollable until tears appeared in the corners of his eyes. As he wiped them off and gradually recovered his breath, he began to splutter: *"Motan'-nari, kaaro o. Wo r'igi? Are. Wei r'igi. Mu suuru. Sipe a ko' gi ru e. Waa ri'gi, waa ri kunmo!"** As Osibo made out his meaning, he held his sides. The laughter waxed so furious that they did not hear the little girl enter and stand in the doorway, making the pharmacist nearly jump out of his skin.

"Good God. Look at her, just like a fairy. Does she want to give me a heart attack?"

"Sorry, sir. Good evening, sir."

"Yes, what is it, Bose?"

"Mama says food will soon be ready. She says she hopes Mr. Pharmacist is staying to eat."

"Of course, girl. What do you think I've been waiting for all this time while your papa was working. Tell Madam I shall be ready whenever she deigns to summon us to the dinner table."

The girl left. Chuckling in spurts, the Genie continued: "But you are right, you know. You don't know how right you are. Sipe will shave clean their heads. In a straightforward way, I mean, not crooked. Sipe plays straight. But he will shave their Italian heads just the same."

"Oh yes," agreed Akinyode. "But you do see what I mean. Their names sound like Yoruba names. Look at this Benito Paserelli . . . *B'eni to pase r'eni!*† Padua . . . look, even that one—*p'adua . . . B'eni to p'ase r'eni p'adua.*" He paused suddenly. "Why does that sound familiar? Padua . . . Padua . . ."

---

* Montanari, good morning. You say you can see wood? Wait. You are yet to see wood. Be patient. Sipe will load your back with timber. You will see wood, you will taste the cudgel!

† As one who can feast us into a state of exhaustion. As one who feasts us so dead tired, we fall to prayers.

"If you don't know that, Mr. Schoolteacher . . ."

"Really. Should I? We never teach Italian geography, you know. Only that of the Empire."

Osibo shook his head. "Padua. If you don't recall it, you will need an *adua* to make me stop when I start to broadcast this ignorance to the world."

"Wait wait wait . . . Padua . . . Padua. Oh dear, where where where? History. Let's see. It has to be history. The treaty of . . . ?

The dispenser shook his head. "You are in trouble."

"Not history? What other subject could it be? Religious knowledge . . . something about the popes? Look, ours is an Anglican school. Did they teach you about popes at school?"

The pharmacist shook his head, firmly. "Not religious knowledge. And you have only one more chance. You miss at the next attempt and I will tell you." He rubbed his long fingers together and gloated, "And you know what that means."

The teacher suddenly exhaled a deep breath of relief. He had been looking out of the window, concentrating hard, when he saw, emerging from the gates of BishopsCourt, the ample figure of the circuit preacher's wife, whose presence in St. Peter's Church the previous Sunday had created such a stir. She had insisted on sitting in the very front pew, which, like two or three others, had its own side doors with latch and was the exclusive seating right of one of the oldest families in Egbaland. The politics was local; it was not a matter in which the teacher had felt obliged to dabble. As sidesman, however, he had had to act, bringing all his diplomatic powers to bear on the circuit preacher's wife even while the husband, sitting in the choir stalls, pretended that nothing unusual was going on in the elevated transept. Akinyode offered the woman his own sidesman's chair with its narrow bible-and-hymnal podium. It was all one unit, down to the kneeling platform, unpadded. This had the distinction of such exclusivity that she was soon mollified and proceeded to occupy her new status. Until she tried to squeeze her bulk into the single-piece contraption, clearly built with a more frugal frame in mind. Then a new commotion began. The event was not lost on the organist; he rose in the sidesman's estimation by playing so loud that only a handful of the congregation—and even this was limited to the occupants of the transept pews—had any notion of the scale of the disaster.

The Genie had noticed the change in his demeanour. "Well?"

"Providence is kind. I knew I deserved some divine reward for my handling of last Sunday's—er—situation."

"Make your guess."

"Shakespeare. *The Taming of the Shrew.*"

"Damn damn damn! But what's all this about Providence?"

"Look out of the window—keep your head low! Don't let her see you."

Osibo raised his nose to the level of the lower door.

"It is the woman?"

"None other."

"And that went into that contraption you normally occupy?"

"She tried to."

The Genie nodded slowly. "Now I know what Jesus saw before he pronounced his 'verily, verily' on the camel and the eye of the needle."

The teacher's wife came in to cut short their mirth, bringing the dispenser to his feet. He took her hand. "Good evening, my dear Mrs. S. My guess is that you have come to summon us to dinner?"

"I am sorry I took a little longer than I had planned."

"Don't give it a thought, Mrs. S. Don't give it a single thought. Your husband has kept me fully entertained, after he took his nose out of his desk, of course."

The Genie stood up, plonked the open journal down on the table, face down. "There's another of your countrymen in there. Let's talk about him after dinner."

The teacher could not contain his curiosity and he turned over the journal, a recent issue of *In Leisure Hours*. The face in the picture that stared up at him was cut from a different cloth than were the imagined shop-corner salesman faces of a Beila or a Paserelli, though he did share a common Christian name with the latter. This Benito was that no-nonsense face whose antics on the continent had formed the theme of impassioned discussion within The Circle, cropping up again and again as his latest manoeuvres or pronouncements came to their notice. Some, like Sipe, had interest only in the fact that this alien enigma had been photographed sitting astride one of the most modern motorcycles to roll out of the Italian motor industry. Could they not import Italian machines? For nearly ten years this face had popped in and out of the news that filtered through to West Africa, appearing even in *The Nigerian Teacher,* but mostly in *The West African Review.* Was he a diabolical tyrant or simply a MOUTH? What drove the man? Was it greed or power? The Circle debated Mussolini endlessly.

The teacher discarded the journal and led the way to the dining room. "At heart," he said, "he is only another one of them."

"Of course. He's Italian, isn't he?"

"No, I mean—another businessman. Trader. He is busy looking for markets for expansion, just like everybody else."

Osibo did an about-turn, snatched up the journal, and stabbed the picture with his long forefinger. "Take a good look at that face. Does that look like the face of a haberdasher? Can you see that one dealing in gentlemen's apparel—shoes, ties, shirts with detachable collars, two- and three-piece suits in worsted wool? This is a man of iron and steel, sir. If Sipe moves near him—which he never will, not even by correspondence—this man will chew him up."

Akinyode admitted that this was not in dispute. The ex-Ilés had long ago accepted that Benito Mussolini was not a figure to be trifled with. And he continued to haunt their discussions, thanks in the main to the editors of *The West African Review,* who, in their Gold Coast colony, appeared also to find his personality irresistible. He emerged sometimes as the very antithesis of those euphonious names of Sipe's partners—calculating and domineering. What had he not done to bring Haile Selassie, the lone African emperor, under his dominance? The diminutive ruler cried for help to the League of Nations—in vain. Step by step, Mussolini proceeded to harry him into the Red Sea. Some claimed that he had routed the Abyssinian forces by the foul use of poison gas. The soldiers breathed it in and simply keeled over without firing a shot. "Activity," the scoutmaster, undertook to commence recruitment for a brigade to fight Mussolini, confident that the colonial government would give its blessing. He was acquainted with several veterans of the last war, he declared, and could field a company of West African Volunteers within a week. Prominent on the wall of his living room was the framed reply he had received from the colonial secretary. The matter, declared the letter, was being effectively arbitrated by the League of Nations. Activity still waved the letter round the town, and it was difficult to decide whether this was an act of pride—that he had actually received a letter from an official in the governor's office in Lagos—or that the lukewarm letter provided proof of collusion among the colonial powers. Even after he had framed the letter and hung it up prominently in his home, his visitors found it impossible to resolve the nature of his invocation of that august piece of recognition.

"Have you noticed something?" the teacher remarked, turning the journal at different angles. "He does bear a resemblance to I.O."

Osibo looked down over his shoulder. "I.O.? You mean our own Daodu?"

"Yes. Take a good look. Same disciplinarian expression. They would make a match, I suspect. Daodu could handle him. If anyone can, it is Daodu."

For a long while, Osibo contemplated the photograph. "You may have something there. Maybe it is Daodu who should be sent to confront him in the League of Nations."

A soft voice broke through their schemes for high diplomacy. It was Akinyode's wife, retracing her steps to express anxiety about the dinner slowly congealing on the table.

"Let's go, let's go," urged the teacher. "Or we'll get blamed if the food has been burnt."

Laughing, they proceeded to the table.

"You know," the teacher resumed, "I never did obtain those books from Foyles in London."

"Which ones out of many?"

"The ones by the German writer Mussolini referred to in that speech. No, not the one you were reading just now—a much earlier speech in *The Elders Review*, more than five years ago. I spent a fortune on stamps sending reminders."

"But Foyles are usually so reliable."

Surgically, Akinyode sliced his *eko,* spiked it with a piece of crayfish, plastered it with bean pottage, and rounded it off with a rind of pork. It finally had acquired the desired shape and submitted to its onward transfer to the mouth. He chewed methodically, integrating his speech into the normal working of his jaw muscles.

"My suspicion, Mr. Pharmacist, is that those books did not arrive for the same reasons that Activity was dissuaded from forming his volunteer brigade. Sabotage. Or censorship, if you prefer."

"I don't understand. Who was the author?"

"It is not a familiar name; I only read of him that once—Gerhart Hauptmann. You see, he is German."

The Genie frowned. "Well?"

"Don't you see? The British, Italians, and Germans have always been rivals, even when they collaborated against us with one another. Remember how we used to argue the possibility of Mussolini reaching for one of the British possessions if he failed to grab Eritrea?"

"Yes, but—"

"Now, if you were the British, would you have encouraged your subjects to have access to the nationalist propaganda of your potential rivals? You wouldn't wait until hostilities actually broke out before sealing up the minds of your colonial subjects against the voices of competitors."

"Could be. Sometimes I think they even carry it into the field of medicaments. Hardly ever did we run into German drugs during our training."

"Oh yes, they kept the boundaries tightly closed once we were carved up. No trespassing. No poaching. Honor among thieves. You never see any German teachers—in fact, any German professionals in any field in this corner of the protectorate. Only priests. And those are confined to interior missions."

Osibo chewed his food thoughtfully. "You think this writer . . . er . . ."

"Hauptmann. I don't know if that is the correct way to pronounce it."

"All right. Do you think he might be a dangerous writer, then?"

"I wouldn't know. I never read him. But he is German. He may be a strong supporter of Hitler. Like Mussolini, Hitler wants more slices of the continent. Well, let's hope that when they really get down to business they'll be so exhausted that they'll all go home and leave us alone."

Startled, Osibo looked up. "Surely you don't mean that!"

"Why not? Oh, I don't mean pack up lock, stock, and barrel. It's too late for that anyway. But look, how would you feel each time Empire Day comes round, and you have to prepare your pupils for the schools' parade in Ibara, teaching them to sing:

Victoria, Victoria,
Aiye re l'awa nje!
O so gbogbo eru d'omo
N'ile enia dudu. *

We've been colonized, agreed. But really, sometimes I feel that is carrying things too far!"

The young wife ate little, contenting herself with ensuring that both husband and guest tasted from every dish. Nor did she take part in the conversation, though she listened intently. When she paused in the motion of refilling their glasses, arrested by a remark being made at that moment, the Genie could not resist noting her attention with approval.

"Madam, I see, shows keen interest in the vicissitudes of our world?"

She smiled shyly while her husband responded, "Ah, you don't know what I have to put up with. She is not Daodu's niece for nothing. In the end, maybe she is the one we shall send to confront Hitler while her uncle takes on Mussolini."

They laughed uproariously. The food sank rapidly, and soon gleaming patches showed in the interior of the white porcelain. This always sprang the wife to action; she seized the bowl and went to the kitchen to replenish it. The dispenser seized one such opportunity to whisper: "The first question I should have asked, but you were then busy. How is Iyawo? Do the pills agree with her?"

"There has been some improvement. She still has those bouts of pain but . . . yes, definitely some improvement."

"And the cramps?"

"Not for over a fortnight now. I think the pills worked for those cramps."

"I have a new consignment from Lagos. German, as a matter of fact."

"German? How—"

---

* Victoria, Victoria,
  What a life of ease we owe you!
  You turned all slaves into free beings
  In the land of the black peoples.

"I have contacts. Sipe is not the only businessman you know. I am really interested, professionally. Some say French medicine is the best. Others say German. No one ever says English. Not one mention of Italian medicine either, come to think of it. Well, what do they say across the border, I mean, in the French colonies? Do they believe there that English medicine is best? Or Italian?"

The teacher smiled. "The pasture on the farther bank of the river . . ."

"That's it exactly. Always lusher than the one behind one's backyard. I really must find out. We shall see if the British are really keeping the superior things from us. It will be a rough road, but I have made up my mind. A colleague in Lagos has opened up the channels."

With a mischievous grin, the teacher asked, "Where do we come in in all this?"

Osibo was puzzled. "Come in? Who?"

Mrs. Soditan returned with the replenished dish.

"We. You and me and all the rest. Before you began to stock your pharmacy with all that *oyinbo* stuff, didn't we have our own curatives?"

Osibo shook his head, firmly. "No, thank you. I am not getting drawn into that argument all over again."

"But we did. And still do. All I am asking is your professional opinion. Does our medicine come after the Germans? In front of the British or French? Or don't we rate at all?"

The pharmacist transferred a full serving-spoon load of bean pottage to his plate, passed some into his mouth, and masticated vigorously, staring stubbornly at the wall.

"Just an informed opinion," the teacher persisted. "If you don't answer I shall send my father to you the next time he comes round with his potion for my indigestion."

The wife remonstrated. "Dear, let him eat his food."

"Madam, don't plead with him. Let him continue to pose his combative questions. I remain mute, firm and impregnable as Olumo rock. Let him continue to waste his breath."

"But why should any of our local herbalists not come to your shop with a bottle of his concoction and ask to become your supplier? No, not even to stock it, just to ask you for a professional opinion. Right?

What"—and he raised his gaze to the ceiling, conducted an invisible orchestra with fork and knife as he posed the question—"what would be so unusual in two professional colleagues exchanging learned opinions on the art of the apothecary?"

The Genie fell for the taunt. "It would not be two professional colleagues but a pharmacist and a jujuman. A trained chemist and a mumbo-jumboist."

"A-ah, but which is which? Let us ask ourselves in all sincerity: What does the local herbalist think of Osibo, the dispenser of white men's medicines?"

"Dear, your food. And do let Mr. Osibo eat."

"No, no, madam. Let him be. I knew where he was heading all along. Some people simply do not like progress. We shall ignore them and persist in our march towards civilisation."

"But you do stock *Gbogbonse?* That is a local product, invented, if I may mention with modest pride, by an Ijebuman . . ."

"*Gbogbonse* is produced in Lagos under hygenic conditions, bottled and labelled according—"

"A-ah, I knew it. The label maketh the drug."

"Labelled according to accepted pharmaceutical usage. It is not a mixture of the powdered nest of the praying mantis with drops of chicken blood and lizard's—" He quickly caught himself.

"Lizard's what?" Akinyode insisted.

"Not at the dinner table. And certainly not in the presence of Madam."

"All right, but don't say I didn't warn you. Sipe will reap all the benefit of your prejudices. His latest proposal includes starting a patent-medicine store, dealing mostly in local potions."

"What?"

"Aha, I thought that would shake you up. He is already securing premises in Yaba. So, if we end up stocking medicines that are not fit for human consumption—"

"You don't mean it. Seriously, now."

"I shall show you the letter. It's all there, in detail. Worsted wool from overseas, patent medicine of our own manufacture. He's worked it all out. He is going to make us rich men whether we like it or not."

The pharmacist glared at the schoolteacher for some moments, heaved a deep sigh. "Well, I suppose if there is no other way of stopping you reckless young men from becoming murderers—"

"Good. Sipe plans to come over during the holidays. He will be glad to learn that he now has a consultant pharmacist."

Osibo shook his head somberly and returned to the business of eating. Mrs. Soditan smiled secretively while the teacher tried to conjure up a mask of innocence; it did not fool his wife.

Pa Josiah's letter lay on the table between them, an unsought and unwelcome marriage test—or perhaps simply a test of faith. Their visitor was gone, the table cleaned, and they were finally alone. Soditan and his wife sought each other's thoughts in the dim light of the kerosene lamp, the wife more desperately than the man. He appeared far less troubled; if anything, his thoughts had ranged much farther away than the immediate challenge posed by his father's letter. What he sought more, indeed longed for, was a resumption of the steamy, raucous debate with his circle over the entire question of cures. The debate was unending; they returned to the same subject again and again, never resolving anything but feeling mentally elated afterwards. As he glanced round the compound, however, he reflected that they were probably all asleep. Indeed, his was the only lamp still flickering in that compound of some twenty families— mostly teachers like himself, but with a sprinkling of court clerks, a pharmacist, the catechist, and one other government employee of indeterminate functions. In his household, the only sound that broke the silence came in the form of angry spasmodic grunts from the direction of the curtained door of his wife's bedroom, produced by the second child of their five-year marriage. The mother knew at once that he had got his legs tangled up as usual in the bedclothes, so she got up and went into the room. It was a warm night like most others, but she would as soon dream of exposing a newborn child stark naked to the rain as leave the covers off a sleeping child. Even in burning heat, COLD—she thought of it in menacing letters—cold was the eternal enemy of infants and must be kept at bay with wrappings drawn up to the chest. Soditan had long ceased to argue, but the baby did not give up the disputation.

In the bedroom, she gently disentangled his limbs, keeping a firm hand on the chest so he would not spring fully awake. It worked, it always did. He continued to sleep peacefully until the next bout of wrangling. In the front room, the husband marvelled at this unending ritual.

When she returned, she found that he had picked up his pen and was dipping it thoughtfully in the inkwell, wiping the excess against the rim. She read the decision on his face correctly and remarked, "Father will think it was I who refused to come."

"I shall make it clear that the decision was mine. In fact, I shall not even admit that I discussed it with you. Come to think of it"—his face opened wide in a mischievous grin—"what are you talking about? I do not even know what you're talking about."

She refused to be sidetracked. "Oh, he won't say anything. But you will see it in the way he sulks at me when next we visit."

"That's if he doesn't show up to take up the fight in person."

Then his mood changed abruptly, betraying a deep underlying concern. He stared hard at her for some moments, then demanded, "But how are you *really* feeling? Really really."

She spread out her hands and shrugged. "It is still too early to tell—I no longer jump at these improvements in my condition. It always waits a few weeks, then starts all over again."

"So you don't feel this has been different from the other treatments?"

"I don't know. I really don't know. I only hope and pray it is. I haven't felt any pains so far but . . . well, I don't know. We'll just have to watch and pray, that's all."

"Your appetite has not fully returned," he insisted.

She laughed at that. "That's what you think. You weren't home when I had my *amala* this afternoon. That was why I couldn't do justice to our supper together."

"That never used to stop you, not a small afternoon snack."

"Oh, it was late. I thought you would be returning late, not before evening, what with the meeting of your Auxiliary Committee."

"That turned out to be more routine. We didn't take up the financial matter I told you about. The accounts were not ready."

After that, they both fell silent. He kept the pen poised over the writing pad, his mind busy on the best phrasing to mollify his father; the letter had to be ready for the courier who would leave very early in the morning. As he began to write he pursed his lips as his mind returned to yet another nagging thought.

"Anyway, we must wait quite a while before the next child."

She understood. Deinde had come quickly after their first child, a daughter. And those pains had begun soon after Deinde's birth; for Soditan the two things remained connected. In vain she reminded him that this was nothing compared with the pace at which other women gave birth, so rapidly that the nurses would sometimes joke that the new pregnancy must have taken hold on the eve of the last labour pains. In her case, it was over six months after the birth of Tolu that she had again become pregnant—they had not planned it so but . . . She shrugged. It happened, so, it happened. And there was certainly nothing complicated about that birth. The pains were longer than expected, but, no, no complications.

The result lay peacefully—for now—on the large bed next door, and besides that troublesome seizure which sometimes wrenched her insides and went on for days, she foresaw no problems with the next. Her husband continued to write, speaking at the same time, shaking his head in continuing bafflement.

"Not even that white specialist from Lagos. And the Massey Street Hospital with all its modern medicine. So where does one try next if it starts all over again? All these tests and drugs and injections —*otubante!* what exactly have they been treating? I think it is nothing but trial and error. They don't know. They simply don't know."

She seized her chance to return to his earlier remark. "They are all agreed on one thing—at Sokenu, at the Catholic Hospital, the consultant who came to McCutter's—they all say it has nothing to do with Deinde's birth."

"So what do they say it has to do with? They know what it isn't. Now let them tell us what it is. The medicines they keep giving you, what are they supposed to treat? The hospital cards don't tell me anything. Uncle Segun, with all his training—he is just as baffled. All right. I'll tell you what I am replying to Father. You are not going to Ìsarà for now—we are both agreed. In principle, we are going to stick to this European treatment." He nodded emphasis. "In principle. It's over a year now, and that is a long time to be kept anxious. I simply do not like it. After this last course, we wait and see. We'll see if the miracle has finally happened. I shall give it one week, a month—but only if the pain doesn't start all over again! If it does, Father will be set loose to place his *ebo** right against the church gates if that is what his *onisegun* recommends."

The wife looked worried. It was difficult sometimes to divine his true intent. "Are you sure we would be doing the right thing, dear?"

He grinned, pleased to find himself on favourite grounds. "Oh no, *we* won't be doing anything at all, right or wrong. It is Father who wants to do something, so let him do it. He is not going to force any medicine down your throat, and what he does won't stop us going for fresh consultations with any European clinic or specialist anyone recommends. Only this time, I am withdrawing the monopoly."

She shook her head in continuing doubt. "This pagan business . . ."

"Pagan? Why pagan? All right, what if it is pagan? Tell me, don't Christians make *saara†* on occasion?"

She sensed she was losing grip on the central issue. The battle light was already in the head teacher's eyes, and soon there would be no stopping him. She had grown familiar with that sign of the flaring nostrils—oh yes, Soditan's adrenaline had begun to pump, ready to take him into the early hours—into the next week, indeed, if he could find stimulating opposition which also possessed his staying power. Still, this was something she felt strongly about, so she braced up for a fight, however brief.

"Let me say this, dear. The way I see it, *saara* is a kind of thanksgiving. A child has been ill, recovers, so we make *saara.* Or, let us say, after a successful childbirth. People have a good harvest, or they arrive safely after a long journey . . . all that is different. What Father is saying in this letter is something else; *etutu* is like a secret ritual."

"Why secret?" He pushed the letter towards her. "Where does it say so in the letter?"

"Oh, you know what I mean," she protested.

"No, I do not know what you mean. There is nothing secret about it. Or we can go to Ìsarà if you like—that would take the secrecy out of it. He has invited us—or rather, you. So, go and find out what it's all about. If he embarks on anything that contradicts your Christian teaching, you withdraw."

---

* Ritual offering.
† Ritual feast.

She threw up her hands in desperation. "I am trying to be serious, dear. This is a serious matter—"

"So am I," he protested, "So am I. The old man says he wants to make *etutu* for your recovery—there is nothing secret about *etutu*. It is less secret than a surgical operation. Those doctors, do they allow anyone in the theatre when they start cutting up people and sewing them up and removing their insides?" He paused. A new idea had occurred to his mind, which now entered its playful mood. "Come to think of it, we don't even know what they do with those organs they remove, do we? How do you know they don't use them to make some white man's *etutu*?" He raised his hand to forestall her protestations. "Hm-hm, you answer only if you know exactly what they do with those organs. They don't replace a thing; all they do is cut things out. Right? What happens to those organs?"

Confidently she said, "Yes, I'll tell you. They put them in bottles in some kind of preservative—that's right, formaldehyde. Probably to study them. I have seen rows of those jars with my own eyes."

That checked him only for a second. "Including amputations? You have seen legs and arms, even tiny hands and feet, in those pickle jars?" Then the grin reappeared. "But tell me, when you go to the market and see all those dried snakes and lizards, mice, monkey skulls and pickled bats and so on, what are they for? And why do these Europeans look down on them as instruments of devilish rites?"

"You are changing the argument," she accused. "You are twisting everything. I don't know which ground you are standing on right now."

"That's because I haven't landed," he cried. "Be patient. I am going to land in a moment. Let's go back to *etutu* for now. We will say that it involves slaughtering a goat. The officiating priest takes bits and pieces out of it—you do know that, of course. Certain parts of the animal are reserved for him as of right. Very specific they are in these matters. Nobody else can take them. Other parts belong to, let us say, the Baale, or the chief of the compound, the head of the family. If there is an *abiku** in the family, his or her part is equally guaranteed. To the celebrant himself belongs this or that chunk,

---

* A child that repeatedly dies—mythical.

while others still are distributed to friends and neighbours. The helpers make sure no one does them out of their own allocation. Right? Now let's return to the white officiating priest—or if you like, the surgeon. What does he do with his own portion, those bits and pieces which no one else sees? Not *everything* goes into those jars! Amputations, for instance—what happens to those limbs?"

Morola did not hesitate. "The surgeon eats them, of course. He takes them home and gives them to his wife to cook."

Soditan sank back in the chair, deflated. "I must have told you that one before."

She shook her head. "No. But I am getting used to the pattern."

"I shall have to take out a patent. When I see Sipe he'll advise me what to do. A man can't have his wife stealing his best lines."

She laughed. "Let me leave you with your letter. And if it's a ram, don't forget we could do with some meat in the house."

"You think I'll forget that? I want half the entire beast. You forget who is going to bear the cost in any case."

"Oh yes," she sighed. "And that is the other thing, dear. These things cost money, and what you have spent so far is hardly child's play. The hospital bills—"

Soditan sat back suddenly. "Ha! How could I have overlooked that? I know why you are so dead against Father's kind of cure. With European treatment, you eat all the medicine by yourself. In our own, we all get to share in it. That's it! Selfish woman. And me fooling myself that your appetite has not yet returned!"

She shook her head with a despairing finality. "I am going to bed. Your letter—don't let the courier miss the early morning transport."

For the husband, it would not be bedtime for a while. Mopping-up operation, he called it, as he completed and sealed the letter, then turned to grapple with outstanding matters on his desk. The annual school report came first. Sighing, he drew thick lines over most of the draft composition—clearly the young trainee teacher, eager to impress, had decided to engage in an essay competition, or an article for *The Nigerian Teacher*. The item on Ogunba especially he rewrote completely. Ogunba, his favourite colleague, was leaving, the one teacher he always considered irreplaceable. He now stressed the urgency of replacing him, certainly before the commencement of the new school year.

The official part over, Soditan let himself sink into doleful thoughts; the impending loss of his friend had long oppressed him. The weekend afternoons, spent alternately in each other's home . . . the rare privilege of a friend whom one could actually take for granted. He cast his mind round others in The Circle, shook his head. With none other did he feel this special bond, neither within The Circle nor among the inner sect of the ex-Ilés, those children of Ìsarà who had also trained at Ilesa and called themselves the first rank of trained exiles from Ijebuland. Ogunba was a personal loss. Even if he were sent the most efficient, most experienced ex-Ilé, could he again, whenever his duties took him from his station, could he ever leave his station again without a twinge of unease? With Ogunba in charge, Akinyode admitted, he would sometimes take an extra day on his journeys, confident that the affairs of the school were in capable and trusty hands. That was it—trust. That really was it, that deep *trust* which bound them together.

It could not be helped, but the head teacher felt cheated. Ogunba was going to take charge of a school in Ijebu-Ode. That was the only consolation, the tiny crumb of solace. Ìsarà was close enough to Ijebu-Ode, so he could look forward to more delightful holidays in Ìsarà. And was it not typical of his friend to leave the elder son, Jimi, behind in his care, so that his schooling could continue under his tutelage? "I don't know how good that Ijebu-Ode school is, but I know it will take us years to bring it up to this standard even if we were together; how much more with me alone . . ." It was Ogunba's way of admitting the wrench he also felt at his departure. I really am absurd, Akinyode admonished himself, as he found a film of tears dimming his sight. He hastily completed his notes, which again urged the mission to arrange Ogunba's replacement quickly, certainly before the school reopened in January, otherwise, "the task of maintaining our standard of education in this school cannot be achieved." He turned to the next item with some relief.

Akanbi Beckley was a truculent eleven-year-old, much too old for the Standard III Elementary, which he had barely managed to attain. Spoiled by a wealthy father, one of the "established" families in town, he should indeed have been expelled from school three or four times over, but interventions from above managed to thwart the teacher's iron code. What he would not accept, however, was that in matters of discipline the same kind of intervention should be countenanced. Akanbi often stayed behind at school to perform some physical chores as punishment—scrubbing the school floor or cutting grass on the playing fields. It was no more than others underwent for like offences, but of course young Akanbi would first refuse to touch anything, sometimes keeping up his defiance until dusk. His father (or mother) would come to fetch him, and the process would continue the following day. Akanbi would stand in the allotted field, banned from classes until the punishment—plus its accumulated interest—was fully carried out. This process might persist for a week, since the head teacher was never known to remit a sentence, once delivered. Finally, the father would come with Akanbi to school, having cajoled him and brought his birthday forward by several weeks or months, then stand over him while he carried out the task. Two or three times a year this comedy was played. Then Akinyode decided that he had had enough.

The teachers had chafed and fumed. They could not resort to the far less protracted form of punishment—flogging—because the doting father had obtained from one of his doctor friends a certificate of ill health. Young Akanbi's constitution was declared extremely fragile, unable to withstand the shock of corporal punishment. Since one of Akanbi's favourite sports was engaging in physical fights, especially in the classroom—fights from which he usually came off best, since he always chose his opponents very carefully—Akinyode had quietly registered his own opinion on that subject.

The day of reckoning dawned at last, not unexpectedly, as school drew to a close. This was Akanbi's open season. He would commence his round of crimes and refusal of punishment near the end of term, after which the holidays would intervene and the whole episode, he reasoned, would be forgotten. He was very wrong about that, but Akanbi's little mind could never stretch to embrace past lessons concerning the head teacher's infinite patience. On this occasion, however, Akinyode was not even prepared to adopt his usual measures. These involved withholding the miscreant's class report or refusing his fees for the following term until the punishment was served out in full, usually in the final days of the holidays, with papa in attendance. This time, as soon as the fracas broke out, with Akanbi's unique vocal register penetrating the partitions between the classrooms and distracting other pupils who were dutifully sitting their examinations, Akinyode summoned both teacher and pupil to his office. He asked no questions. He simply reached into the corner of his office and ordered the teacher: *"Gbe pon!"*

The teacher stammered in confusion. Was their H. T. out of his mind? He did not even recall that such a role had never before been given a teacher—the norm was to make one of the bigger boys carry the victim piggyback—so preoccupied was he with the enormity of the event. This was the delicate egg no one dared touch. Mr. Soditan flexed the cane while Akanbi gave him a look of utter contempt. The head teacher further underscored his intentions by locking the door to his office, then turned round and repeated, "Hump him! Are you deaf?"

The child with the delicate health put up the fight of his life. It did not save him. His arms were pinioned round the neck of the teacher as he was hoisted onto his back while he twisted and wriggled, tried to kick his mount, the head teacher, the walls, and the ceiling. Soditan thereupon took the tiny head in one hand, yanked it round to face his own, and spoke above his screams.

"Now, it is in your own interest to lie still. If by chance this cane misses you and hits your teacher, when I have finished, he will himself give you three strokes for every one that touches him. Anywhere he pleases. You understand me? I will not be carrying you. I will simply hand him the cane and he will give you a general flogging. I hope that is clear."

Young Beckley, seeing that he was clearly doomed, began to whimper and beg. Too late. Akinyode gave him, as he was fond of putting it, "twelve of the best," then sent him back to class to complete his interrupted papers. When he reached home that day, he took a shower, ate his supper, and selected a very stout cane, which he placed beside him in the front room. Then he sat down to await the storm.

He was surprised that it took so long to arrive; Beckley Senior also probably believed in having his supper before embarking on a confrontation. He had, however, also taken time to have his son examined by his doctor and had received a written report on the state of his back and his little bottom. Armed with this potent document, he stepped onto the raised concrete entrance of the head teacher's house and was astonished to be received with fussless courtesy. Soditan rose and opened the door for him.

"I've been expecting you, Mr. Beckley. Please take a seat."

Mr. Beckley eyed the teacher with undisguised hostility, which he extended to an inspection of the front room. The left half of his face, especially the region between his left nostril and upper lip, squeezed itself together to indicate his disgust at being compelled to be in such surroundings. He faced Akinyode squarely.

"I think what we have to say to each other will not require my sitting down, thank you very much, Mr. Head Teacher. All I want to know from you is whether you wish to deny that you were responsible for inflicting those inhuman injuries borne home upon his back by my son Akanbi. Not surprisingly, he is now seriously ill, confined to bed, and may even have to be hospitalized. I have come merely to hear what you have to say in your own defence."

Soditan sighed, resumed his seat, and leaned back comfortably.

"I hope you have no objection if I sit down myself, Mr. Beckley. Actually, I think this may take some time. I would seriously urge you to sit down."

"I am NOT sitting down, Teacher Soditan. I am asking you very simply—did you or did you not inflict those inhuman injuries on my son?"

The teacher did not immediately reply. He took out a folder from under a stack of papers, opened it carefully, and began to turn over the sheets.

"Your son, I think I am correct in saying, is Akanbi Beckley. This file contains all the reports which his teachers have made on him over the past four years in two classes, as he spent two years in each class, where a normal pupil spends only one—"

Mr. Beckley exploded. "I did not come here to ask for a school report on my son. Did you or did you not savagely attack the child, knowing full well that his health is most delicate at the best of times? That is the only issue I have come to discuss with you."

Soditan closed the file and carefully put it back in its place. "I thought," he began, "that this was to be a sort of parent-teacher meeting. I was under the impression that you were so concerned about your son's future that you decided to encroach on my private hours and impose on me for a few minutes' discussion. Since, however, this is not the case and this still happens to be my house"—and with that Akinyode brought out his cane from its hiding place—"I will give you five seconds to remove yourself. At the end of that, I shall proceed to do to you what I have unjustly done to your son. Because you see, Mr. Beckley"—he rose slowly from his chair—"it is you I should have flogged, years ago. Then perhaps we would all have been spared the disgusting nuisance of your delinquent dullard of a son." By the end of his speech, Akinyode had squeezed out of the confined space behind his desk, his eyes glinting like a fanatic's. Beckley spluttered, raised his arm in a warning gesture, but finally let himself to be persuaded by the mad gleam in Akinyode's unblinking eyes, fled the house and the compound without a backward glance.

The result now stared Akinyode in the face: Beckley's letter of complaint to the school board, with a covering memorandum from the schools inspector. The matter had become formalised: Every exchange was being forwarded and copied in triplicate. It was likely—and this was nothing less than he had anticipated—that the bishopric in Lagos was already in possession of the facts. Beckley's connections were of the very highest. In a separate folder lay Akinyode's ultimate response: his letter of resignation, which lacked only his signature and the date. But that would come only as a last resort. It was prepared as an expression of his stand in the matter of young Beckley. This far, the folder said, I am prepared to go.

He took up his pen and prepared a draft response to his querry. It stated the facts very simply and reiterated his view that Akanbi's conduct merited instant dismissal from the school; he had been flogged as a lesser punishment. Finally, he wanted to know in writing from Mr. Beckley how he would like his son to be treated in the future. Beckley, he wrote, must anticipate every conceivable situation based on his son's past conduct and the moral welfare of the rest of the school. He set the draft aside for further ideas in the morning. A smile played on his face as he tried to imagine Sipe's reaction when he came to learn of the episode. Working for the likes of Beckley—I told you! Abandon that post! As for teaching itself, I don't know what you see in that thankless, graceless, unrewarding profession . . .

He turned to the folder marked PERSONAL—FOR REPLIES. News of the death of his cousin Akinsanya's father continued to plague him. The reply was written, but should he visit him in person? But for these year-end chores he would already be on his way to Lagos. To Lagos? His cousin could be at Ìsarà that very moment, then be on his way back to Lagos while he sat in an Ìsarà-bound passenger lorry. He decided to await news of the funeral plans. And if his work load lightened rapidly, why not a visit to Lagos. Saaki would appreciate it. And he must not forget his lemons this time.

Tailor Famade wrote from a new address at the Nigerian Railways, Kaduna Junction, where he had gone to set up a tailoring service. He was beginning to get worried about the influx of tailors. Word seemed to have gone round that Kaduna was becoming quite a fast-growing civil service and business enclave, what with its increasing importance as a junction for the two main rail lines—from Enugu in the east and Lagos to the south. A new barracks for the West African Frontier Force had also recently been opened. They required uniforms; so did the police, which had been proportionately expanded. Every two-bit tailor, he complained, was heading north with his Singer sewing machine. Trade was expanding at the same time, and a number of wealthy traders required new *buba* and *agbada* outfits. He was surviving, having got into the main chance early, but the encroachments were becoming quite heavy and determined. He was thinking of coming down in the New Year to have Akinyode's advice.

A letter from a former teacher-trainee under his instruction brought a twinge of regret. *My dear old pedagogue,* she began. What a mischievous bundle of seductive energy she had been! A trainee teacher, she had been attached to his school for some months for practical experience; he had ended up wondering who was the teacher and who the pupil. Pretty, provocative Olarounpe was one of the most capable trainees that had ever come to his school. She hardly ever required help or needed supervision. After her practical sessions she would write up her notes and bring them to him in person—then the game began. A little difficulty encountered, she would claim, in her English class; she could not make her pupils master the rules of Direct and Indirect Speech.

For instance, "I set the class this simple exercise, and I was most disappointed by the results: *Put into Indirect Speech the following sentence: The teacher said, 'What I most admire in a man is discipline and dignity.' "* Looking at him in a way which neither Direct nor Indirect Speech could ever hope to convey. Then wistfully, "I have a feeling that the results will always be the same, disappointment?" But most unnerving of all was when, under the pretext of translation problems in the Yoruba class, she left him, in her own handwriting, the passionate speech of spurned love by Kako's wife in Fagunwa's *Ogboju Ode!* That, he admitted, had made him sweat. Now the letter in his hand resumed the tease: *I am still as weak as ever in my Direct and Indirect Speech. I wonder if I should come for a refresher course with my dear pedagogue but fear the results will never change.* Then, as a dutiful afterthought, *I nearly forgot, do give my love to the fortunate Mrs. S. and the entire family. My very best wishes for a Happy Christmas and for the New Year.* The season was her excuse for renewing this correspondence, subtly restating her attachment.

Soditan sighed, turning the letter over and over in his hands. Deep in the pit of his stomach, he knew that this inconclusive affair would continue to haunt him for a while. Sipe, who was his main confidant in such matters, chided him for his cruelty and swore to uphold Olarounpe's interest as long as she showed interest, and as long as her claims did not try to monopolise the rights of the many "butterflies which flutter around your deceptive, coy candle that hides its flame under a bushel."

Despite his inner conviction, he leaned out of the window, struck a match to Olarounpe's letter, and watched the paper curl up, charred, letting it drop only after nothing was left of the white-lined "love-blue" sheet. He regretted now that he had not addressed to her one of the Sipe-ordered Christmas cards, then again decided that it was a good idea not to have done so. He turned his attention to the remaining item for the night, the hard nut which he had deliberately reserved for the quietest hours of the day—an address to the Owu National Society. Heaven only knew why he had succumbed to this hazard of proposing a toast to the Owu elite. He considered himself a poor substitute for J. S. Odunjo, whose textbooks were in such wide use in the country. In any impromptu debate the teacher could hold his own, but delivering formal speeches always gave him stage fright. Reading the lesson in church was easy, but addressing an audience of mostly strangers? What did one say? In the first place, he was not even an Owu, he was not related to Owu by blood or water. He had, in effect, been blackmailed into accepting the dubious honour. J. A. Ladipo, the headmaster of Igbore High School, was Owu, and Soditan had requested his services at the prize-giving ceremony of his own school. It was a special occasion for which Soditan wished to gather all the local heavyweights. He needed them as balast to offset the presence of the principal guest, Mrs. Melville Jones, wife of the director for education. Ladipo, ever the blunt Owu man, put it to him quite directly:

"Ah, God is good. J. S. O. can't come to honour our gathering after all in December and we desperately need somebody who is close enough to his stature. You agree to come and do us the honour; I agree to come and help you balance Mrs. Melville Jones at your own do. Agreed?"

The teacher was so taken aback by the opportunism of the man that he found that he had shaken hands on the deal before he knew it. And now he could not even think of a theme for his speech. He had given himself today as the absolute deadline for the first draft. His notes on Owu history lay beside him; they included even some bloody clashes with the Ijebu, that is, with his own Remo and Ìsarà ancestors.

But first, the joke to break the ice—he had that ready selected. No sensible speaker plunged directly into his subject; a joke must oil the way. An immaculate script which never deserted him, even in the drafting stage, began to cover the paper: *I was taken aback to find myself asked to be the proposer of the toast of the Owu National Society in place of the well-known educationist and textbook author J. S. Odunjo, at these famous educational premises. I felt I would not be a good substitute, more so when I recollected the story of the Viennese scientist who, with as much pride as could be conjured, announced to his audience: I have discovered a substitute for human blood. After a brief silence, a man from within the audience shouted: You can see that we all here very much doubt it. And don't imagine the income tax people will be fobbed off with that!*

The pencil paused. His original idea was to link the story with his own unpaid appearance there or with the Owu's reputation for hard-headed business. Or else find some connection with the reputation of the Ijebu for being tightfisted. And the story—transpose the story to an Ìsarà herbalist, perhaps? An Ìsarà herbalist announces that he has successfully concocted a substitute for blood. The hardheaded Owu man consults him after falling off his bicycle and losing a lot of blood . . . No, the roles should be reversed. An Owu herbalist invents the blood substitute; then an Ìsarà man falls off his bicycle and consults the Owu man for treatment. On being offered the blood substitute . . . what happens next? Enter Sipe, who works in Inland Revenue. No! Better still, that glorified tax collector should be the one to fall off his bicycle. Come to think of it, was he quite certain he had read the joke? Wasn't it likely that it was from Sipe's unlimited repertoire of stories? No, he felt reasonably certain that it had come from a book, although he could not remember which one.

He turned to his notes on Owu history and character. Begin all over. Given: The Owu are known to be tough, hard bargainers, but they do not appear to come even remotely close to the Ijebu reputation for extracting money from stone. Or blood. Yes, take blood . . .

Fifteen minutes later Soditan admitted failure. At least, deferment, until The Circle could meet and help him out. Jokes, he admitted, were not really his forte. They did not spring to his mind with that spontaneity which he admired in others. So he left a gap for later inspiration and proceeded to the substance; there was no shortage of material in the history of Owu people. But first, perhaps a little more on the theme of his own inadequacies, then contrast them with the virtues of Owu people? *I do however consider myself highly honoured to be asked to speak here, being neither Egba nor Owu, being blessed with neither a sweet tongue nor a good voice. Since you must have known all of this before asking me, I hope you will overlook the inadequate manner in which I set forth what little I have unearthed to redress my ignorance of the many achievements, not only of the Owu National Society, but of Owu people themselves.* He read it over, permitting even his strict judgment to admit that that was as good a transition as he could hope to make between preliminary remarks and the main burden of his speech. Next, to reap the harvest of his diligent research: *The Owu National Society, founded some years ago, no doubt from patriotic reasons, is a society fit to be compared with a tree which has strong roots in the ground and shoots out so many branches at the top. There are, of course, many societies with your own aims, ambitions, and branches, but ask your-*

self which of them has achieved a fraction of what you have achieved since the few years of your birth! Is it not within living memory, evergreen memory, the part you played when a decision was taken that the late Olowu of Owu would henceforth go and collect taxes from the farm? By your unity and steadiness of purpose you put an end to such a step that was fraught with danger to peace, containing as it did a threat of repression to the poor peasants of Owu. Can anyone deny the role you exerted in the selection and installation of the present Olowu . . ." Soditan paused, a little bit uncertain. Would this not be considered an impertinent interference by an alien in the affairs of Owu? He had no means of ascertaining if all of Owu were quite united behind the decisions of the Owu National Society. After all, the former Olowu must have had his own supporters. Again the pencil paused for some minutes. In the end, he left a gap for the achievements of Owu and went into the safer grounds of Owu's role in the Ijaiye wars. The next instant the pencil was flung down. Safer? Was it really that much safer? The Ijaiye war was a war which could awake bitter memories in some of the immediate descendants of the tragic participants of that war. A glancing reference, perhaps, just to insert a historic sense—no more. He filled out the remaining space on that page, took a fresh one, and embarked on the controversial character of Owu people. It was time to draw on his little notebook of quotes, some ready ticked for this address.

Owu people have earned a high reputation, one which makes them frequently contrasted with their neighbours, of sticking to their guns, never being scared to utter their conviction of the truth. Thomas Henry Huxley, the great educationist, it was who said, "Every word uttered by a speaker costs him some physical loss and, in the strictest sense, he burns that others may have light. So much eloquence, so much of his body resolved into carbon acid and . . ." Oh dear! Was that much different from Adeniyi-Jones's approving description of a teacher as a "candle which lights others, while consuming itself"? Would his use of Huxley's quote not suggest that he agreed with that patron of the teachers' union, whereas the truth was that he, Akinyode Soditan, most emphatically did not? No, he must not appear to select for praise airy attributes that he himself considered extravagant to expect in the commitment of a teacher. Akinyode began to wonder if he had not taken on more than he could chew. Still, he found that he had already put together nearly two pages. He returned to the records of the young society for guidance in directions of a less controversial nature. Such as? Pity he had never seen an Owu masquerade, or more accurately, he did not know which of the masquerades that paraded the streets of Abeokuta were from Owu quarter. Some comparative remarks—Owu versus Ìsarà masquerades, perhaps—would have moved his address to areas of culture. Culture would be a less risky subject. He went over what he had written and took his decision: He would leave in the early sections to spike things up a little—a bit of political ginger did no harm— but for the rest, deal with the Owu National Society through its cultural life. . . . He yawned, replaced his files and writing materials in the planned order of resumption for the following day, and retired to bed. On the whole, he reflected, it had been a day well spent. He was well ahead of his working schedule.

By dawn the courier was rendered superfluous. When the maid opened the front door in the morning to sweep out the dust, she let out a scream that took Soditan clean out of his early-morning dream and sat him bold upright in bed. Simultaneously, he heard his wife's voice raised from the adjoining room. "Who is that? Who screamed just now?"

The maid's footsteps came pounding into the parlour, then stopped. Morola could hear the heavy panting as the girl tried to recover some measure of control.

"Bose, is that you?"

"Yes, Ma."

"What were you screaming about so early in the morning?"

"An old man, Ma. He was sitting right against the door."

A loose pair of slippers slapped their way into the front room and their owner voiced his umbrage at the maid. "Is the girl mad? Who is an old man? It is your father who is an old man. Get me some water to drink, you fool."

Later she would tell her mates that she had opened the door that morning to find a *sigidi** squatting by the door. It was all very well to punish her for screaming, she complained, but she dared anyone,

* Incubus.

anyone, even Teacher, who was the most unflappable man in the world, she dared him to open the door in that early-morning half-light when it was neither dark nor dawn, encounter a waist-high object in *agbada* propped against the wall, and not think it was a *sigidi* which had been placed there during the night. Oh yes, she declared. Anyone would have screamed and taken to his heels. It was a wonder she had not fainted. Mama would most certainly have fainted, she with her frail health.

She had good cause to be apprehensive. The head teacher's wife had already decided her punishment; such loss of control admitted of no mitigating circumstances. For his own part, Teacher Soditan, who had been subscribing to the publications of the Rosicrucian Society and sometimes experimented with some aspects of its regimen, regretted that he would have to miss his morning meditation that day. He recognised the voice at once, even though he refused, for some moments, to believe his ears. When he emerged from the bedroom, still trying to fasten his coverlet round his waist, his father, Josiah, was comfortably seated in an armchair in the parlour. The maid returned at the same time with a glass of water that spilled onto the tray held in her trembling hands.

Soditan walked slowly into the room, prostrated himself carefully, and took a chair opposite his father. Then he waited while Pa Josiah drank his water.

"I did not mean to wake the household—this foolish maid. I thought I would sit there quietly waiting for the house to wake. In fact I dozed off. I haven't been to sleep all night. And then she screamed in my ear. Did she think she was seeing a spirit?"

"Never mind the girl, Father. Has something happened at home?"

Josiah refused to be mollified. "Screaming her head off like that! She nearly scared me to death!" His baleful glare followed the girl's departure. "Iyawo nko? I suppose she is awake too, and she really ought to have as much rest as possible. She has to stay home for some time, get plenty of rest, you understand? Forget all her trading up and down for a week—that is what Jagun says. She needs to be strong."

Soditan looked puzzled. "How did you know she was back? Even in your letter—"

"Efuape's son told me. He sent his wife home ahead of the New Year, with some goods just cleared from the harbour in Lagos. Everything works together at the right time, just like I always tell you. How do you think I got here so early? The transport that brought Sipe's wife and goods was a produce lorry going to Omi-Adio to collect a load of palm kernels. It was to leave Ìsarà hours before dawn, so I decided to follow my messenger here. The driver didn't even charge me anything." He chuckled admiringly. "Efuape! There is nothing that one can't get away with. Diverting a whole government vehicle to Ìsarà on the way to Adio. That boy will either end up a millionaire or end up in prison."

"Didn't he pay for the hire, then?"

"Of course," Josiah said. "But, you know, private arrangement. Bringing me here without paying was the *eni**—he knows how to drive a hard bargain, that boy."

"He takes risks," Soditan commented. "But he was born lucky. Well, what about breakfast?"

"All in good time. I didn't come here just to push my message, you know. Something happened. If Efuape had not arrived, you would have seen me later today anyway. You see, last night, Jagun sent for me. I was with him till about two o'clock this morning. I haven't had any sleep at all."

"About that matter, Father—"

"I know, I know. I already know what objections you would have. Don't think I didn't anticipate all your doubts."

"I have written it all in the letter. Do you want me to read it to you?"

"Wait, just wait. I am telling you that something else has happened. Jagun sent for me to tell me that he had seen something. Just in the normal course of consulting—not for anyone, just for general well-being. And he came across something which he recognised as touching me. He sent his servant for me and we looked into it together. Don't say anything. Just wait until Iyawo wakes up and I shall ask her some questions. Then we shall see."

Soditan spoke as gently as he could. "Of course, Father. You ask her anything you want. But I have to tell you, we don't think she should come. Anything you want to do over there, that's fine. I won't even try to stop you. But Baba, you know how we think already, so why involve us in this thing?"

* Bonus.

"Wait, I tell you. Wait until you've heard what we found. It is quite weighty. You say I am trying to involve you? Not me. Blame the person who really involved you."

He turned in the direction of a noise and saw Morola emerge from her bedroom.

"Ah, Iyawo. I knew that *alakori* of a maid must have woken you up!"

Morola knelt before him. "Papa, you are welcome. And don't worry about my being woken up. I was already wide awake."

"Then you should not have been. And I don't want you doing all that travelling around for a while. You have to keep your feet in one place."

"Anything you say, Papa. What of breakfast? I shall go and prepare something."

"Sit here." Josiah's voice had gone very soft as he patted the chair beside him. "We'll get to breakfast soon enough. I want to ask you some questions."

Morola cast a quick glance at her husband, who shrugged slightly. She took her seat and waited.

"Tell me, Morola, do you share your shop with anyone?"

She shook her head. "No. No one at all. The shop is hardly big enough for me."

"Not even the pavement?" he asked. "There is no woman who displays her wares anywhere close to your shop? Someone you allowed to—"

"Oh, the pavement. Yes. There is a woman there. I allowed her to place her *ate* there. Sometimes she is still selling long after I have closed up my shop."

Josiah glanced triumphantly at his own son. "*Alate. Iya alate.* * That was what Jagun saw. One *iya alate* whom she brought there herself."

Morola tried to correct him. "No, I didn't bring her . . ."

Josiah shook his head indulgently. "You don't understand. You did. She doesn't pay you rent, does she?"

"Oh no, God forbid."

"That's it. You brought her there. She is there because of you. Because you gave her permission. *Iwo ro gbas'ile. Ota ile de ni.*"†

---

* The woman with a tray (of merchandise).
† It was you who brought her indoors. And she is an inside enemy.

Akinyode broke the silence that ensued. "And Jagun holds her responsible?"

"No question at all. The letter I sent you, I said that we had already found that Iyawo's illness was not *oju lasan*. That was obvious. We didn't need to look into anything to see that. Twelve months in and out of hospitals, and no one knowing what it is. All those clever overseas doctors? But we looked anyway, just to make sure. Then, last night, Jagun sent for me—I told you. When we looked together, it was there, and Jagun read it out. I tell you, when *awo** wants to take a hand, it takes a hand. Ask yourself. Your wife was in Lagos, that is what we all thought. Efuape's wife brings news that she has returned to Abeokuta. That same night, Jagun sees something. Then it so happens that Efuape's lorry is waiting to go on to Omi-Adio, passing through Abeokuta. A child can see it all. It is not just that it was time that something should be revealed; it meant that it was time something should be done. The evil work of that woman is itself ready to be undone. Its power is on the wane."

Soditan smiled. "Well, in that case—"

Josiah rounded on him. "In that case you are about to talk like a child. Leave everything as it is, right? Wasn't that what you were about to say?" He shook his head in annoyance. "I keep reminding you—I knew what I was doing when I let those people baptise me. It wasn't that I meant to turn my back on everything I knew, just you keep that in your mind! Twelve months! Up and down, in and out, here and yonder. Do you think I can sit all that time with my hands folded? And now that we know what has been going on, you want us to leave things to take their own course?" He paused, turned from one to the other. "Just why do you think these things are revealed to us at all? Why? If they could take their own course for good, without our own participation, why would they be revealed at all? So that we can boast and feel clever for having known? Oh no. *Awo* is far too busy for that kind of indulgence!"

Soditan gestured surrender. The contest had been merely symbolic, anyway. Josiah had to be kept somewhat at bay, just sufficiently to make him understand that his son was resolved to lead his own life,

* Divination.

no more. He respected his father's stubborn will; they were both alike in that respect. The difference was that the teacher disliked open clashes and would walk a circuitous route to avoid them. Not so Josiah.

"All right. What do you want us to do? Of course," he casually added, "as you yourself have just advised, Morola won't be travelling anywhere for some time. I am glad you reinforced what I was telling her only last night. So, whatever you want us to do here, we shall do. If it is to be in Ìsarà, then it must be done on her behalf."

The elder man glared at the son, a suspicion stealing over him. Could it be that he had trapped himself? Not for the first time, he was compelled to cast baleful thoughts in the direction of that Ilesa seminary, which he held responsible for the slippery tongue his son had acquired when it came to an argument. Of course he had to get her to Ìsarà. Going to Ìsarà was a different matter from running up and down on trading errands. In fact, the point of saving her strength was to save it for the visit to Ìsarà and a full *etutu,* with all that would entail. Well, he would just have to be cadgy with this son. Seminary or no seminary, he Josiah was still the head of Ile Lígùn.

"I have the list of things I am taking back with me." He said it with finality. It was clear that the old man was in no mood to permit any new grounds for argument. He ticked them off on his fingers. "A shawl, one she has used since it was last washed. In other words, I don't want one fresh from the washerman. Also one of your own discarded slippers."

"My slippers?" Soditan thought it was a slip of the tongue.

"Yes, your slippers. A very old one, worn through at the sole. He says he prefers one through which the sole of your foot has actually touched the ground."

The son laughed. "Suppose there isn't one?"

Josiah's reply was unsmiling. "Then you will simply have to make a hole in one, put your foot in it, and walk round the house. Stop asking me these foolish questions. I also want one of the coverlets you use for your children." He dug into the pouch of his *agbada* and brought out a scrap of paper. "Here is a list of the other things— snails, two doves, alligator pepper, and the rest of it. Morola must buy them from the market with her own hands—I am sure you will find them all at Itoko." He handed the paper to the wife, who cast a hurried glance over the list.

"Yes," she nodded. "I am sure I can find them."

"Good. While you are getting them, I will wait for you in the shop so I can get a good look at this woman. She can thank her stars that we are all Christians now. If she had tried this when I was as I was, I would be doing more than just taking a look at her. Now I have to settle for simply protecting my own and rendering her powerless to do further harm."

Morola stood up. "Shall I get breakfast now?"

"That is a good idea," Josiah consented. "But first I need a wash."

"I'll have some water for you in the bathroom in a moment."

She left the two men together. Josiah leaned back in the chair, a feeling of partial achievement leaving him somewhat dissatisfied. Still, the battle was not yet over; he would find some way of ensuring that his son did not hide her away during this New Year season, as he did the last one. Not that it mattered that much; Jagun had merely wanted to take a look at her, and pass his hands over her head, the hands which had carried out the *etutu*. The teacher, on his part, remained watchful; it was too early to breathe a sigh of relief that all had gone so smoothly. His father was not the kind to give up that easily.

"So, how is Foluso doing? Does he appear to improve at all?"

Akinyode threw up his hands. "It's the same as I reported to you the last time. The evening classes are a waste of money. And as for the tailoring trade he is supposed to be learning, his master complains of him every day. He is not serious."

"*Oloriburuku!*"* He let out a long hiss. "Did he ask you before making that request he sent me in his last letter?"

The teacher frowned. "What request?"

"A wife. He wants us to find him a wife. That idle one who has no work, no trade to his name, no money to even feed himself, he wants us to find him a wife. To condemn some poor girl from a hardworking family to a life of hunger."

"He asked you for a wife?"

"If I had not been in such a great hurry, I would have brought the letter with me."

* Ne'er-do-well!

"I don't think that boy is well in the head," the son observed at last.

"Forget his foolish head. Let's talk of better things."

"Pity. I had to send him to Lagos with some things for Saaki. I would have liked to see his face when you mentioned that wife business."

Josiah waved off the subject impatiently. "He will meet his deserts soon enough. I am glad you mentioned Akinsanya because I have to tell you that he did nobly over his farm. He sent a pound to pay labourers when I was ill for some weeks and couldn't go on the farm myself. But for him, we would have lost most of the harvest. Too bad about his father. You will come for the funeral, of course? All of Lagos will come to Ìsarà, I am sure."

"I am waiting to be told the date. He will have to fix his car now; he's been having problems with it or he would have brought Morola back himself. He sent a note through her though," he added, smiling, "asking for fruits."

"Fruits? Is he also trading in fruits in Lagos?"

"No. To eat. He has developed this craze for fruits, and just when he gets to Lagos, where they are so expensive. He has gone mad on things like oranges and lemons especially."

Josiah shook his head dolefully. "I feel sorry for our people in that Lagos. I feel really sorry for them. They should come home more often than they do. And tell Akinsanya to take care with those white men. They say he is secretary of a union for people with whom he is working. Isn't that dangerous for him? You do remember what we last spoke about?"

Soditan smiled. "You know Saaki. He is like Sipe—in a different way. He was never meant to lead a quiet life."

"Not like you, enh?" the older man teased.

Soditan waved a hand in the general direction of the compound. "All this place is noisy enough for me. And it keeps one more busy than you can imagine."

Josiah nodded. "I know. I know. Your friends give me all kinds of good news. Oh, and talking of your friends—"

The maid interrupted to announce that water had been placed in the bathroom. Josiah got up, waited for the girl to be out of ear-shot.

"Yes, talking of your friends. Don't lend them so much money."

Soditan was flabbergasted. "Who told you that?"

"I know. I hear these things. They couldn't try it with someone like Sipe. But they take advantage of you."

"Oh, Sipe. He told you?"

"Who said he did? Hasn't he also borrowed money from you? He has eyes on business even though he too is working for government. But these people all know you have a steady job, you don't risk money in all sorts of dubious ways. They know you save steadily, so they know you always have some money in hand. And of course, you lend it to them. You don't know how to say no. That's right. Just like your father."

The son made disparaging noises; then he spoke, rather shyly. "Well, I don't know. I was actually thinking of coming to ask for your advice. It's about Sipe. He wants me to go into business with him."

Josiah stood open-mouthed. "Efuape? Sipe asked you? I thought he had too shrewd a business head for that. He knows you have no head for business."

"Oh yes, he does. But he wants me to invest. He will do all the hard work."

"A-ah. That sounds more like him. What sort of business?"

"Anything. He has so many ideas, that's his trouble. But first he wants us to form a syndicate and put aside money for whatever enterprise we decide on."

Josiah thought over this for a while, then shook his head sadly. "I don't know. I don't know what advice to give. I have never tried that route myself, I have no head for it. But I can't help thinking, sooner or later you will have to start thinking of earning something outside your teacher's salary. The children will grow up. You will want to send them even farther than St. Simeon's. That is the way it is. We all pray that our children go farther than we did, and we try to help God answer our prayers. And if others of your own group start sending their children to study overseas and you can't, you won't forgive yourself. Isn't that the way your mind is working?"

The teacher nodded. As usual, his father had read him accurately. The old man grunted, "Hm-hm," as if to say, "I thought so," then went off for his bath. As usual, he had avoided giving an opinion on the real issue, one way or the other.

V

HOMECOMING

F irst to call was the widow, Mrs. Esan, taking the fight to Akin-yode for leaving Morola behind. She had travelled directly from Saki with bales of *eleto eto* cloth and, with great pride, samples of the Saki variant of the imported velvet *petùje,* whose influx on the market had threatened the local weave from Iseyin and Saki. A former trainee teacher under Soditan, she had imbibed some of his resent-ment at the claims of this cloth, which the Lagosians had named, with such disloyalty, "the cloth which eclipses *etù.*" *Etù,* that noble cloth whose warp and weft spun the very fabric of the history of the Yoruba! Isolated in the Women's Training College to which she had been posted, she thought often of this outrage wrought against the local product by the insensitive elite of Lagos. It was bad enough that this so-called *petùje* should command outrageous prices yet be so much sought-after, but to lord it, in addition, by the sheer power of naming, over a passive product of undisputed worth—this was aug-mented thievery, aided and abetted by the shameless children of the house! She was in charge of homecrafts at the training school, and aided by the weavers of Saki and Iseyin, she set up her looms in the school, unravelled the velvet impostor along patterns borrowed from the disparaged *etù,* then filled them in with cotton yarns, based on the original colour motifs. The result was lighter, more porous, and therefore more suited to the climate. She named it *èye etù.* She had come home with two full sets of *bùbá, ìró,* and *gèlè* for herself and Mrs. Soditan, sewn from this cloth. Its outing was to be at the New Year in Ìsarà, and what a sensation they would have caused, just the two of them in *èye etù.* Now she was faced with bitter disappoint-ment.

"She is in hospital," Soditan informed her, quietly.

Mrs. Esan was immediately contrite, accusing herself of every crime in the world, as if she should have known in advance. This was followed by renewed alarm at the state of Morola's health. Had no solution been found even now for her recurrent illness?

"She is recuperating," Soditan explained. Her illness was finally diagnosed—it was pneumonia all this while, suppressed from time to time by the prescriptions but never fully cured. It all came to light when she returned to the maternity clinic for routine testing . . ."

"The maternity . . ."

Soditan's smile carried a tinge of sheepishness. "Yes, I'm afraid she is pregnant again."

And Mrs. Esan dropped her bag, took off her headtie, flung it round her waist in a loose knot, and began to dance, accompanying herself with her voice.

> *Mo fe e su're o*
> *Aa se*
> *Mo fe e sure o*
> *Aa se*
> *Iku o ni wo'le to wa*
> *Aa se*
> *Arun ko ni wo'le to wa*
> *Aa yun aa yun a bi rodo*
> *Aa se*
> *Aa bi aa bi a bi rodo*
> *Mo fe e sure o . . .* *

In vain did the uncertain father-to-be try to shush her, succeeding only when, now fully carried away, she threatened to extend her joy into the street and join up with one of the roving bands of masqueraders whose treble voices identified them as children. Akinyode shut the door firmly on her and proposed instead a glass of Dimple. Restoring the sash to its proper use, Mrs. Esan accepted a glass of pineapple juice instead, toasted the expected child, recited an endless litany of blessings, and predicted the sex on the spot.

"It's a boy, you will see. And you can only name him Obatunde."

---

* I wish to pronounce a blessing
  So be it
  Death will not cross our threshold
  Illness will not cross our threshold
  Our wombs shall grow big and rounded
  Our wombs shall deliver again and again . . .

"Sit down, sit down," Akinyode urged. "What is happening in Saki? I felt annoyed with myself afterwards. I should have written to tell you I was making that bicycle tour—"

"Yes, just imagine my feelings! I would have stayed behind to welcome you. Oh, I felt so cheated! I had kept some salt, too, but had no one through whom to send it. Since I have only a maid living with me, I always have surplus from my ration. And I had cartons of Guinea Gold and Capstan cigarettes. Those are the favorites of the *akowe*. Bicycle brand is everywhere, I think—no problem there. You know Saki is near the Meko garrison, so the soldiers usually sell us their unwanted rations. Or maybe they steal from stores—that's their own worry. Those favorite brands are scarce now, so I kept some for her. I've left them with Mama at 'Gborobe."

"I shall take them with me when I go back. Thank you."

"I haven't been able to obtain the black thread she wanted—the flat-packed kind for braiding hair. Only the spindle type is available. She wrote me months ago saying she had run out in the shop—she should come over, Teacher. As soon as she is better, let her come and stay with me. Then she can choose all the things she wants. There is so much scarcity down here, but we don't do too badly upcountry, you know."

"I'll tell her," Soditan promised. "As soon as she can travel, she will pay you a visit."

Mrs. Esan sipped her juice thoughtfully. Exhausted perhaps from her gyrations, she gradually sank into a pensive mood. It was a good while before Soditan had to admit that her mind had travelled elsewhere, as thoroughly as during her earlier outburst of joy.

"Is there something the matter?"

The visitor sighed. "I don't know, Mr. Soditan. I simply get worried sometimes. You know, we who live on the way to Meko, we see all the movements of these soldiers. We feel the war a lot more over there, perhaps more than in Lagos. And those of us in the trade—even we part-timers—we know how everything is affected. Farmers know it, business is undependable. And the training schools—education, technical, or whatever—when the students leave, there is no job for them. Even secondary school learners. Well, Teacher, the question I have been asking myself is this: Whose war is this? What is our stake in this quarrel between white people?"

Soditan smiled ruefully. "I wish I could tell you. All I know is that we are caught in it. Unfortunately, we cannot even choose between two evils; one of them has already enveloped us."

"And afterwards?"

"Afterwards, Mrs. Esan, I think you will find that people like Onyah, Akinsanya, Mrs. Kuti, Enahoro, are right. You should read *The West African Pilot* if you can get it in Saki. And the *Daily Times* also. They sometimes echo what Mahatma Gandhi says on the other side of the ocean—they are in the same boat as we are, you know. One way or the other we all have to choose our destiny—ourselves. The war will bring things to a head—for the colonies, and the colonisers. That is what they are saying, and I think they are right."

"But that is the very thing which troubles me, sir. Will these people let go of us? I read what many of our own people have to say about the win-the-war campaign, why they are supporting it. They give that very reason, that the war will set us free. I like to believe it; sometimes I say it myself. But you see, sir, it is that very hope that takes my mind to the many things the white people themselves have written and said. Will this war help them to change their mind? That is my question. Will they have a change of heart? Do you remember, sir, when you used to send me your old journals?"

Soditan nodded.

"Well, I used to copy out some things before returning them—I won't say from whom I acquired that habit!" Her laughter filled the room as she dug into her handbag and brought out an envelope. From it she extracted two sheets of paper, both copied in her handwriting. "You'll be surprised how many of your former students imitate you in that respect—and in other ways too, but I won't tell you which. One of us reads his Bible religiously every night, then follows it with a passage he stole from your notebook—night after night, the same passage, his wife tells me. He sneaked into your office when you were out—he was much too scared to ask your permission."

Soditan shook his head to dispute the last point, but she stuck to it. "Oh yes, we were all a little scared of you, sir. Except maybe Miss Olarounpe." Her eyes danced wildly with mischief. "Do you still hear from her?"

"Sometimes, she sends her old teacher the occasional Christmas greetings."

"Oh no, not so old!" she protested, smoothing out the sheet and holding it to the light from the window. "Shall I read it to you? I am certain it is from *The Elders Review,* although I did not make a note of the source at the time—not a pass mark, I must say, but I was too emotional over the matter, so I forgot. May I read it, sir? It will help me practise my English—my pronunciation, I should say. Out there, I have no one to keep me on my toes. I can bomb the English language worse than Hitler and no one will complain." She cleared her throat self-consciously and began to read: " 'The average West African whom I have met is a good chap. I love him. But he has his limitations. He is a merchant, an electrician, a farmer, or a grocery boy; within his bounds he is excellent—but only within those borders. Occasionally, he shines as a lawyer, a doctor, or a padre—but only very occasionally. You never find the West African who can invent a big business, such as a steamship line, or a bank, or a railroad. The white man steps in there. The average West African is no more fit to govern his own colonies than the average English member of Parliament of today is to handle any part or portion of the British Empire. If the African were allowed to try, and we, at the pull of our silly sentimentalists, withdrew the home stiffening, how long would it be before chaos reigned? Five years? One? Six months?' "

She looked up. "Does it ring a bell, sir?"

Akinyode nodded. "Of course it does. That is a constant theme of the colonial tune. Surely you know that."

She nodded vigorously. "Yes, of course, sir. In fact—"

"Wait. I even think I remember that particular article. That was quite a long time ago. There was heavy correspondence on it afterwards—mostly from Sierra Leone."

"There was. And most of the letters were from other colonial officers who took that writer's side. I wanted to reply myself but it was around that time you stopped sending me journals."

Akinyode looked rueful. "I'm sorry I didn't keep it up."

"Oh no, there is nothing to be sorry about. You did your work; it was up to us to carry on as best as we could. But then we get married, have children, acquire extended families with all their problems. But you see, sir, afterwards something happens, like this war. And one's mind goes back to things one had forgotten, and all the old questions return. If you don't mind, I'll skip the middle and read you the last paragraph. Here it is now. The man says, 'The West African would be well-advised to hug his present vassalage, and indeed pray for it to be firmer in points. Nobody who knows has the smallest idea that the West African Negro can govern himself efficiently. We are not long removed from the blood bath and the crucifixion tree of Benin city.'

"So, there you are, sir. Somewhere in between, the man even says that he couldn't care a bean if virile nations take us over, just like property, that if native West African rule were set up, it would be . . . please, let me just find that place . . . yes . . . he says it would be a 'blood-and-iron affair' which would apply 'whips and scorpions with a steady hand.' The long and short of it, Mr. Soditan, is this, to my way of thinking. If these people have already made up their mind about us, why should we worry about who wins their war and ends up with us as property?"

Soditan walked over to her, took the lined, handwritten sheet, which showed its nine or ten years' aging, and reread the entire extract himself. He felt strangely moved. "And you copied it at the time?" he asked.

"Yes, Mr. Soditan. You see, you underlined it. In red. If I had the magazine in my hand now, I would point exactly where the paragraphs were on the page, even if I was blindfolded."

He laughed. "And you want to tell me that in between trading in *eleto eto,* dried fish, yams, and *gari* together with my wife, plus your teaching schedule, you actually found time to recollect these . . . er, jottings and engage in battle with colonial powers?"

"And the matter of Abyssinia, Mr. Soditan. What sort of a place is that League of Nations? Yes, they should be called that. They are all in league against us, the black people!"

Soditan nodded slowly. "When you next come to Abeokuta, tell your partner to take you to meet Mrs. Kuti. You know Beere, don't you?"

Mrs. Esan's eyes sparkled. "Who doesn't, Teacher, who doesn't?"

"I am sure the two of you will have a lot to say to each other."

"Ah, sorry, sir. I forgot to give you this." She handed over the other sheet of paper. "Please find time to read it, and let me know what you think. I tried out parts of it at the synod last week, in Lagos. I hope you won't disown me when you learn of the reactions. Please look it over for me before I send it to *The West African Pilot.* I really would appreciate your corrections, Mr. Soditan."

"All right. I will."

She stood up, looking elated. "Now I must go and catch my home customers. They are all waiting for their Christmas stock and if I don't get rid of what I've brought before the Lagos people come in—"

"Of course, of course. I am only sorry again that Morola could not come. I know you would have done your rounds together."

"I'll manage. And I've kept her own goods separate. I have sorted out the ones which are for New Year sales; I'll sell them for her and send her the takings."

Soditan watched her depart, then remained by the door looking out into the village as dusk gathered. He felt very strange after the visit. He could not remember when he had exchanged so many words with the woman alone; usually she came to see his wife, who was perhaps her major trading partner. Beyond a comment or casual exchange over some immediate event or news, they had not spoken much together since she completed her practical teaching course under him and was sent off to Saki. There she met and married her husband, a native of Ondo, also a co-teacher. He contracted tuberculosis and later died. For a number of years afterwards she would not even return home, so terrified were people of the disease and its reputed contagion. To make matters worse, they had lost their first two children, although not to the same disease. Later, as a year passed, then two, and it became clear that she had not fallen victim to the disease—which, it was widely assumed, she must have caught from her husband through living together as man and wife—her return became easier and she reintegrated herself into the community, fully. But to have noted and kept that article, which had so outraged him at the time, yet divided his feelings on the cautionary grounds of that dire prediction, the "whips and scorpions," stolen from the Bible . . .

He looked up and saw the familiar figure of his erstwhile colleague Ogunba coming up the road and felt a surge of childlike happiness. Ogunba suited the tranquil part of him; they would meet, greet, and simply sit, commenting desultorily on any subject that happened to cross their minds. As the figure drew nearer, however, he saw that it was not Ogunba at all but his cousin, who so much resembled him as to be sometimes taken for his brother. He drew level with the door and stopped.

"Sir, my cousin asked me to come and greet you."

"Where is he himself?"

"Still in Ijebu-Ode. He hopes to be here tomorrow."

"He will have to pay a fine. I hope he knows that."

"He knows it. And he sent it ahead. This is yours, sir." He handed over a small raffia bag. Opening it slightly, Akinyode beamed with delight, taking out the little packets of seeds, which were neatly labeled in capital letters.

"Gossypium Brasiliense . . . Ishan type Gossypium . . . South African U4 . . . Vinifera Afri . . . Hey, this is what Akinsanya's son promised to send me from Achimota. He must have sent it through your cousin, that's all."

"I am only the messenger," the cousin grinned.

"All right, wait till I see him. If he thinks he can pass this off as his fine . . ."

"He'll be here tomorrow," the messenger promised.

"Yes," Akinyode grumbled. "Leaving me to cope with Efuape all by myself."

A mere trickle to begin with, the human flow through footpaths and surrogate roads would swell gradually into a torrent over the remaining days before the New Year. Ìsarà was filling up. The native sons and daughters came on foot, in lorries, and on bicycles which served more for porterage of personal belongings than for human conveyance, vanishing into bulging sacks, tins, covered baskets, and boxes, weighed down on both sides like donkeys. Singly and in family groups, lorries disgorged the returnees at the motor park. A few vehicles struggled bravely up the sole laterite road, which pierced the very heart of township, past Node's compound and onto the field of bamboo poles which served as the central market, coating the last vestiges of green in an all-pervasive rust. There were a few cars also; their entry brought admiring heads out of doors, peeking through windows, eager to know whose son had finally brought the wealth of Lagos or Kano into Ìsarà—never mind that the motorcar may have been hired for the journey. It was the difference that mattered; someone had actually aspired to a private sedan; the reflected glory enhanced the status of the town.

The push-trucks had the hardest time of all. Every foot gained up the hill had to be secured by thick wooden slabs before it was lost to a backward roll. When the pusher's feet slipped, a disaster was almost inevitable. And it was the traders who needed the trucks, so the loads were predictably heavy. Patiently, the hirer, usually a woman, walked beside the tensed, muscular figures, caked in dust and sweat, and clad—when they were not half-naked—in the most outlandish gear, usually copied from a favourite figure in the cowboy film going the rounds of Ijebu-Ode or Sagamu. The headgear was always the most distinctive; their cheerful banter was incomprehensible to all but one another since it was a unique dialect of Lagosian Ijebu twanged through the nose in the manner of their favourite stars. Clearly they were strong, but it was mostly their humour that got them up the hill.

A patronizing smile broadened on Wemuja's face as he perched on the bonnet of the Commer near Node's compound. Self-consciously he alternated between picking his teeth and puffing on a clay pipe, a new acquisition which he had made only a few weeks before from Mariam's stock. His scoutmaster hat was thrust forward over his forehead, his eyes narrowly calculating whether or not the space left by his Commer on the choked road would suffice the *omolanke,* or would he need to wake up his apprentice, Alanko, to move the vehicle out of the way? Certainly he, the Master Driver, was not going to stir himself for a mere push-truck. As the crude contraption inched nearer, he made his decision. After all, it was nearly a month since Alanko had his last driving lesson. He shouted over the wall of Node's yard, slid down the bonnet onto his bandy legs, and strolled off towards the palm-wine shack near the marketplace. That, he shrugged, was how his own master had taught him. Whenever a chance occurred for a manoeuvre of some five or ten yards, his mentor simply threw the keys at him and left him to sink or swim.

A festive anticipation pervaded the streets, the households, even the churchyard and the marketplaces, where the goods already on display were clearly *oja odun,* not the humdrum, everyday affair of basic needs. The push-trucks had not creaked up the hill for nothing, nor motor passengers paid the extra fare to tempt their driver to risk stalling his engine up the sheer cliff face of the only motorable road into Ìsarà. Already rival explosions of cap guns could be heard outside the houses—homemade "cannons" devised by the local blacksmiths:

The metallic cup was filled with matchheads scraped off matchsticks, a nail was rammed into the cup, and the charge was detonated by striking the nail against a stone or a concrete wall. The larger the charge, the greater the explosion; sometimes the entire weapon split all the way down and had to be taken back to the blacksmith for repairs. And the same children donned their masquerades, took to the streets, jigged from house to house, accompanied by their band of stick percussion and tin-can drummers, though some actually boasted the occasional talking-drum, usually borrowed according to size. They danced as if possessed, inventive, while others augmented their fervour further by loading up, sneaking round to the nearest wall, and detonating their weapons. The dancing grew even more frenzied as the chorus threw its challenge to adult powers—a challenge unanswerable at this universal season of the year—urging half-pennies from reluctant pockets:

> *Olopa ko le mu wa.*
> *Odun to de la nse.* *

Far, far different was the dance of the adults. The mood of levity of groups which drummed past the house of the regent, Olisa, for instance, was on the surface only. More than one war fever had gripped Ìsarà. The capers in the open grounds raised more than dust, and the masquerades emerged for a far deeper purpose than to enliven the days of waiting for New Year revelries to commence. *Orin ote,* the songs of intrigue, had taken the place of the usual sounds of *sakara* and *agidigbo.* Familiar tunes and lyrics were changed or amended subtly as each band of strolling minstrels approached certain frontages or encountered the relations of marked individuals. The Odemo was long dead. The battle for succession was now joined. The war being waged in faraway Europe was relegated to a background noise as rival bands, armed to the teeth with *agogo, sekere, omele, gangan,* and *dundun†* took to the streets.

> *Aafa, a gbe'ke yan*
> *Labalaba oluwo*

* No policeman can touch us.
  It is this festival that we celebrate.
† All musical instruments.

Aafa a gbe'ke yan
Oko iya Talatin. *

Not that Hitler's war was ever permitted to be totally forgotten. Sipe Efuape's first port of call was Pa Josiah's home, where his problematic son would be found, he swore, probably digging a deep hole for his savings to prevent them falling into the hands of the "big bad wolf" from Germany. Akinyode, a smile on his face, watched him drive up the hill in his borrowed Morris, consoled by the fact that he himself had arrived in Ìsarà three days before the seasonal invasion began and had at least enjoyed the very last spaces of tranquility Ìsarà would offer for the rest of the year. Sipe stepped out of the car and smoothed down his *buba,* his glance swept the surrounding houses casually to savour the admiring looks cast in his direction, then he strode grandly into Pa Josiah's living room, overwhelming it completely with his vitality.

"So, you got to Ìsarà before me."

Akinyode shrugged. "As usual."

Sipe looked up at the ceiling, inspecting the house minutely before settling himself into a seat.

"He seems to have missed," he concluded.

The teacher stared at him. "Who did? What did you hide here anyway that you kept looking for?"

"Hole in the ceiling. Hole in the ground. You mean Hitler hasn't bombed Ìsarà yet?"

When the laughter had subsided, Sipe proceeded to upbraid him. "But really, Yode, you are just too much. I write to you on serious, straightforward business matters and what do I get? All sorts of procrastination. Seemingly erudite but merely pedantic wigwagging—"

"Oh-oh-oh-oh!" Akinyode held up his hands, palm forward to mime a shield. "My head, Sipe, my head! You are breaking my head."

"No, no, this is serious. What am I to do with you? You are stuck in that backwater called Abeokuta and your temperament has become one with her rock of ages. Nothing can move them—same with you."

* Chief Priest, vaunting his hunchback
Butterfly with horns
Chief Priest, vaunting his hunchback
Husband of the mother of Talatin.

"Lagos, for me, is—" Akinyode began.

"Forget that! Why do you like to travel backwards? I know why! So that you don't have to face the real issue. I have already given up the whole idea of your coming to Lagos. I tried, yes. But finally I said to myself, Sipe, son of Efuape, give up on that man. He is a stick-in-the-mud, a man of inexhaustible excuses and self-justifications. He will not move. All the efforts you have made on his behalf, all the openings you have obtained for him with the aid of friends, greasing that palm or using 'long legs' here and there—oh, did I tell you that that fellow ended up in jail?"

"No. What happened?"

"He overreached himself. Tried the same trick once too often. Imagine, pretending to collect bribes on behalf of the European supervisor. Anyway, this applicant was a messenger in Joe Allen—"

"Saaki's territory?"

"Yes, that is where our slippery Aiyedipe made his mistake. Ten pounds from an ordinary messenger! How much would a messenger earn in a whole year, much less talk of saving such a huge sum. Anyway, the fellow found the money, paid him, and began the long wait. Come today, come tomorrow . . . three months, then four, five, six. He got desperate, naturally—At least give me back my money, he kept crying. Doesn't the song say 'Orisa, if you cannot save me . . .' "

" '. . . leave me at least as I was.' "

"A-ha. Well, to cut a long story short, the messenger and would-be clerk took his case to Saaki. Hm. You know our man. He fired a formal letter directly to that supervisor in his hottest English, made it double-barrelled by signing S. A. Akinsanya, Secretary, Lagos Motor Workers' Union, and Secretary, Nigerian Youth Movement, then took it personally to the man."

"Ho ho. Sangba tu s'epo!"*

"Precisely. The supervisor quickly called the police. The end of it all . . . eighteen months. And another wasted opportunity."

"Yes, it's sad. When someone in such a position throws away his future just like that!"

Sipe looked at him with his perfected mocking tilt of the head. "Who are we talking about?"

* The bean-cake has scattered in boiling oil.

"Aiyedipe, of course. Who else?"

"You! You, you, you! I am talking about Akinyode *omo* Soditan! That was another job open, free for the taking. Vacancy created instanter—Aiyedipe out, Soditan in. Senior accounting clerk, Lagos Town Council. You would be right in the centre of action, where all sensible men with an eye to the future congregate."

Akinyode stood up and moved to the cupboard. "I have some Dimple left from that bottle Opeilu sent me."

"Oh yes, go ahead. Change the subject. Who wants you in Lagos, anyway? Wasn't that the very point I began to make? There is no longer any need for any of you to come to Lagos. But is that the same thing as refusing to *invest* in Lagos? What is wrong with investing in Lagos?"

The teacher smiled and Sipe sneered as they both gave the answer at the same time. "The—war."

"So why do you continue to bother this born provincial?"

Sipe sighed. "What a pity. What a pity."

He continued to shake his head, recollecting the many lost opportunities. He had himself bought property, indifferent to Hitler's bombs which might choose to fall on Lagos. If Lagos was indifferent, then so was Sipe, son of Efuape. Until the governor began to pack out of his residence, he considered his investments safe. He had taken only one precaution—removed what money he had in the post office savings account and transferred it to a proper bank, advising all the ex-Ilés to do the same. The post office savings could be commandeered for the war effort, compulsorily acquired in return for war bonds. That was one of the few advantages of working in government service—one gleaned such bits of vital information and acted in time to forestall such awkward developments. There were a few other pleasant by-products too, all of which he did his best to share among his intimate circle. Somehow Sipe had long since come to the conclusion that none of the others were worldly-wise, that he had been uniquely chosen to help them find their way in an inhospitable world.

As if reading his thoughts, Akinyode, handing him a glass, a bottle of soda, and the whisky, enquired, "Anything going in 'private treaty'?"

Efuape hissed. "What is private treaty to you? Do you know how many chances you've wasted?"

"Don't worry. It's not for me; Osibo says he might be interested."

"Private treaty" was another unwritten bonus of working either in government service or within or near Lagos. It brought an enterprising mind—not just everyone—into contact with government and licensed auctioneers under whose hammer passed landed property. Private treaty meant prior arrangement, with the public hammer only providing the formal show. The auctioneer took his cut, and so did the middleman, if there was one. Sipe had succeeded in putting together a treaty or two; the rewards had been sufficiently lucrative to enable him—aided by the same contacts—to do a private treaty on his own behalf. The result was a modest bungalow in Ebute Metta, one wing of which had, until a few weeks before, borne a signboard announcing the birth of his long dreamed-of COASTAL HERBAL INSTITUTE. The dethronement of that board—which Sipe swore was only temporary—was the result of concerted efforts of the Medical Association and the only slightly less prestigious body called the Qualified Dispensers' Association. That argument which ran lightheartedly in the head teacher's home in Aké between Osibo and Soditan had finally been transferred to the public ring, carried into a realistic confrontation with the young entrepreneur. A herbal institute? What sort of a monster was this supposed to be? Sipe could only rage in the background. As a civil servant he could not even enter the fray directly, since he had acted against his terms of employment by engaging, in the first place, in private enterprise. Everyone did it, of course—who wanted to retire on a niggardly government pension? The essential thing was not to get caught. A front managed the business, erecting barriers of files to camouflage his principal. The affair rankled deeply in Efuape. Not once, however, had Akinyode even linked Osibo with the actions of his professional union. Now Efuape slowly put down his glass, staring at the teacher as if at a madman.

"Did you say Osibo?"

"Which one?"

"The same. You know, the Genie of the Bottle."

"And you want me to help him to a private treaty?"

"Sure. Isn't that your favourite hobby? Lucrative hobby, I should add."

Sipe appeared to pick his words with difficulty. "You—want—me—to help—that—dispenser?"

"What is the matter?"

"Did he actually send you to me? Or are you just asking this all on your own?"

"Sipe, what's wrong with you? What has he done?"

"What has he done? What have they not done, all those Europeans and their black quacks calling themselves Doctor this and Dispenser this and that? Have you forgotten . . . ?"

"Oh." Akinyode, belatedly remembering the unfinished warfare. "Well, even so. What has it got to do with the Genie?"

Sipe waved his hands furiously, as if to ward off the subtly gathering forces of assault which he could already divine in Akinyode's mind. "You can forget everything already seeping into your mouth. This is no joking matter and I am not listening to your arguments. Tell your Genie he can squeeze himself back into one of his dispensing jars, preferably one of those labelled 'Poison.' That is, if his European nose can fit in. Typical. Only a person with a nose like that will choose to be a dispenser anyway; it fits the white company into which his job takes him. No—don't say anything. What is wrong with our medicines? They all turn up their noses at our native medicines—what did their grandfathers use to bring them up? Dare they come to Ìsarà and tell me not to set up a herbalist shop in Ita Oba? Do they dare close down the herbalist stalls even in Ereko market in Lagos? No. They cannot. They know their fathers' heads will end up in the *salanga** behind the nearest compound. But a proper shop in Lagos is too good for herbalists, not so? The streets of Ebute Metta are too European for black man's medicines!"

Akinyode sipped his whisky and water slowly, waiting for him to wind down. "Have you done?"

"No!" He exploded. "Do you know, my clerk and the agent were both arrested! They were taken to the CID and interrogated!"

"You wrote me. You bailed them out, didn't you?"

"And they were charged to court . . ."

"Oh. I didn't know that . . ."

"That happened last week! But they don't know who they've taken on, oh no, they don't! They are fooling with the son of Efuape—God willing, a millionaire in his own right before white hair makes its

* Pit-latrine.

appearance on his head and long before the first spot of shiny skull begins to show."

"Resolute Rooster!"

"Cock of the Walk."

"Mephisto-Rooster."

"Death to the Beestons of this world and their native allies. Anathema and Maranatha!" And his mood changed abruptly, dissolving in self-deprecating laughter.

"Wait, wait, wait. I missed that. What was that terrible curse you just pronounced?"

"Anathema and Maranatha! Plus fire and brimstone and the Seven Plagues of Egypt!"

Akinyode shook his head. "I know the others. But which one is Maranatha?"

"I don't know. But we had this magician who performed in Glover Hall. And that seemed to be his all-powerful conjuring code. Apart from the regular 'Abracadabra' and 'I conjure you in the name of' and so on."

Akinyode tested the phrase in his mouth, chewing the words. "Anathema and Maranatha! He must be from India."

"They all claim to come from India. Or at least to have trained there. Anyway, those dispensers will find that Ìsarà medicine is stronger than theirs. We will shrink them down to size, seal them up in their own medicine bottles, and float them back to England."

"All right, all right. You know Osibo had nothing to do with it. It was obviously government action. If Uncle Segun had been home, he might have prevented it. He works with the General Hospital, so he has influence in government circles."

"That Rosicrucian? He only eats vegetables, you told me."

"And what has that to do with herbal medicine? If anything, it should make him more sympathetic."

Efuape ruminated. "Maybe. Maybe. All I know is that he is almost the opposite of his brother, I.O. Anyway, what news of the dandy? England must suit him—he can have all the tea parties he wants. And bow ties. Still, I don't envy him. I only hope he is dodging the bombs in London. People like him don't bother with protection before they leave. They don't bother to arm themselves with *egbe* and the like."

They fell silent. The war was both remote and near. They had been part of crowded scenes at the harbour, had looked in on preparations when a son of Ìsarà, or indeed any friend or colleague, joined the select band of those who would leave "in search of the Golden Fleece." The prayers were now more fervent and frequent, no longer the routine send-off services at home or in church, the parting benediction was far more passionate as the well-wishers were finally persuaded to descend the gangway and the boat began to weigh anchor. The thanksgiving services that welcomed them back were riotous celebrations of the heart, not merely hymns of pride at the numerical growth of the local challenges to European control of Nigerian life.

His face clouded and solemn, Akinyode said, "Suddenly, Ashtabula is full of new perils."

Outside, the haunting chant of a girl selling *ebiripo* floated in their direction. But it was drowned moments later by a more aggressive tune, and as both men picked out some words, they realised that the faction of the regent was on its way to pay Pa Josiah's house a glancing visit. Akinyode shut the window that looked out on the road but left the top half of the door as it was, open. The revellers' passage was mostly good-humoured but the challenge was undisguised. They paused directly outside the house, pounded the road on jubilating feet, as if already assured of victory. The name of their candidate was sufficient motif for their improvisations: How, indeed, could an elephant be shifted by a child?

> *Atari ajanaku*
> *E mi s'eru omode*
> *Eni ema a m'erin yi'se*
> *A r'orun bo, a f'ina bori.**

But not even this ongoing skirmish succeeded in banishing for long the other, whose reminders had become woven into daily existence. And it was not simply the usual run of rumours, which once brought the war to Lagos and, later, Meko.

---

* The head of the tamer of forests
  Is no load for a child.
  Whoever will turn aside an elephant's stride
  Will first visit heaven, he must wear fire on his head.

After the first bombs fell on London, the war effort was stepped up even more intensely in the colonies, a spirit of patriotism for the colonial powers calculatedly whipped up, even taken to a competitive dimension. The Spitfire Fund, for instance: rallies, concerts, exhibitions, dances, and plays organised to raise funds to purchase a Spitfire fighter for Britain. Both within their hometowns and operating through their town unions in Lagos, Spitfire Clubs vied with one another to prove themselves loyal subjects of the crown and defenders of British possessions. The Residents, the District Officers, toured the country, encouraging the numerous events, announcing the progress of the collections, and spurring others to greater efforts. Spitfire badges were distributed to the deserving; the more successful organizers were honoured with invitations to tea parties at the Residency.

The dissidents were censored. The intrepid Mrs. Esan seized her chance to declare that the war would free Africans, that Africans "can set the Thames on fire." It happened during the "free session" of the synod in Lagos, after the official business of the gathering was over. She had begun harmlessly enough, delighting her listeners with her imagery of the institution of marriage as the union of the shuttle and the loom. As she warmed up, however, asking into what role the African family should fit in the war, the assembled prelates became restless. Glances were exchanged with increasing intensity, notes were passed. The presiding bishop tugged at his round collar but there was nothing anyone could do until the well-known trader-teacher of Saki completed her thesis and sat down to restrained applause.

The war even bred expectations. Would government really pay the rumoured "war bonus" of forty percent of the salaries of civil servants? A twenty-six-thousand-pound outright grant to teachers was no rumour. Denounced by Onyia as grossly inadequate—it was meant to compensate for the sharp rise in cost of living—it was yet to be shared out. And in any case, shared out on what basis?

And salt turned to gold dust.

It was a mystery. How could common salt suddenly vanish from the markets? Where it was available, its price had jumped tenfold or more. And finally, it was now being rationed. Salt! Rationed? How could such a thing happen? Not even in those ancient wartimes was such an event recollected, and this was a war thousands of miles away. Was salt also part of the war effort? Was salt used to manufacture guns and Spitfires? Or could it be gunpowder?

But the tailors were doing well. In a different corner of Ìsarà, Tailor Famade was awaited in vain; he would not be home this New Year as there was far too much money to be made. Over two hundred tailors, he wrote, had been hired by the government to make army uniforms. He would simply have to celebrate the New Year another time, not this year, thank you. This was boom time for his trade and he would not be a proper child of Ìsarà if he threw that chance away to come and feast at home. The war might end the following week, and then would he not bite the fingers of regret?

It was boom time also for enterprising lorry owners. Private lorries were seized to transport goods and soldiers, and there was compensation at thirty shillings a day. And so began the scramble to hand over lorries. Bribes to the police, to government officials, by lorry owners: Seize mine, please, won't you please seize mine? Food prices, the cost of utensils, clothing, farm implements, even of local foods, rose until the pulpits rang with denunciations. Money is the new idol; the spirit of religion is dead in us! Why, why is this war bringing out the worst in us? So what would it do to those who are actually engulfed in it—will those mothers now begin to sell their children for a quick profit?

And there was panic within some Ìsarà households. That Osode should join the army was only expected. He was heavily in debt and there was no other course for him. Mind you, he had astonished even his loudest enemies; his first paycheck was sent to Akinyode to pass on to some of his creditors; so was the next. And he wrote, enclosing a picture of himself in full uniform, braids and all, proudly announcing his promotion to the post of ammunition storekeeper. While the rest of the country scrounged for salt wherever they could, Osode revealed that there was no shortage of that commodity in the army. He sent the head teacher a bag and promised to send more if needed. Books were what he needed in turn; he was also seizing his chance to study shorthand in the army's vocation school. He wanted to increase his vocabulary. Would his friend the teacher kindly send him any unwanted books?

But that was Osode, always a wild one, which was no wonder, as he had a drunk of a father who had even sold his family land (includ-ing farmland) in order to remain in Lagos and crawl from bar to bar. But what would one say of the son of the Reverend Opelami, a well-brought-up son, lacking nothing, who had even graduated at Yaba Institute of Health and was obviously destined for greater things! Everything was prepared, his admission to a higher institution in Bristol confirmed. His passage was booked, a new wardrobe pre-pared by the "London-trained, etc., etc.," men's outfitters in Broad Street. Even the farewell services had been held—both in Lagos and Ìsarà. All that was left was for the liner to dock in Lagos and young Opelami, escorted by a galaxy of his father's friends, relations, and their relations, would be consigned to the merciful hands of God of the high seas. Only . . . Opelami went mysteriously AWOL, and it took a letter from Osode, his childhood friend, to reveal that he was with him in Kaduna, enlisted in the infantry. The wise heads of Ìsarà shook their heads; no, there was no doubt about it. Envious enemies of the family had done it. They had worked at his head and turned it in the wrong direction. *Efun!* Even a child could see it—*efun!*

"I suppose," Akinyode enquired suddenly, interrupting the direc-tions of their individual reveries, "I suppose you would have thought of publishing?"

Sipe's snort of dismissal required no elaboration.

"The reason I ask," the teacher persisted, "is that I received a very interesting proposal from—you will never guess who."

"It can only be a woolly-minded teacher like you. Look, I have given it plenty of thought. Leave publishing and printing to the government and the Church Missionary Society. Publishing is no way to real business for people like me."

Akinyode sighed. "D. O. Fagunwa doesn't think so."

It sat Sipe up with a jerk. "Fagunwa? The *Ogboju Ode* man?"

Akinyode nodded. "The same."

"And he wants to set up publishing?"

"No, not quite. But he has put forward a—well, something a young entrepreneur like you might want to consider. At sixpence a copy, he believes he can provide a background to the war, just to help our people understand what is going on. And of course it can become part of our history textbooks, proving—maybe—as popular as his *Ogboju Ode.* Just a small pamphlet. So he is looking for a printer. He already has the backing of the Resident of Oyo province, but that one cannot guarantee the use of the government printer."

Sipe's shake of the head was quite dubious. "Hm. I doubt it will prove that popular."

"Even from the pen of a famous writer like Fagunwa? And he plans to do it bilingually, you know, English and Yoruba. And that is only to start with. Later, it will have other bilingual versions— English-Ibo, English-Hausa, maybe even Tsekiri and one or two other languages. He'll call it *Iwe Itan Ogun."* Soditan paused. A smile broke out on his face, mischievous. "We should recommend Mrs. Esan to him, I think—you know, she could write the foreword."

"Eparipa!"

"Well, just an idea. Two warring heads in a book on war—why not? Anyway, he is thinking of an advance subscription drive—he cites the example of Dr. Azikiwe's *West African Pilot,* which already had a sale of five thousand copies guaranteed before he printed the first copy."

Sipe snorted, derisively. "You see, you are all the same—teachers, fabulists, and innocents. You are comparing a war pamphlet with a newspaper? Who really cares about the war? Oh, just because we are all doing what we can for the victory of the Allies—heh, you think people like Onyia and Esan and that Saro man Clinton are in the minority? You can count the son of Efuape among those who swear that this war will give Africans and Asians their freedom!" He sprang up, tiptoed to the door, and glanced melodramatically to left and right. "But don't say you heard it from Sipe's own lips because he will deny it and swear on his grandfather's bones! The law does not recognize hearsay or—indirect speech." And he threw his head back and rocked back and forth in uproarious laughter. "Do you still hear from her, by the way?"

The door was flung open and a compact tornado erupted into the room. Neither of the two young men expected Pa Josiah. Seasonal homecoming, as this was, generally meant that he would abandon his home completely to his son and his friends, taking refuge with his wives in turn, but mostly staying with Jagun. Especially in the first few days of reunion, when they all moved from one house to the other, drinking the spoils of their prolonged sojourn away from home and swapping tales. Josiah's forehead was creased in violent furrows as he swung from one figure to the other and released a compressed snort, then jerked his head backwards to the figure of Jagun, standing in the doorway just behind him.

"They are laughing," he said. "They have come home for New Year and all is well." He marched into the room, fixed them both with baleful eyes. "You have cause for merriment, not so? You don't even care that war has broken out beyond these walls?"

Sipe and Akinyode exchanged puzzled looks, which seemed to infuriate the old man all the more.

"Yes, war!" he virtually screamed. "While you sit there talking grammar—and you, Akinyode, you, whom I relied on to warn them in Lagos, did I not tell you the matter was getting desperate?"

Hitler! Was he in Lagos already? Chaotic thoughts raced through the teacher's mind. Well, he was right, after all. By now Hitler's storm troopers were probably sequestering Sipe's "private treaty" properties and carting off the occupants to slavery. The agent and clerk would wish they had not been bailed out after all by the Resolute Rooster. The police cells seemed suddenly safer. There was only one thing he could not understand: What was he supposed to have done to halt this Teutonic invasion?

Sipe's mind had raced even farther. Once again, he had failed to anticipate! So much for careful planning, so much for all the gibes at the cautious Yode. Next came the question: How soon would Hitler's conquering hordes march into Ìsarà? To make matters worse, he was still based in Epe, and if there was one thing they had all learned, it was that the first target of an invading force was the harbour. After Lagos, Epe had to be next. He had not built a house in Epe but had already secured a piece of property—and on the waterfront. Indeed, Sipe's next project was a simple canoe with outboard motor, nothing like the Resident's yacht nor a simple canoe with outboard motor, semidetached, but still an integrated vessel, the model of which he had seen in Epe's burgeoning shipyard, and on which he had made a modest down payment. Now it would be commandeered, just as the British had seized the lorries, only—if Hitler's reputation was to be believed—without even the mention of compensation.

"Well, are you just going to stand there staring at me like *ileya* rams? Get inside that tin-box motor you have left outside my door and let Lagos know what is happening. The Olisa faction has installed its Odemo!"

Yelps of disbelief, horror, and anguish were rent from his bewildered audience of two. Jagun had come fully inside the cottage; he led Pa Josiah to a seat by the window and sat on the chair just vacated by Efuape.

"They have. It is true what you just heard. It happened this afternoon."

The elder Josiah hissed a trickle of snuff-black juice through his upper teeth onto the floor. "Yes, the regent. The one we named regent after the death of the Odemo. But I know where he got his courage—it is that senile old man Agunrin Odubona, calls himself Agbari Iku!* Odubona, who doesn't even accept that the railway or motor lorry exists in this world!"

Sipe raised his hands. "Enough, Baba, we will leave tomorrow. Awobodu will still be in Lagos. And Akinsanya. We will round up our friends in the newspapers and cry havoc in the ears of the governor himself!"

"It is an abomination," Jagun persisted. "They could not even perform the proper rites. How could they? But Olisa took his creature into *iledi* . . ."

"Who?"

"Who? Erinle, of course."

"I just wanted to be sure it was still the same person."

"Who else could it be?" Josiah snapped. *"A nki, a nsa, o ni oo m'eni to ku!"*†

"His supporters have sung past the house," Akinyode explained, as if to mollify him, "but we still could not assume that Erinle would agree to such an illegal step. It is so foolhardy—"

"It is worse than foolhardy. Erinle has committed *eewo.*‡ To put on the regalia without the correct rites! He thinks he is riding on the reverence we all have for Agbari Iku, who supports anything that is toothless like him!"

"We will leave before dawn," Akinyode promised, nodding towards Sipe. "Tonight, we will meet with the others. Some will go to Ibadan and report the matter to the district commissioner. Another

* Death Skull.
† We call out his praise-names and recite his lineage, yet you continue in ignorance of the identity of the deceased.
‡ Taboo.

delegation will visit the Resident—everything will be arranged; leave it to us, Baba. In fact, we should start thinking of a lawyer. I can see the whole affair ending up in court."

Sipe spoke next. "There is only one thing. The whole town knows who Olisa's candidate is; we've all known that for some time. But all we have regarding the choice of the other side is mere rumour. The last we heard was that five names altogether were sent to the king-makers, including Erinle's. Who are the other four?"

"The other four?" Jagun stared, open-mouthed. "We farmed past that stream a long time ago."

"You mean you don't know?" And Josiah regarded his own son with unbelieving eyes.

"All you said, Baba, was that the matter concerned us in Ile Lígùn. That we had an interest in the outcome."

Jagun looked at Josiah, who threw up his hands but nodded assent. "All right," he said. "Come closer."

Ray Gunnar was a young middle-aged Trinidadian of Indian origin and adventurous bent. He woke up mid-ocean one morning in October 1939, overwhelmed by a belated realisation that he had committed the greatest error of his life. The torpedoes had so far ignored him, but news of their depredations came daily over the radio and were reinforced by daily emergency drills on board in which both crew and passengers were compelled to participate. Over the wireless he had also heard the torrential harangues of the man with the unique moustache, and even though Gunnar did not speak a word of German, he had become convinced that this little man, a total stranger, had a personal, single-minded design against his life. Gunnar's dreams became sessions of emotional torture, from which he often woke up screaming and sweating, invoking the aid of his personal *obeah* and the hundred and one deities of his forgotten ancestry, which was Hindu, for the security of his existence.

England, the "mother country," was—if all reports were to be believed—herself quaking under this menace, so who was he, a mere deckhand, barely above the status of a stowaway, to refuse to take this threat of annihilation to his very existence seriously and personally?

His presence on this cargo boat—which took also a dozen and a half steerage passengers—was clearly a result of compulsion: Ray Gunnar had only that choice or a stretch in prison, for reasons he preferred to forget. But the violent contractions of his stomach on that sea voyage soon made him look back with longing to the abandoned prospect, which certainly did not include flying bombs and torpedoes on the wide-open seas. Before he got to Liverpool he had made up his mind that the return journey home would be his last. When his ship docked, however, and he felt the firm, secure contact of good mother earth beneath his feet, he knew that he had sailed on his very last voyage for a long time. Ray Gunnar jumped ship. The Liverpool air was a dirty fog but it smelled infinitely healthier than the mists and squalls of the open seas, whose depths were constantly threaded by invisible torpedoes seeking out his heart and no other, no matter where he chose to hide himself within the bowels of the boat.

To Ray Gunnar, making friends was second nature; no one who tended his life with such disarming candor and affection could fail to evoke sympathetic feelings. He was especially drawn to West Africans, who were not much different from the Trinidadian blacks, whose cultivation had landed him in that small trouble with the police. A series of menial jobs took him to the black centres one after the other—Birmingham, Hull, Glasgow, and eventually London. His West African acquaintances were fascinated by his store of scratchy but authentic calypso records, and he also appeared to have an inexhaustible supply of a brand of marijuana which, they swore, was more aromatic than any they had ever smoked. In return, when he decided to move to London, his African friends provided him with a letter of introduction and the address of the West African Students' Union, a home from home for the increasing band of African students in London.

Ray Gunnar was impressed by the organization of the students. No less than an authentic princess, the daughter of a paramount ruler in Yorubaland, the Alake of Abeokuta, held the office of the union's treasurer. Its secretary-general, a brilliant, articulate lawyer called Ladipo Solanke, actually held liaising meetings with important officials at the Colonial Office in Whitehall, and their news journal did not hesitate to castigate British colonial policies in incredibly robust language. As for the League of Nations, a debate on the conduct of the League of Nations towards Abyssinia in its dispute with the premier of Italy, Benito Mussolini, literally took his breath away. Some were self-declared communists. One Nigerian prince had fought with the International Brigade. "Hats off to Hitler" was the title of a lecture that Gunnar attended. The students obviously did not fear the wrath of the British government. Nothing was sacred to them, and to tell the truth, Gunnar was more than a little bit intimidated by their lack of regard for the sensibilities of their host government.

Before long, Gunnar had obtained a job as cleaner and general odd-job man at the African hostel in Camden Road, London. He got to know the students very well, their problems and their ambitions. He had of course long since made a stunning discovery: The preeminent obsession of the West African, both in Britain and at home, was—studies. It did not matter the subject or the end qualification: London matriculation; bachelor's or master's degrees; higher, elementary, or primary examinations in the various professions—law, medicine, pharmacy, accountancy, economics, etc. The West African paid vast sums to famous and reliable correspondence schools like Wolsey Hall, Oxford, but even more to fly-by-night schools which simply collected the cash and fed the students useless instruction papers. Such schools, unlike the accredited ones such as Wolsey, did not even mark course papers or assess the students' progress.

Gunnar was very interested in the potential of this educational hunger. He studied the wording of advertisements placed by correspondence schools and tried a few tentative compositions himself. He was impressed by the results. He took a bus to the opposite end of London, Kennington, and paid for a post office box. Then he had leaflets printed, which he stuck on the notice board of the African hostel, left on dining tables, in the common rooms, and under the doors of the students' bedrooms. Avoiding the journal of the students' union itself, *WASU*, he obtained the addresses of other journals, such as *The West African Review* and *The Nigerian Teacher*, and invested some of his accumulated savings in advertisements on their pages. Then he sat back, carrying out his humble chores at the hostel, running private errands for students and visitors alike, while he waited for the postal orders to flow in.

It was purely by chance, as he browsed through old copies of *WASU* in the reading room, that Ray Gunnar learned that a great Negro bass named Paul Robeson had actually visited the student centre during those years of his duels with the Trinidadian police. Paul Robeson had then delivered a speech which still formed a subject of enquiry in students' letters to the editor and was variously described as "invigorating," "a cultural manifesto," "a summons to the black Renaissance," etc. What had become of this great project, they demanded? Gunnar's chick-pea eyes popped out of his head as he read the rollcall of African elite who had graced the occasion and who in turn graced Paul Robeson with the accolade Babasale, in effect, the Grand Patron of the Union. His wife also earned the female equivalent, Iya Egbe. So Ray Gunnar laid his mop and pail aside, tracked down the famous speech in the sparse library of the reading room, and studied it. The great man had not minced his words, nor did he confine himself to misty rhetoric, no! Paul Robeson actually launched a project, and this project touched a creative chord in Ray Gunnar: Robeson would create a Negro Theatre in the West End of London.

Theatre was a field to which Ray Gunnar instinctively felt he was born—his life, after all, had been nothing but theatre. In his next advertisement, therefore, "Professor" Gunnar was pleased to announce that the Ray Gunnar Inter Correspondence School would also provide courses in all theatre and cinematic skills and was setting up an actors' school in the very heart of London. But it would serve more than actors and future film stars; Gunnar's school would teach "confidence, public personality, poise, and public speaking, to lawyers, preachers, executive officers, princes, and politicians." At the bottom of the advertisement was boxed a quote from Paul Robeson's speech:

> Out of these traditions will grow with spontaneity and power an art perhaps comparable with that of Elizabethan England— but unique art, Negro art, yet as far removed from the Negro art we know as modern British poetry is from that of Chaucer. I do not think this is an impossible dream.

Ray Gunnar then wrapped up his copy with a ringing annunciation in bold print:

THE DREAM OF BABASALE, PAUL ROBESON, HAS FINALLY ARRIVED! BE PART OF IT! CREATE THE GREAT NEGRO CULTURE!

In faraway Sierra Leone, Gold Coast, Liberia, or Nigeria, no young reader of this advertisement had any doubt at all that the school project was the authentic product of Paul Robeson's brain. The R. G. school also promised scholarships, for which application forms were available for the modest sum of one guinea—postal orders only.

For most aspirants, their contact with Ray Gunnar began on the pages of the journal and ended with their dispatch of the fee for an application form. There were, however, the exceptions. These were the stagestruck cases whose thirst for the boards could not be assuaged by the eloquent silence that followed the dispatch of their one pound, one shilling. They accompanied their fee with passionate pleas, expressing their readiness to stowaway to London if a scholarship was not forthcoming and to undertake the most menial of jobs to keep alive during their training. Ray Gunnar sympathized, offered them the desired scholarship, which, however, required further deposits "for the completion of formalities as required under British law." In many cases, though it sometimes took up to six months to a year, the deposits would be painstakingly saved and sent to Ray Gunnar Inter for Drama.

Efuape was too earthy an individual to be affected by the malady of the stagestruck; nevertheless he had long realised the business potential of theatre in an entertainment-hungry Lagos. Having watched a few Christmas and Easter "cantatas" and the odd historical play or biblical story dramatised by amateur groups, counted the heads of the audience, and estimated the production outlay, he began to give periodic thought to exploring this avenue of obtaining capital for his greater ventures. Moreover, he had watched Akinyode's efforts in Aké, as his versatile friend assembled a team to prepare the pageant celebrating the one-hundredth anniversary of the entry of the first missionary into Abeokuta, an event that would last two days and promised to be elaborate. It would involve almost all the articulate adults of Abeokuta and even their children. Sipe had also taken to heart the stirring performance of *Faust*, when he had been one of the young blades who created such a sensation among the audience. Again, the observant young man had noted the arithmetical lesson of the audience multiplied by the entrance fee minus the probable cost of production.

Fascinating as Aké's centenary pageant developed, it was the drama of Akinkore, the librettist, that mostly intrigued him. Sipe had taken his annual leave during preparations for the pageant. Spending most of that time with the teacher, he had obtained a ringside seat at the unfolding of this drama and been bemused by the intricacies revealed in the nature of the dramatic muse.

First, the organising committee (appointed by the Anglican diocese) met and selected what should be the highlights of the drama. The first visit of the Reverend Henry Townsend was accepted as the starting point but it was his second visit, in company of Reverend and Mrs. Gollmer (reduced to Goloba in Egbaland), which would form the centrepiece of the drama. It was this second visit which led to the establishment of the churches; and even more significantly, the visit took place at a perilous moment for the Egba, who were then at war. Such potent ingredients of history could not be celebrated with a mere thanksgiving service, and it was indeed this fact which had led to the commissioning of the pageant.

The head teacher tracked down the wandering minstrel, Mr. Kilanko, to assist him in composing the music. Various individuals had been marked down for various roles—Osibo, the dispenser, was, for instance, a natural for one of the white visitors; his long face and hooked nose eliminated most of the competition. So did the light-skin complexion of the shy, normally retiring court registrar from Igbore, Bandele Dosumu. And Sipe, bored with merely watching his host pump the pedals of the harmonium and issue instructions on numerous details, accepted a small role as the ghost of Chief Sodeke, who died just when news came from Badagry that the nasal preachers were on their way to Egbaland, their purpose being to establish a Christian mission. Sipe would have to take casual leave for the performance week and travel back for the event, but Akinyode rehearsed him in this newly created role before his departure.

The search for the librettist was easy: Akinkore, a health officer with creditable experience in the writing of Christmas and Easter cantatas. He embarked on his assignment with enormous enthusiasm, drew up a vast list of dramatis personae, unearthing minor characters whose involvement everyone else had forgotten, even inventing others in order to accommodate new aspirants to the Thespian crown. Chiefs, civil servants, tax inspectors, nurses, policemen— all were ordered to stand by. The Egba nation had need of them! This was an event which would resound not only in Lagos but in the Home Office in London. Akinkore split up the times and places of action in the best professional style:

Act I, Scene i: at Badagry.

Act I, Scene ii: at Ado.

Act I, Scene iii, had as yet no location but this was compensated by the subtitle: OKUKENU INSTALLED THE SAGBUA OF EGBA IN PLACE OF SODEKE THE BALOGUN OF EGBA.

Act II, Scene i, continued the action: in Abeokuta Town.

Act II, Scene ii: at the Town Hall.

Act II, Scene iii: a divine service at Oso Ligegere's house.

The final scene was presumably somewhere in Abeokuta because its synopsis was given as: REV. AND MRS. TOWNSEND'S DEPARTURE FROM ABEOKUTA ON THE GROUND OF MRS. TOWNSEND'S ILL HEALTH.

After which, Akinkore seized up. Overwhelmed perhaps by the wealth of historic detail, his mind ceased to function. At meeting after meeting of the preparations committee, Akinkore turned up with the same sheet of paper, except for once when, in a sudden explosion of creativity, he was able to reveal progress in two specific areas. First, in Act I, Scene iii, he had scratched off "in place of" and replaced those words with "to succeed." The synopsis of that scene therefore read: OKUKENU INSTALLED THE SAGBUA OF EGBA TO SUC-CEED SODEKE THE BALOGUN OF EGBA.

The second development was truly dramatic. Akinkore finally presented a sample of typical missionary dialogue—as he explained to the meeting. It was now only a question of fitting this sample to the general action, situations, and even unforeseen events, and the play was ready. The sample dialogue was duly read to the committee by the dramatist:

REV. TOWNSEND *(to Chief Ogunbona)*—Good afternoon, Chief Ogunbona. Information has just reached us at Badagry that the Egba people are at war at Ado, and as we have an intention of proceeding to Abeokuta very shortly, we therefore decided to visit you. We are also very sorry to hear that our friend Sodeke is dead.

Akinkore insisted that this was how the nineteenth-century missionary spoke to Egba chiefs, and there was no one who could gainsay him. Akinkore then disappeared again for two weeks, and all the news that could be obtained about him was that he was ill. He, however, sent a message that he had created a new character—the ghost of Chief Sodeke.

When a crisis meeting was summoned three weeks after the creation of the model dialogue for Reverend Townsend, all the dramatis personae, it was clear, were now struck mute by a historic virus caught from Akinkore's muse. Since he caught it first, he was unable to attend the meeting. His confinement was spent mostly wondering why Christmas and Easter "cantatas" dealing with God, his son, magi, and saints should be so easy to write, but not an episode of Egba history dealing with mere mortals, like chiefs and missionaries.

Akinyode Soditan, composer and chief impresario, took it all with calm resignation. "Perhaps he should have undertaken the Ray Gunnar course," he sighed.

"What is that?" asked Sipe.

"Oh, haven't you seen his adverts? He runs one of those *gbogbonse* correspondence courses. As a matter of fact, our union has been asked to investigate him."

"Is he a phony?"

"We don't know yet. Daodu wrote to the director of education on the matter. We are waiting for his reply."

Sipe departed for his station in Lagos soon after, somewhat sad that he had had to abandon his friend in the middle of such a crisis. Still, the teacher seemed quite capable, and he had taken over the role of the librettist as well. Efuape also penned a few verses—plus music—of the kind of lugubrious threnody that he felt should emerge from the throat of the Ghost of Sodeke when he appeared to the Egba army camp in Ado. He had become rather taken by the spirit of the whole enterprise, much to his surprise. He was even more surprised that his friend found his song unsuitable, eventually excising the Ghost of Sodeke from the pageant altogether, as being neither founded in history nor essential to the drama. Since he did not believe in wasted effort, Sipe stored away his lyrics. Long before the two-day epic of the missionaries in Egbaland could materialise, they formed the cornerstone of Sipe Efuape's own debut on the Lagos stage—in the "native opera" titled *Ali Baba and the Forty Thieves!*

Sipe had, however, been greatly troubled by the phenomenon of Akinkore. With such a panoply of events spread out before him, how could any man simply dry up, his mind refuse to function? Unable to resolve the mystery and determined to avoid such a set-back in his own case, he wrote to Akinyode for the reference of the journal whose professional offering he had referred to in such a flippant manner. Perhaps Ray Gunnar held the key to theatrical success. A guinea was a reasonable investment, in any event. So Efuape bought his postal orders, cut out the application form, filled and mailed it, but also commenced preparations for his own strictly business theatrical venture. Weeks passed without a word from Ray Gunnar. Sipe gathered his troupe together—these consisted largely of his office colleagues, the agent for his private business, two or three ex-Ilés and their lady friends, plus a local Lagos runaway member of the Tunde Young juju orchestra who was seeking wider fields of fulfillment.

Assisting Sipe with backstage management was a young Lagosian who had simply drifted in during rehearsals. A clearly starstruck youth, he never missed a film show in Lagos or on mainland Yaba and Ebute Metta. He haunted all the performance halls and collected cigarette postcards of film stars, Shirley Temple being his favourite. Soon he was handling the publicity for Efuape's company and managing the front of the house. He had access to many of the "expatriate" Yoruba of Lagos society and guaranteed their attendance when the music drama *Ali Baba*, tired of waiting for the expertise of Ray Gunnar's school, finally took to the boards. Young José Santero, as de facto manager, had, however, taken over the pursuit of Ray Gunnar and had indeed entered privately into the second phase of correspondence with him. The scholarship prospects threw him into a fever of anticipation, with which he also infected his fellow Thespian Kolawole, the runaway musician from the Lagos band. The financial success of *Ali Baba* was stunning, and it owed much to the dedication of young Santero, and his plans for his own future.

As the Morris trundled its way to Lagos, Sipe turned to Akinyode and gave him advance warning of an additional chore they would tackle once they had taken care of the main business of the succession.

"Do you know the Santeros?"

"Oh yes, I've heard of them. There is a branch of the family in Abeokuta."

"Good. It's not too bad actually, this unexpected trip to Lagos. We can kill two birds with one stone."

"Which is the other bird?"

"I'll tell you when we have finished with Akinsanya. I tell you, the gods are taking our side over this matter. But let's plan our campaign. First, Akinsanya, how exactly do we tackle that one?"

"Yes. We should decide that before he gets a chance to be difficult."

Sipe smiled. "Oh, I am leaving you to deal with that. He's your cousin, after all, so you take care of him."

"Why do you think I brought the lemons? While he is salivating at the sight of them, I shall let go at him with both barrels."

"Good. Still, I wish Job had arrived in time to come with us. He seems to know just what to say to cool down that fiery head of his."

Akinyode chuckled out loud. "Job is right. What was his affliction the last time he wrote?"

"His wife. Before that, it was boils. With an *s*, you know. Not for him a solitary boil, even though it sprout within an embarrassing divide, like that of Sipe, son of Efuape. No. Opeilu would be content with no less than plural boils, preferably accompanied by piles and maybe *sobia* as bonus. Then a clash with drunken soldiers from which he rescues himself by reciting Psalm 21 . . ."

Sipe cast a sidelong glance at his companion, reminding himself that this otherwise tedious journey provided the best chance for sounding out the teacher on the matter of the Spirit of Layeni. No distractions or possible interruption. Akinyode could indulge in his favourite sport of arguing for the sake of argument till he was sated. But at least he would know at the end of it all where the teacher stood. Then he could proceed to take his own decision.

There were also any number of other matters, far weightier, which he sought to preview with Akinyode before they came to formal airing at the seasonal gathering in Ìsarà, when the other ex-Ilés were home from Kano, Port Harcourt, Saki, Samaru in Zaria, Lagos, and everywhere! The change of status of the colony districts to Native Administrations was one—five new administrative units from Ijebu-Ode district alone! Ìsarà now belonged to Remo. But not even this momentous event agitated Sipe as much as the planned road between Ìsarà and Ibadan. All the work that the Ìsarà Road Committee, spurred on by the Ìsarà Auxiliary Society in Lagos, had done was being frustrated by the Alake of Abeokuta. He had ordered the surveyor to work on the route between Asa, Fidiwo, and Ìsarà instead of Asa, Ipara, and Ìsarà, as decided by them. They were the ones who collected funds, wrote petitions, made the preliminary surveys, and mobilised public opinion, especially in the newspapers. But the Alake single-handedly decided to re-route everything through Fidiwo, leaving out their close kin in Ipara. That was a major fight for which Sipe had braced himself, and he meant to deal hard with the ex-Ilés of Abeokuta when he had them all under one roof in Ìsarà. Perhaps their closeness to the Alake had sapped their will; well, he would remind them that they were Afotamodi, firstly, daily, and lastly. They were born in Ìsarà and would return home to die. This was war; no other attitude would do. He felt like pouncing on Akinyode there and then but decided that this should wait. He would conserve his energy for a massed onslaught. Or maybe begin on the return journey, when he would have the support of Awobodu and Akinsanya, though that one had become too involved in national politics and trade union activities to pay sufficient attention to what was happening at home. Well, he was in for a shock. The thought of the jolt which was coming to him from the clear sky gave Sipe a thrill. After this, let him dare give second place to the affairs of Ìsarà!

Events were moving too fast, Akinyode thought. Would they even have time to go through the plans for the maternity clinic Otolorin had helped him design for Ìsarà? There was always the problem of priorities. The Lagos group, he knew, was obsessed with the Ìsarà–Ibadan road. This was only a logical extension of their even more ambitious plan to link Lagos, Ikorodu, and Ìsarà by a year-round, all-weather motorable road. The pace of events had outstripped all routine programmes, however; it was doubtful if even the usual rounds of convivial gatherings would take place, or the ritual reviews of the year and planning for the new. This was beginning to look like a New Year for children only; he now regretted that he had left his children behind. At least they would have enjoyed the seasonal reunion with their cousins and age-mates and wallowed in the indulgence of their aunts and grannies while the men tackled this immediate hard-eyed business of local politics. Still, he gave silent thanks that Morola's illness had been finally diagnosed. His father and Jagun would have schemed their way into making her undergo their *etutu*, and once she was in Ìsarà, all the advantage was theirs. Then his grandmother—three days already he had been in Ìsarà, but he had kept walking right past her cottage each time he set out to visit her. That macabre performance was something he never wanted to see again. Instead, he had gone to the plot of land on which he proposed to build his own house, stood there for long stretches of time, planning the building in his mind, costing it, setting a timetable for its progress. Pity Ogunba had not arrived before his father's eruption into the house. He would have been on this journey also. No matter, he intended to place the construction of the house in his charge, now that he was in Ijebu-Ode, much nearer home than Abeokuta. Opeilu was the one whose arrival most of them awaited with some impatience. Even more than Efuape, he was at the hub of economic trends because of his job as produce inspector; he could predict the pattern of price fluctuations, he knew what commodities would become scarce or prove a glut on the market and how the war affected everything. Opeilu would advise him whether to buy corrugated iron sheets at once and store them or wait until prices came down. And bags of cement, nails, even the treated timber . . .

"You know," Sipe began slowly, "it's all very well to laugh at Opeilu's misadventures, but sometimes I can't help wondering. And then, of course, his remedies for getting out of scrapes and illnesses. I mean, Yode, I ask myself sometimes, one hears so much about the Sixth and Seventh Books of Moses. Have you never been curious what they actually contain?"

"Of course. I once tried to order it from that same Ray Gunnar. He has a sideline in educational and oriental mystery books and so on."

Sipe nodded grimly. "Yes, he would. Anyway, even if the books exist—"

"No question at all. I am sure they do."

"Well, what could be inside them beyond what is already in the Bible? And if one uses verses in them to conjure good luck or riches, would that be any different from, er . . . well, from Opeilu, for instance, reciting Psalm 21 anytime he is faced with danger?"

"What of the other things he's done to counter his wife's—well—plots against him? Hardly what you would call biblical remedies!"

"So? Isn't one permitted to fight fire with fire?"

Relaxing after a spirited and successful defence of Oduneye before
Bishop Vining in Aké parsonage, Opeilu had good cause to be proud
of his loyalty to his friends. Oduneye was convicted of keeping
shoddy accounts, but beyond that—he was innocent on all counts.
Vining went even further: He accused his main accuser, D. Kuye, of
a vindictive attitude, "unchristianly and ungodly." Vining had been
so impressed with Opeilu's objective concern that he asked him to
spend the night in BishopsCourt so that he could consult him on a
number of decisions. The Location Committee would not meet again
until Passion Week of the New Year and there were transfers to be
made before then. Opeilu, as produce inspector, travelled a lot and
worshipped wherever he found himself. His gentle, benign face,
lightly marked by a childhood attack of smallpox, was familiar to
most of the parishes in the south, especially those served by the
railway line. He was known to be above church politics and was
therefore often invited to arbitrate internal wranglings. But it was
the first time he had been asked to testify for a friend, and by a white
bishop at that. Bishop Vining began to unburden himself, asking
advice. Oduneye, for example. It was clear that he could no longer
remain in the Ibadan diocese; he had far too many enemies. Did
Opeilu think he would be happy in Abeokuta? Or should he go
farther afield to Ondo? Reverend Alalade was old and had earned his
pension. Vining would make recommendations to the Patronage
Board—did Opeilu think the decision right? And then there was
Archdeacon Phillips, who did not wish to go to Abeokuta for love nor
money. Opeilu was close to the head teacher in Aké—would he
discreetly find out why there was such bad blood between him and
the Director of Education, Melville Jones? Reverend Adegoroye was
being difficult. Igbara-Oke was a good station—why didn't he want
to go? He had even threatened to leave the Church if he was transferred from his present station. You mustn't take offence, Mr. Opeilu,
I hope you won't take offence, but our African brothers in Christ
sometimes strike me as being deficient in their sense of mission. Are
you not all one people? Why does an Ifo priest fight tooth and nail
to remain within shouting distance of his hometown? We go wherever we are sent, in England. After all, look at me. I was sent all the
way to West Africa from across the seas—of course I obeyed. We

must all go wherever our mission is needed. Even the Methodists are having problems, from what I gather. Young Mr. Ogunbayo has just resigned from their mission, and all because of his transfer to Ilesha. Somebody must serve the Methodists of Ilesha, not so? Oh oh, you mustn't think that I am painting a gloomy picture of everything. We have quite a good number who can hardly wait to pack their portmanteaus and head for their new positions. Mr. Okusanya set a very good example, for instance; he heard the news of his transfer to Owo just as he returned from vacation and he simply picked up his bags and went. Of course, he is not a prelate—you know him, don't you? He is the new principal of the teacher training college. Perhaps teachers are more adventurous than prelates—do you think that's the truth? Ogunba left willingly for Ijebu-Ode, didn't he? I received Mr. Soditan's letter asking for his replacement. I gather from other sources that they are very close friends; they certainly made an excellent team in St. Peter's. But that's the point. We need good workers as pioneers. Tested workers. The same thing goes for the cloth, of course—that is what I wish they would understand. Look at the way I. O. Ransome-Kuti has taken Abeokuta Grammar School by the scruff of the neck. He's performing the same miracle there as he did in Ijebu-Ode. A remarkable man, a remarkable man. He is Soditan's in-law, isn't he? By the way, I hope people were not too upset that I couldn't personally officiate at Elliot's wedding. It was the event of the year for Ibadan, from what I gather. Bishop Akinyele told me all about it, gave me a copy of his sermon. Over two thousand people, bicycles jammed all over the place. And of course quite a number of motorcars. Well, I hope they didn't forget the Spitfire Fund; that is the kind of God-given chance for the war effort—very well-to-do modern and professional Nigerians. Quite the cream of the Nigerian cream, wasn't it . . . ?

Opeilu did not mind. He felt a deep serenity sitting with this white benevolent face, which seemed to glow as dusk gathered in Bishops-Court. It had been a hard day but he felt satisfied with what he had achieved. His only regret was that Soditan had already left for Ìsarà; it would have been pleasant to spend the night with him and recount the day's battle over Oduneye's case, into which he had been brought as an impartial witness and, of course, as a man with some commercial expertise. He was never really at ease with the Europeans, but Vining struck him as almost native to England with his easy familiarity with everyone and a boundless, gossipy energy. He appeared ready to indulge himself in the respite of talking to someone outside his normal field of engagement, all night long if that was possible.

And so, Opeilu recognized, was he. BishopsCourt was a different world from Ekotedo quarters in Ibadan, which he had to pass through every day on his way to work. Ekotedo was the notorious sector of Ibadan, patronised by prostitutes and now, of course, by soldiers in search of amusement. The drunken street scenes through which he had to pick a careful course when he returned late from his produce shed in Adio, he was certain, must have something to do with the frequent eruption of boils and other afflictions on his body. And it had been a trying year, which did not really do much good to his general state of health.

If only his own problems were as trivial and easy to unravel as the minor infraction of Oduneye—a technical one, at that. But his work involved great personal risks; he had begun to wonder if the protections on which he depended would really survive a determined assault. The war seemed to bring out the beast in everyone. Forty-eight bags of salt at a blow, snatched from the store right under his nose! The labourers thought he had left for the day because he had locked up the store and his office. So he caught them red-handed—forty-eight bags in all, and the mastermind was none other than his assistant. He thought of how much that would have fetched in the open market, when even a fairly senior officer like him had to manage with the official allocation of a pound and quarter each fortnight. And only last week the government announced that this would be further reduced to four ounces. Now, how was a normal family with all dependants supposed to manage with that? And that was without reckoning with friends who were not in the government service and therefore received no allocation at all. The profiteering on the open market had really reached unbelievable proportions. Even so, forty-eight bags—the attempt was bold! Well, so was the punishment. Three years for Mr. Kadiri Toye, plus two for the assistant inspector of police with whom he had planned to subvert the course of justice. The labourers were freed—that seemed quite just; they were, after all, only obeying the orders of their superior.

But then, soon after, the entire store was burned down. The arsonists were yet at large. Had it been part of the main plan? To burn down the store so as to cover up the fact of the missing bags. Or was the burning down an act of revenge for the apprehension of the villains? Was it a warning to him? It was no wonder that he began to cough afterwards. Probably he had breathed in too much of that unhealthy smoke—all those fumes from God knows how many different commodities. Still, it was a relief when he went to the doctor and he found that he had not contracted tuberculosis, as he had feared. TB was rumoured to be raging through the country at the time; perhaps it was the soldiers who brought it with them and were spreading it.

The soldiers! They were the greatest menace. It was possible—maybe they were behind the arson. The inspector, or even Toye himself, could have instigated them. After all, did they not break into the warehouse at Ilaro on their way to Meko when they were being transferred to the border town, supposedly to stem the rumoured invasion? Nobody bothered anymore about the kegs of palm oil and bags of *gari* removed by the soldiers. Life was at stake, and anyway, who cared about looted shops when even the government warehouse could be raided by soldiers. His dysentery, which followed that unresolved attack, had lasted two weeks, continuing even after the rumour of invasion was scotched and some of the loot recovered from the soldiers.

Those soldiers had become the bane of Opeilu's life. His most scary fever had begun after their display in the seedy passages behind the cinema in Ekotedo. Nothing but physical exhaustion could have made him take the shortcut, but it had seemed safe enough at that moment. A number of late-night drinkers were out on the street, but there was no sign of soldiers. He was halfway through the passage when they burst out of the Starlight Konkoma Bar, staggering from wall to wall, all fifteen to twenty of them. There he was, trapped, and if he hadn't quickly recited Psalm 21, he would never have seen the obscure doorway, which could hardly hide a child, but he had forced himself flat against it anyway, praying like mad and psalming soundlessly. One of them gave a shout, which must have been an order because they all tried to gain some form of balance, then began to unbutton their trousers. Another shout and they all began to urinate, against the walls, into the passage, on themselves, so drunk and unbalanced were they. But the strangest sight was still to come.

When the next order came, they buttoned up—that is, those who still remembered that their "objects" were still dangling out, because some were so eager to obey the next command that they forgot. And that order, it appeared, was that they should take off their belts. And they began to flog one another! Opeilu knew all about *egungun* festivals, he had seen all types of masquerades, and he knew that there were those outings in which men held flogging contests, using palm stalks and the springy *atori*, applying the whips only to the legs, which were usually covered anyway by thin trousers. But these soldiers were applying the buckle end of the belt to one another—and everywhere! Blood flowed copiously, but on they went, nonstop. Those who collapsed were simply left lying in their urine puddles. The exercise—for what else could one call it? Opeilu had demanded in his letter to the teacher—the exercise lasted some three quarters of an hour. Onlookers had gathered at a distance from the centre of action, but there he was, trapped in the middle, nothing between him and the certainty of death on discovery but the narrow space in that doorway and the power of Psalm 21! When they were finally wearied of the exercise, their "panic-sowing and alarming show of barbarity," they flung their empty beer bottles against the houses, shattering them against the walls and smashing windows, then hauled up their wounded and staggered to their barracks, singing at the top of their voices.

Opeilu's fever was prolonged, even though he had to report to work every day. He wore a thick scarf around his neck, and a generous whiff of mentholatum surrounded his presence. Only his illness had prevented him from dealing more severely with his new assistant, who had taken over from Kadiri. This new Bolaji was incompetent. His grading of cocoa beans and palm kernel was so atrocious that he, Opeilu, had to do it all over again to avoid scandal. In fact, it was so bad that he suspected him of taking bribes. But what really riled Opeilu—and what he suspected had probably made Bolaji last this far in the civil service—was his disloyalty to his colleagues. Only this individual, as far as he knew, had refused to join the civil service union. He refused to sign the membership circular and seemed to take pride in being a yes-man. Without stooping to such tactics, he,

Opeilu, still had the best report in the handing-over notes of the European head of Oyo division. Thank goodness for Otugbile, whose staunch alliance offset Bolaji's depressing presence. Yes, Opeilu had finally realized that Bolaji was the main cause of his recurring migraine. He was not accusing him of doing anything deliberate—no, not yet. But one could not help observing a link. He certainly did not suffer from migraines until Bolaji assumed duty at his station . . . And suddenly Opeilu realized that he was in a unique situation from which he had not yet profited. Perhaps some other psalm would prove even more potent than Psalm 21 against the likes of Bolaji. He opened his mouth to enquire, but the bishop beat him to the draw.

"Well, then, Mr. Opeilu. Who is going to be the next Odemo of Ìsarà? Or is it a secret?"

Their knocking went unheard, so Akinyode opened the door and entered. They had heard raised voices from the moment Sipe parked the car against the raised pavement in front of the house and cut off the engine. Akinsanya lived in Denton Street, not far from the edge of a lagoon inlet with its brackish water and mudskippers. Fish traps lined the bank, a few yards from the cemetery at Alagomeji. The lagoon border—one could hardly call it a shore—oozed forth a black sludge, as if every sea-plying vessel discharged its wastes of oil and tar into that marshy bay, which curved through from Ereko waterside on the island to the depot of Zarpas Motor Transport, a mile and a half from Iddo railway station. Across the stretch of mudflats one could see the boats and the timber pontoons heading out to sea to join the vast oceans, heading towards ports that would turn them into Spitfire frames and ship hulls for the war against Hitler. Children raced across the road, trying to catch the soft-shelled crabs which sidled out from their dank holes, crossed the street, then raced back to their underground shelters for safety. A short distance away, an Aladura church had already commenced its evening service, with bells and chanting, swinging incense burners, and the slap of bare feet on concrete floors. This part of Yaba was a different township from the main body of Lagos, as if it were a waterlogged Ìsarà, completely remote from the island itself with its violating sense of noise and motion. Its sole link to the island colony was Carter Bridge, a replacement for the old Bailey Bridge constructed by the West

African Royal Pioneers. It gave off such an air of eerie desolation in the evenings that children stayed close to their doorways, playing their games within sight and hearing of elders in the house. And the story was told—so complete was the dependence on Carter Bridge—of one of the earliest Lagosians to attain a position in the senior grades of the civil service, who once attended a party on the island in his brand new Austin sedan. It was his first drive at night over the bridge. He returned home late, drunk. His wife put him to bed, took off his clothes, and left him to sleep it off.

The following morning, the civil servant woke up but refused to leave his bed. It was long past the time to prepare for office but he remained asleep—at least so thought his wife until, alarmed by the lack of movement in the room, she looked in to see in what state her husband was. To her astonishment he was wide awake; he lay on his back, eyes wide open and staring at the ceiling. The poor woman became anxious; was the man ill? She moved closer.

"Darling, are you all right? Are you going to miss work today altogether?"

The man turned his head towards her slowly, appeared to recognize her, and beckoned her to come closer. She moved forward with trepidation. "Shall I call for a doctor . . . ?"

The husband's response was quite emphatic—no. He took her arm, invited her to sit beside him on the bed. Gently, with the weight of one divulging a secret, the details of which he was as yet uncertain about, he confided: "I am still trying to recollect the route, but do you know, dear? Between our mainland and the island there is actually an alternative route. I used it last night. One doesn't need to go over Carter Bridge at all. And it's quicker. It takes less than a quarter of the time one would normally take using Carter Bridge. The trouble is, I cannot recall how I gained access to that hidden route."

The wife did not remain puzzled for more than a few seconds. Then her eyes popped. She rose slowly from the bed, stood rooted to the spot for a few more moments, then let out a soft sigh and keeled over backwards in a dead faint over her husband's body.

They could distinguish two voices in the inner room as they stepped unnoticed through the front room, a sparsely furnished and narrow room with framed photos hanging on the wall, and a few more of obviously superior technical finish on a round table in a corner. Soditan spotted the latter group at once, stepped round the leather pouffes neatly arranged on the perimeter of a fibre mat, and picked up the photograph of a smiling young man in a heavy overcoat. He stood in front of a fountain, while an equestrian statue on a plinth towered over him and pigeons fluttered through a soft gray haze, some of them perched on his outstretched arm as if in dutiful response to a request from the photographer.

"Look at S.O." he said, holding out the framed picture to Efuape. "The one he sent me was taken on a pier; he said it was Brighton."

"Hn-hn. Whose turn is next?"

Akinyode did not answer the question. "This must be the famous Trafalgar Square. Or Picadilly Circus. He's probably written it on the back."

Sipe replaced the photograph on the table, sighed. "What annoys me about young Awokoya is that he won't cooperate. All I ask from him is a short list of reputable firms; instead he sends me descriptions of snow. Who cares about snow!"

A wistful look came over Akinyode's face as he glanced around at the other photographs on standing frames on that table. Each background was alien. It bore a forlorn air like some unattainable distance, despite determined smiles on the faces of the subjects. The structures were like nothing that existed in Lagos; the streets were broad and looked antiseptically clean, unwelcoming. Glancing round the parade of these doubly exiled ex-Ilés, he sighed.

"Ashtabula podium."

Checked in his stride, Sipe cast a quick glance around the display. "Ah, yes. All those who have braved the seas and come to harbour."

Akinyode jerked his head in the direction of the voices. "Shall we wait or join them?"

An angry voice rose from the other side of the closed door. "Bowen has to go. I don't care what their teachers do in their own public schools. But no European comes here and attempts to sodomize an Ìsarà son and gets away with it. That King's College must be cleaned up once and for all."

"I assure you, Mr. Akinsanya, the matter has been officially reported."

"When? When? Every day he stays in this country is an affront!"

"I am sorry, sir." The other voice was very subdued. "But it was the only thing I could do . . . I would not affront your sensibilities for anything—"

"No, no! You are still taking it personally. Look, McEwen, it was decent of you to come to me and admit that you have given him refuge. You did a Christianly thing and I do not hold it against you. Do get that clear. But the Ìsarà union has lodged a formal complaint and demands action. I am speaking now of official action, and you can take my words to the education department. We would do the same if such an abomination had affected any other pupil! And I can tell you right now that the Nigerian Youth Movement has also taken up the matter! Bowen must leave the country. How do we know how many others he has attempted? Perhaps even succeeded with! Sodomy! Is that the kind of civilization these Europeans want to inflict on us?"

"I understand, Mr. Akinsanya, I understand. It is all most unfortunate. We are trying to avoid a scandal—"

"Who wants a scandal? You know the man who left here just now? That was J. V. Clinton of *The Eastern Mail.* If I had wanted the matter to reach Calabar by next week, all I had to do was tell him. Not to mention the *Daily Times* and *The West African Pilot* closer to hand. We want Bowen off these shores, that is all. But if the education department drags its feet, then there will be a scandal!"

There was a scraping of chairs, followed by a sigh of resignation. "All right, Mr. Akinsanya. I shall pass on your message."

"Be sure to state it as a condition. Bowen goes or I cannot guarantee what will be our next line of action."

The door opened and the owners of the two voices emerged. One was a wiry, light-complexioned man, obviously a mulatto. He held a trilby in nervous hands and, although quite young, was clearly balding down the middle of his head. As they came out, the other, somewhat paunchy, as black as the other was off-white, broke into a delighted shout on seeing his visitors. His massive head was split by a grin as broad as a generous slice of pawpaw. He wore a loose shirt over a local-weave wrapper bunched up at the waist, and this lounge ensemble was topped by an *ikori* cap which swung down over one ear, flapping in his excitement like the loose patterned slippers on his feet.

The man called McEwen took one look at the pair and cast a

worried glance back at his host. Akinsanya understood and hastened to reassure him, though it was not quite the kind of reassurance he sought. His face had lost its smile and he spoke quite sternly.

"If you are wondering if they overheard, you needn't worry. Because I shall tell them anyway. These are close friends. They also have sons who will probably find their way to King's or any of the other government schools in the country. And I already told you, this assault was against a son of Ìsarà. Nobody tries to make a woman of an Afotamodi, Mr. McEwen. Nobody."

A faint plea hovered in McEwen's eyes as he took a polite leave of the two men. Akinsanya waved him good-bye at the door and turned, with evident relief, to his townspeople.

"Was that McEwen of the secretariat?"

Akinsanya nodded yes. "You know him?"

"By correspondence only. We've been dealing with him over this matter of the teachers' war bonus. The government seems to want to back out."

"Let them dare! And as it happens, I have news for you. Pity, you just missed Clinton. He sailed from Calabar expressly for that purpose. He wanted to talk to Kuti. Sit down, sit down. Let's stay out here. I took that man into my study only because of the dirty matter we had to talk about. I'll get some glasses—oh, did you bring me any lemons?"

Sipe and Akinyode exchanged glances. "They're in the car. When we have spoken, I'll decide if you deserve any."

Akinsanya stopped dead in his tracks, inspected their faces carefully. "Yes, come to think of it, shouldn't you both be at home already? In fact, Sipe, I ran into H.O.D. only yesterday and he told me you detoured through Lagos to see him on your way to Ìsarà."

"Hn-hn. I wanted him to intervene in the matter of Santero."

"So, how is that going? Is the mother going to bail out that scapegrace?"

"I don't know yet. Anyway it's been overtaken by events. I have since thought up a way of breaking the deadlock. During this very last night, in fact."

"Wait a minute, wait a minute. We'd better take everything one at a time. First, the drinks. Johnnie Walker or Haig? And there is Keo of course—both brandy and sherry."

"No Bristol Cream?" Sipe pretended to be hurt.

"Leave my sweet tooth alone," Akinsanya barked and went into the study. He was back a moment later with an armful of bottles. From a cupboard stuck high on a wall of the living room, filled with porcelain plates with intricate designs along the rims, he extracted three glasses, darted back again to fetch a jar of water and bottles of fruit juices. Then he stood, legs apart and hands on the waist, surveyed the array, and proceeded to nod with satisfaction.

"Right. We don't have to get up for a while. If you came back all that way after settling yourselves in Ìsarà, the matter must be serious. Ah, wait . . ." He dashed back into the study and returned with a letter, and a piece of paper. "Clinton left this for I.O. He also wants to spend New Year with his family, so he could not afford to miss the ferry. He had hoped he would catch Daodu here in Lagos—somebody told him the synod would not break up until tomorrow. Imagine that! Something which finished last week! But we discussed what is inside the letter, and I took down some notes. In fact, I am going to undertake the same exercise for my union; it is such a brilliant idea. Let the Colonial Office contest the power of statistics if they can."

"Well, what is it about?" Akinyode demanded.

"It's all in here"—slapping the notepaper. "He wants the teachers' union to prepare a list of the ideal menu for a family of teacher, wife, and two children. The menu must contain—it's all listed down—all the necessary vitamins, protein, proper quantity of carbohydrates, roughage, salts, etc., etc. It's to be used in what would be a union pamphlet of advice on nutrition. It will have the backing of the Medical Association, of course—they must endorse it! Then we itemize the average cost of rent in the given area of the respective branches, clothes for the whole family, etc., then total up everything. In a parallel column you will tabulate the average earnings of different grades of teachers. And don't forget emergency expenses such as medical bills, etc., etc. Now, the *Mail* for its part will gather market prices of the essential commodities in different areas of the country . . . You've got the general idea?"

Sipe applauded loudly while Akinyode nodded thoughtfully. "Yes, I think I know what it is aimed at. The Colonial Development Fund."

Akinsaya nodded vigorously. "Correct. It is not only the *Times* and the *Pilot* which are now read in England, you know. *The World Review* even carried an editorial from the *Mail* only last month. Clinton is anxious to influence decisions over there. Of course, we will use the same method, in a slightly different way, to work on the motor firms. Our problems are different. These are private firms. But the *Mail* will run the series over three, four, even six, months, covering one area after another. I like the man's project. It has method." He slapped the arms of his chair. "So, the union man is finished. What brought you two back?"

Akinyode took a deep breath. "Saaki. What is happening with the youth movement?"

"Oh." He sounded somewhat disappointed. "Is that what brought you all this way?"

"It is connected. But tell us, first, what is the position?"

"All right. Here is the latest. We were all pretty riled by that editorial in the *Pilot*—but you know all of that. What you may not know is that Ernest Ikoli has been to see me. He even wrote letters— I'll show them to you later. For me personally, I have put all the provocation behind me, but, well, we have the 'hotheads.' And while they say they will take their cue from me, whenever they get together on their own they become more uncompromising. Zik has also made overtures. I agree with him; the good of Nigeria should come first. But he has to call his own hotheads to order."

Sipe said, "In short, for now one could say that you are not really playing an active role in the movement."

Akinsanya hedged. "The movement is active, that's the important thing. I have enough on my plate, fighting these private firms for new conditions of service."

Again, Sipe and Akinyode exchanged signals and the teacher pressed home the point. "Ìsarà needs you. And it has become now a matter of urgency. The trouble has already burst."

Akinsanya's mind shot straight home. "Over the succession?"

"You guessed right," Sipe confirmed. "The Olisa has jumped the gun. He has installed Erinle and even handed him the regalia. Saaki, charity begins at home, if you don't mind me stating the obvious. You have to forget the movement for a while—and we are not speaking just of the movement, all the politics attached to it. You have to come home and face this crisis with us."

Akinsanya was puzzled. "I don't understand what the movement has to do with the situation in Ìsarà but . . . look, certain elementary steps should be taken right away."

"We've taken them," Akinyode assured him. "We came to Lagos while a different group headed for Ibadan to see the district commissioner. Amoda, Olusoga, and Sowole went; the Akarigbo's clerk accompanied them. My father said that the Akarigbo had earlier mentioned his suspicions that the Olisa might actually take such an illegal step; he said he warned him and thought he had given up the idea. Erinle is an ambitious man. He is weak, so he can be led. This thing is really Olisa's doing. He does not really want to give up being regent, so he wants a pliant material like Erinle as king."

"We must brief a lawyer too . . ."

"Sowole's team have their instructions. Our choice is Prince Adedoyin—we are going to pass by his chambers after seeing you. Then Sowole will come straight to him from Ibadan and report the result of their meeting with the district commissioner before returning to Ìsarà. They will also confer with you."

"Good. That seems to have taken care of everything. Jagun and others will of course mobilize Ìsarà people and I will interact with our descendants' union in Lagos. Fortunately, I had not quite made up my mind to come home this New Year. I may go to Achimota, look up my son, 'Kitunde."

Sipe's smile was thin. "You will have to do more than that. You must demand audience with the Resident and state Ìsarà's position. Then the most crucial role of all . . ."

"Go on."

Akinyode looked him straight in the eye. "Can't you think what that is? Something only you can take on."

Akinsanya cast his mind through every possible step that needed to be taken in this long-simmering crisis, which had now burst open. "No. Every ground appears to have been covered by someone." And then he burst out laughing. "Unless, of course, you want me to volunteer for the throne."

And his laughter suddenly dried up, watching the unblinking stares of his two friends boring into his face.

"Oh," he exclaimed, and went on repeating, "Oh. Oh, oh . . ."

"You see." Akinyode spoke gently. "That is why you must leave politics for a while. That is father's message to you."

"And Jagun's."

"Yes. The majority of the kingmakers agreed on you a long time ago. The others we heard rumoured were merely wasting their time—and money. And you have the support not only of the Aka-rigbo of Remo, but of the Awujale himself. And Chief Ladega in Ibadan. Of the Ìsarà chiefs, we have already told you of Jagun. There is also the Apena—we don't have to tell you. But you know how things are. If you continue to terrify the government with your politics, the Resident will be instructed to get under these people and turn them round: Do you want such a troublemaker as a brother Oba?—that kind of thing. Our chiefs can be quite fickle; even a child knows that!"

Sipe stood up and made towards the array of drinks. "Well, Saaki, it has made my day just seeing you lose your power of speech. Yode, while he is looking for it . . . Haig's? Or the Johnnie Walker?"

"Everything combines together for good for the righteous man," Sipe pontificated, steering the Morris over Carter Bridge into Lagos Island. Akinyode stared at him in surprise. This level of sermonizing was most unusual in the young tycoon. He attributed it to the feeling of elation which must have developed as a result of the meeting with Akinsanya, and the effect of seeing his face after they had sprung the surprise. But Sipe tapped himself on the chest and said, "Me. I am talking about me. The Righteous Rooster. When I think of the entire saga of Ray Gunnar . . ."

Akinyode nodded slowly. "So. You are now the Righteous Rooster."

"Yes. Haven't you noticed? I have not talked or thought business for the past twenty-four hours. But now, we are on our way to settle a business affair. Amicably. And all because of these dramatic developments. Well, drama calls to drama, I suppose. This time it will serve the interest of our friend Saaki. That is what makes me feel righteous."

"Virtuous, I would have said."

"Have it your own way, Mr. Pedantry. 'Seest thou a man righteous and diligent in his works, he shall stand before kings, and not before mean men.' "

Akinyode placed a hand on Sipe's brow. "No. There is no sign of a fever."

"But better still, young teacher, than standing before kings is the thrill of helping a king to his throne. I have not felt such a rise of excitement since I made a hundred and twenty pounds on negotiating three private treaties in a week. As the deal rocked this way and that and finally began to clamber up that last crest of near-certainty, I found myself in a state of unparalleled ecstasy."

"Sipe, please. Don't let us count our chickens yet."

"I know. There is many a slip twixt the cup and the lip—you see how inspired I am this morning—but look at even you. You've lost the Micawberish dillydallying which you normally exhibit in the face of straightforward choices. You have taken to the engines of intrigue like one born to the art. That is why I am certain of success. I know this is only the first blow in a long battle, but you see, I am already tasting victory. You are going to see the old Rooster, a butterfly emerging from a long sleep induced by temporary uncertainties. Yes, I must confess a secret I have carefully kept from you all this while— you, Akinyode, you had infected me somewhat with your spirit of cautiousness, but now—I am myself again!"

"Well, I am happy for you."

"Denton Street! That is where Saaki lives—have you thought of that? You think that is a mere coincidence? Denton! Don't you remember Denton, the agent who tried to bribe the Awujale? Denton! The one who tried to get the Awujale to sell Ijebuland for a thousand pounds. And Saaki lives in the street named after him! Now let any of you dare sneer at destiny after this."

The car drove through Idumagbo, turned through the rutted streets towards Tinubu Square, and negotiated the narrow passage created by the corners of two houses which were evidently built before there was any thought even of horse-drawn carriages.

"Oh, that reminds me. Opeilu had to grease his way with nearly fifteen shillings before he got his building plans approved in Mapo Hall. They dribbled him here and there, querries sprang up from nowhere, from the Town Planning Office. His file would vanish for two, three weeks at a time, 'gone for the final approval.' But approval where? He swore he would not grease anyone's palm—remember?" Akinyode nodded. "Well, I heard from him two or three weeks ago. He said he had to choose between the rashes on his skin and a temporary retirement of his principles."

"How is his body responding to that new situation?"

"No, not body. His soul. He went to Aladura church the next Sunday to make atonement. So far, no news of his rashes. Well, here we are. I don't think this will take long."

Sipe drove through the massive gates of a walled compound, a wrought-iron arch over the pillars at its entrance. It was a sharp contrast to the streets through which they had just driven and also to the majority of houses in the neighborhood. Vines clambered over broken trellises, wisteria and bougainvillea smothered the walls in a profusion of colors. The expanse before the main building was filled with neat rows of royal palms, wild apple, guava, and pawpaw. The manicured lawns almost duplicated those of the parsonage at Aké— which, however, had none of the majestic palms, so suggestive to Akinyode's present frame of mind of an awaited royal procession. The style of the building was distinctly Brazilian. A wide wooden verandah surrounded the top floor, its support beams at diagonals to the wall. There was ample space all round the house on every side, and a row of outhouses with low wide doors lined the wall of the compound to the left, facing the house. Sipe gestured towards them.

"The stalls. Once each one was occupied by a thoroughbred. Now only two horses remain. The family still races one but the other is just a household pet. Spotless white. I've seen young Santero exercise it along the beach." They climbed the steps and Sipe applied the heavy knocker to the door. "What you see before, Yode, is—debt. The entire house is papered with debts. Only pride keeps them going. Everything should really be up for sale. I know one of their money-lenders. What we should do is pick up this mansion stone by stone and rebuild it in Ìsarà for a new palace."

The door swung open into a gloomy anteroom, smelling of a mixture of camphor balls, mustiness, and freshly cut flowers. The maid was dressed in a black skirt over which she had tied a waist-high apron. Her eyes assessed them coldly; then she appeared to recognize Efuape.

"Oh, I . . . do you want to see Mama?"

"Yes. Tell her it is Mr. Sipe, son of Efuape."

"Please wait." And she waved them in the direction of the stuffed sofa, covered in thick purple velvet, its wooden back topped with carved figures like misericords on a baroque pew.

"So this is his background," the teacher remarked. "Then why did he do it?"

"It reeks of impoverishment, Yode. Beneath it all, nothing but proud penury. But it isn't that which does it. Young Santero is no different from our own Sotolu, for instance. Look at how that one threw away such a cushy job in Army Supplies. I ask you, how could a young man of his age be so greedy? Sardines, whisky, gin, cartons of milk—powdered and evaporated—it was nearly a full lorry-load of nothing but luxury items. And he stored it all in his father's house. In his own father's house! If the elder Sotolu had not been so respected in the community, so far above suspicion, who would have believed he was not acting in collusion with his son?"

"I still don't understand. How could he have hoped to get away with it? The hoard was too much."

"Oh, easiest thing in the world. Just continue doing what he was doing, put the word out that he had special goods, and sell them off bit by bit. He was only caught at the second attempt. That was when the police went to search his house."

The maid re-entered, held aside the heavy green baize curtains, and announced that Mama would receive them now.

A lineup of portraits of the Santero ancestry confronted them as they entered the vast reception hall. In massive frames of faded gold-and-cream rosettes, they dominated the reception hall of the Santero family house, redolent of a different time, a different space. The largest portrait was also dead centre; it was that of the Senhor himself, Alveiro Miguel Domingo do Santero, who had brought back the clan from slavery in mid-nineteenth century. New floors and wings had been added to the house since then, porches were attached to the main entrances and the hanging verandahs widened, but this reception room with its raised dais beneath ancestral portraits had remained virtually unchanged for nearly a century. It occupied most of the ground floor and was surrounded by corridors that were generous in space and permitted a constant flow of air in every direction. The portraits behind the raised dais of this main room were dressed, without exception, in formal attire. Alveiro was himself dressed in the full regalia of the Grand Order of the Lodge, his hat perched on a round table to one side. Others wore mainly frock coats, a top hat settled in the angle of a carefully extended arm. A variety of orders dictated details in other portraits—a medallion, a mace extended outwards, a shield in the background emblazoned with the words "Order of the Knights of St. Patrick." Lace trimmings in varying tints of white, yellow, and brown, ending in a knotted rosette at the top of the portrait, singled out those who had passed away. It was possible to tell the order of their departures both by their distances from Alveiro at the centre and by the degrees of brown-rimmed yellowing which the white lace trimming had acquired with age. The living appeared to require no such adornment.

Madame Santero was the last surviving sister of the last male descendant of the Senhor. She sat in a high-backed chair directly beneath Alveiro's portrait, a small, intensely dark woman with hair pulled back tightly in a white bun, which rested sideways on a crochet-work antimacassar. On either side of the chair were round low tables with flower vases surrounded by yet more family portraits, this time of the younger generations. Weddings, christenings, mounted polo players, horse-racing and pavillion scenes—the Santeros were synonymous with horse racing in Lagos and Ibadan. Indeed, it was part of the Santero legend that the family introduced horse racing into the southern part of the country.

Madame Santero gave the appearance of a diminutive queen holding court among subjects who had briefly excused themselves but left behind their shadows. She waved her two visitors into chairs on either side of her and raised her eyes in question at the one she did not know. Sipe introduced him.

"Mr. Akinyode Soditan, school principal from Abeokuta." School principal sounded more impressive than head teacher, and Sipe felt a need to balance this splendour, however decayed.

She held out a fragile hand and Soditan took it. He hesitated for a moment, wondering if the old lady would prefer him to raise it to his lips, as he had sometimes observed among the white officials and their wives. Even some of the Lagos "been-tos" indulged in the practice, and Madame Santero was obviously of that returnee stock from Brazil. He settled for a brief handshake and a bow, murmured the usual "Pleased to meet you," and hastily took his seat. She came straight to the point.

"Well, Mr. Efuape, what have you decided?"

Sipe exhibited surprise. "Mrs. Santero, I thought it was your family which had to decide. When we last spoke—"

"No, no, young sir, I made our position quite clear. We are going to stand by our son, whatever you decide to do. We do not deny what he did, neither do we condone it. But I made it clear that I simply do not have the money to refund what he . . . what he stole from you. And my family is tired of rescuing him from the mess he creates for himself. You understand, Mr. Efuape, we obviously cannot pay. So it is you who must propose some arrangement. Do you still wish to press charges?"

"The case is already with the police."

"I know. But it can be withdrawn. Please, let me remind you of what I said. My son is not dishonest—"

"Mrs. Santero—"

"No, not really dishonest by nature. He gets into scrapes, yes. The point I am making is that he did not misappropriate your theatre funds just to spend them. We have the proofs in the post office receipts—he sent most of it in postal orders to that con artist in London, this mysterious Ray Gunnar. You must, after all, accept some of the blame yourself—"

Sipe's voice rose to a scream. "I, Madame?"

"He would never have learned about him if you had not assigned him the task of recovering your money from Ray Gunnar. That is how he was caught in Gunnar's web. José has always been stage-struck." She rode over Sipe's gasps, wrung out by what he considered the greatest injustice of his life. "But all that is neither here nor there. I am only trying to tell you that the case may go on forever, because we definitely intend to subpoena this Ray Gunnar. And that means awaiting the results of investigations in London. The police have to find him first."

"It is a lot of money," Sipe murmured.

"I know," the lady said gently. "I am aware of that, Mr. Efuape. I am sorry that José is such a romantic fool. He already saw himself as a film star."

A long silence followed while Sipe appeared to think. "I take it you cannot even think of paying it back by installments. We could come to an understanding."

"I wish I could do that. I wish I had the means to guarantee that. But I know the repayments would be irregular."

Akinyode sat up with a jerk at the next pronouncement, which emerged with unmistakable finality from Efuape's lips. "In that case," he announced, "I will take the white horse."

Mrs. Santero's eyes flashed for a brief moment, either with anger or with shock; it was difficult to tell. Then they went soft and gentle, and a sad, brave smile hovered round her thin lips. "Bahia." Her lips trembled slightly as she turned round to look at the photograph of the ancestor directly behind her. "That's the last in the breeding line of the first Bahia, which came with him from Brazil. He named him Bahia. He wanted his descendants to have a live reminder of their other home in Bahia."

"It is a handsome horse," Efuape commented. "Your son brought it sometimes to Glover Hall. I have watched it being exercised on the marina beach."

"Do you like horses, Mr. Efuape?"

Efuape shrugged. She turned to Akinyode. "What about your friend?"

Startled out of his bewilderment, Akinyode stammered that he was not a wild one for horses but that he did admire the species.

"And are you going to sell it to offset your loss, Mr. Efuape?"

"Oh no. A king is going to ride it—into Ashtabula." And he grinned at Akinyode.

She frowned. "A king? Ashta . . . ?"

Sipe nodded. "Yes, a king. An Oba. Ashtabula is a place my friend here knows more about."

"A *future* Oba," Akinyode amended, but Sipe repeated firmly, "An Oba."

Mrs. Santero reflected only for a few more moments. "And this will be in full settlement?"

"Complete settlement."

The lady exhaled a deep breath. "So be it. It was really José's horse; no one else rode it. I think it is only just."

"I believe so, Mrs. Santero."

"In that case, perhaps you can get your lawyer to draw up the terms of settlement . . ."

Sipe succeeded in astonishing Akinyode one more time that day.

He reached into the inside pocket of his coat and brought out a legal-looking document tied with a red ribbon. "I have it here already. A friend, Lawyer Otusanya, prepared it for me last night—in Ìsarà. Everything is in order."

She did not take her eyes from his face as her arm reached out to take the document. Again the faint smile played over her face. "So. You knew what you wanted all along."

Sipe smiled in turn. "What else could one think of, Madame? I had actually asked a mutual friend, Mr. H. O. Davies, to look into the matter for me—act as intermediary, you understand? I had not planned to see you so soon myself. But then certain events intervened to promote a new idea—only last night. I think it is the best solution all round."

Her hand moved towards the bell on the side table. The silvery tinkle sounded unearthly in the gloom of the reception hall. The maid appeared.

"Bring my writing set." The maid left. "I suppose your friend here will act as witness?"

"It is convenient he's here."

The maid returned with a pad built into an inkstand, two pens lying in grooves near the edge. She took it and placed it on her knees.

"Now bring the sherry decanter and three glasses. I'd like to drink with a man who can teach José such an impressive lesson."

VI

ASHTABULA!

E xhausted but filled with euphoria, Sipe turned the gray Morris at last up the sheer cliff-surface that controlled all motorised entry into Ìsarà. Soditan was somewhat pensive. They had called on his uncle, the carpenter, in Sagamu, and now he wondered if this had not been a mistake. Soditan was rapidly developing an instinct for the sheerest threat of new responsibilities; in his mother's brother, he detected just such a threat. The man had to be fetched from his favourite workplace, the drinking parlour at the motor garage. He turned up, his speech slurred, yet sufficiently clear to convey his plans of sending his two "wayward" children to his famous nephew in Abeokuta, to imbibe a little of his tested discipline. Soditan very firmly advised him to postpone such a scheme indefinitely, warned him that if they arrived without his approval, he would send them back on the next lorry. Yet he feared that this would not be the end of the matter. If the carpenter continued to drink his business dry, the children themselves might turn up on their own, or be sent not by the carpenter but by a concerned relation.

The carpenter went into a torrent of excuses, barely understandable, but related to Tenten's death and a message from his sister Mariam. Teacher was not to believe whatever his mother said; he had not even been home at the time and only returned to find a message left by some girl, who obviously mistook his assistant for himself. Anyway he had been told of Teacher's stout assistance and may heaven bless his efforts and didn't he always go on his knees in Sagamu and pray that his own children would grow up to be like this son of Ìsarà of whom everyone was so proud? Akinyode did not even know that Mariam had turned to her brother for help at the time; he wondered why she had wasted precious money sending a message to such a feckless being. Still, what was he doing there himself? Even if the project that took him there was to be a secret from Ìsarà until the last moment, were there no carpenters nearer Ode to whom he could give the commission? He shrugged. One had to keep trying. If the business could be assisted from time to time . . . it was not too much in the way of duty for a nephew. And it was in his own interest. If he did not lend a hand and his young cousins arrived on his doorstep, destitute . . . well, which was the greater evil?

Soditan gave the instructions to the assistant, sketching out in minute detail the contraption he wanted built on the back of Node's lorry for the awaited event. They left some money for wood; the rest would be paid after the frame was mounted on the lorry—probably in a week. While he busied himself with the carpenter, Sipe wandered through the workshop, his gaze fixed on the stacked cabinets, wardrobes, and all-purpose cupboards awaiting customers. In the interior store there were a few coffins stacked on trestles, awaiting orders before being given their finishing touches. Briefly he wondered if the Syndicate should invest in the carpentry trade but deferred a decision until after the kingship tussle was settled. And he stored away the skill with which Akinyode had made his sketches; perhaps he could persuade him to turn his hand to designing for the new enterprise—if that route was pronounced lucrative after he had made his enquiries.

They found Josiah in Mariam's cottage, washing his hands after a meal of *eba* and *ikokore*. He waited impatiently while they greeted Mariam; she cleared away Josiah's plates and the calabash of water, then went to prepare food for the newcomers.

"We saw him," the son reported.

"Hn-hn?"

"He accepts the decision of the kingmakers."

"And the rest?"

"Yes. He will do as we asked. No more fight with the government."

The older man waited. The two emissaries fidgeted and exchanged glances. Josiah looked at them with amusement, appearing to enjoy their discomfort. Finally he said, "You have not told me the rest."

Sipe spoke, somewhat plaintively. "Baba, you know our friend. He agrees to keep quiet until the Resident has settled the matter in our favour. But he says he hopes the elders of Ìsarà are not expecting in him a deaf-and-dumb king. Because if they are, they should search in another house."

Silence followed. Then a low chuckle began in the hidden regions of Pa Josiah's chest, welling out into gusts of laughter that shook his entire body. He slapped both hands on his thighs and rose, still shaking. "I knew it. I told Jagun. If they think that the son of Akinsanya will stop fighting those white men forever, they have mistaken their man." His laughter stopped abruptly. "But he must not breathe—Feem!—until we have won the battle. Not even to fart, you understand?"

Hastily Sipe reassured him. "Oh no. We have his word."

"And the other contacts you promised to make—the lawyer, our people in Lagos . . ."

"We left nothing to chance," Akinyode said.

"Good. I'll take the news to Jagun."

At the door he turned. "Oh yes, Sipe. Jagun has something for you. I heard all about your troubles over the native-medicine store you are trying to open in Lagos, so I spoke to him."

"Oh, thank you, Baba."

"Far too many of our own people don't wish their own kind any good or success. That is why the black man is not making progress in this world. As soon as it looks as if someone is forging ahead, when they see the skin on his body glistening . . . oh, have you heard of Opeilu's cousin, Sorunde?"

"Yes, we heard."

"Well, that is an example for you. Not even one month to enjoy his promotion to assistant inspector, they had to send him to join his ancestors. But there is a God in heaven; sooner or later his enemies will find that out. Now you make sure you see Jagun; he will give you something to hang over your shop. He says, give it six months at the most and that licence will be in your hands."

"Thank you, Baba. I will talk to him."

"He went into the matter, I don't have to tell you, as something that touched his own person. This time, Lagos people will find out whether or not our fathers had their own kind of power. And if they think it died with them the moment white men stepped on our soil . . . You see for yourselves to what straits we are now reduced? I have to wait on the white intruder to decide who is going to sit on the throne of my ancestors. Are we not even supposed to learn from the past? Look at the Oyo and Ibadan—I am talking of the Kiriji wars.

At the end of it all, who did they invite to come and make their peace? The white man. The missionaries. And we are all paying a heavy price for that till today. Now that is the situation Olisa is shamelessly provoking all over again, as if they have no history in his father's house!"

"But Paa," Efuape demanded, "is it not also the fault of us Ijebu? Surely we have a share of the blame."

"Oho, the grammar people have come. O ya, tell me. In what way?"

"Well, didn't Awujale Tunwase sign that treaty with the white man? When he wanted to change his mind, it was too late. Carter said to him, an agreement is an agreement, so he brought soldiers to collect his debt."

"En-hen. How else do you want the white man to narrate the story? That is what they taught you about that affair when you went to school, not so? You should sit down with Agunrin Odubona some-day—when all this is over—and hear what he has to say. The war was before my time, but he took part in it. And he met this man Carter in person. In Lagos. Ìsarà sent him to accompany the Awujale's men when they took their peace offering to Carter. We all remember. But he is now senile, and Olisa takes advantage of that."

A commotion was developing outside. Two men, babbling in ex-cited voices, emerged from the dark, shouting Pa Josiah's name. They stopped when they saw him in the doorway and greeted him with a hurried prostration while the elder panted out their message.

"Jagun sent us to find you, Baba Tisa. Very bad things have hap-pened on the farm."

"What sort of thing? I was actually on my way . . ."

"They have just brought in the body of Jagun's in-law Ba'tola. There was a big fight at Oripe farm; Olisa's men went and attacked them. Ba'tola was macheted to death. Many others were wounded on both sides—they were taken to the hospital at Sagamu."

Josiah stood stock-still, his eyes boring through the dusk. "So," he breathed at last. "Erinle wants to wear the king's slippers with bloody feet? So be it. Take me to Jagun."

"You cannot see him now, Baba. He has gone into *osugbo*. He wants you to handle the trouble at the farm because—and this was his message to you—he is going where he cannot be reached."

Josiah hastily pushed his way through the messengers and stood outside, beyond earshot of his son and his friend.

"Give me the rest of the message."

"What he said, Baba, was that Olisa is fouling up the town only because he has the support of the Agunrin Odubona. So he says he will call him home, all night if need be."

"He said that?"

"Those were his words. He will come out, he said, only when the old man has finally answered."

Josiah was again silent for a long moment; then he spoke softly, as if to himself. *"Olorun a gbu'se."**

He turned precipitately, almost bumping into two figures who had emerged round the corner of the house, directly behind him. The bigger one was Sotikare, the court clerk from Lagos; the smaller was Ogunba. Pa Josiah barely acknowledged their greetings before he disappeared in the direction of 'Gborobe, from where he would send for the men he needed. With Jagun in total seclusion, the mundane duties had clearly been left to him.

Sotikare pushed his way up the step, filled the doorway with his bulk. He glowered down at the two friends, who sat sombrely before the dishes Mariam had prepared for them, untouched. Then Akinyode caught sight of Ogunba, partly hidden by Sotikare's body, and moved forward to greet him. The quiet but severe voice of the court clerk was a lash across his face, freezing him dead in stride.

"I hope you are all satisfied!"

Ogunba tried to remonstrate with him; it was obvious that they had been arguing all the way to Mariam's house. Sotikare waved him aside and plunged into violent denunciations. "I thought young Akinsanya had more sense, and if he did not, that he had friends who could lend him some. An intelligent man like Saaki, he starts competing for a primitive institution like obaship, and you, his supposed friends, actually encourage him. You bring him to the level of ignorant men like Olisa and Jagun."

Soditan's face was grim. "Go on. Don't be afraid to include my own father in that list."

"I did not refer to Paa."

* May God grant success to his endeavour.

"You should. If there is a conspiracy, he is at the very heart of it."

"We don't have to bring personal emotion into this."

Sipe laughed out aloud. "Who is bringing emotion in it? Just look at you."

"It's a disgrace, that's all I have to say to you. And if you have any love for your man you should tell Akinsanya to pull out his candidature—immediately!"

"But why?" Ogunba demanded quietly. "All you have said so far is all you've been saying all day."

"You are all educated men. How could you involve yourselves in such a matter? It should be beneath you."

Akinyode turned to face Ogunba, dismissing the court clerk with the suggestion of a hiss. "Where have you been? What kept you in Ijebu-Ode?"

"This very affair. I heard rumours that our man had been chosen—"

"You mean you knew before we did?"

Ogunba laughed. "What do you people know in Abeokuta?"

"Ho ho, listen to this runaway? He hasn't even settled down in his new station and he's already become the ear of all Ijebu!"

Sotikare walked away from them and sat apart, staring gloomily through the window and murmuring under his breath.

"So when did you hear?" Sipe demanded.

"Not that long before you did. The kingmakers sent an emissary to the Awujale to report Olisa's move. Of course he had known months before what the Ìsarà kingmakers had decided. But when Olisa crowned his own man, it blew things out into the open. I went to see him. He has sent for Olisa and his backer—that old man they called Agbari Iku. And then I stopped to see the Akarigbo—he agreed to summon an emergency meeting of Remo Local Council."

"When?"

"They met this morning. I waited to bring you the decisions but had to leave while they were still at it. My cousin will bring the news first thing tomorrow morning."

"Good. Very good."

Sotikare's voice cut through their elation. "I hope the council finds a way to bring Babatola back to life. Not to mention those others who will be the sacrificial lambs over such a primitive contest."

Sipe spun round angrily but Akinyode restrained him, got up instead, and went to stand over the simmering hulk of Sotikare. "Look, er . . . Sotikare. We are all ex-Ilés here, so we can speak the same language and speak it frankly. State your objections in clear terms. What do you have against Akinsanya's selection?"

"The whole thing smells. He is lowering himself . . . an ex-Ilé."

"We've heard that. But what exactly do you oppose—the entire idea of obaship? Or is it that you think it is okay for illiterate people but not for a Simeonite?"

"The entire thing is too primitive."

From the other side of the room, Sipe swore out loudly.

"Why don't you and Ogunba start eating?" Akinyode said. "I have just one more question for our civilised clerk." He faced Sotikare directly. "Now tell me, what do you feel about the throne of England?"

"What?"

"You heard me. The throne of England. Is it primitive? Did King Edward abdicate because he found it too primitive, or was it simply because of woman trouble?"

Sotikare ignored the loud laughter of the others, a look of disbelief stamped on his rotund face. He managed to stammer out at last: "Are—you—comparing the throne of England to—this throne of—Ìsarà?"

"Why not?" all three chorused.

Sotikare rose. "Now I know you are all lost. You actually compare—I mean, are you people serious?"

"Well, one is obviously bigger," Akinyode conceded amiably. "It even boasts of an empire. We all have to dress up our pupils every Empire Day and march and sing songs of praise to the English throne and all its forebears, Queen Victoria included." He turned to the others and raised his arms in a conductor's pose. "One—two—three!"

> Vikito-ria, Vikito-ria
> *Aiye re l'awa nje*
> *O so gbobo eru d'omo*
> *N'ile enia dudu.*

Sotikare glared at them rolling in laughter after they had ended their cacophonous rendition. But it was mostly Akinyode to whom his attention was directed. "You know, I am seeing a side of you I never suspected before. I always thought you were more sensitive to things of this kind. Look at you, a man has just died . . ."

"Sotikare, we all regret that death. But do you know how many of our people have died to preserve the British throne? Those who have now joined the army for this war at least made their own choice—thank God for small blessings. But whose throne are they really fighting and dying to preserve? It is certainly not that of the Odemo of Ìsarà!"

"Talking of the war," Ogunba said, "the radio predicted this morning that the war will certainly reach Senegal. Something about treachery by one Admiral Petrain."

"Hm-hm. It creeps nearer and nearer," Sipe agreed. "Let's eat our dinner before Hitler snatches it from our mouths. Come on, Sotikare."

"I don't want to eat!"

"It is *ikokore,*" Soditan warned, taking him by the arm. "We can eat and plan how to stop the violence before it spreads. You will come in useful there."

"I've told you, I want no part of it."

"As court clerk to the British crown," Yode said soothingly, "your voice will carry plenty of weight." He led him to the bench and sat him down before the dishes. "And you are already close to the Rokodo House—Erinle's people, from where Olisa made his choice."

Ogunba nodded in agreement. "We mustn't leave things to Jagun and . . ." He chuckled, glancing at Akinyode.

"And my old man, you are right. We will have to tell them that Akinsanya is one of ours, and he must not be made part of any violence."

"You see, Sotikare, something which seems to have escaped you—everything is being transformed. Adjustments are being made to a new age, and the obaship is only one of the institutions that are affected. It is wrong to think that the former Oba were 'illiterates,' by the way; that is very, very wrong. Very narrow-minded. Akinsanya is merely representative of a new breed. Of course, if you are saying that the whole thing should be scrapped . . ."

"No, I never said that."

"Well then," Ogunba continued, "as long as that position is there, let's make sure that we help to fill it with an enlightened person."

"Talk to the Rokodo family," Soditan said. "Let them see that violence will only bring the full weight of the government down on Ìsarà. And it is wartime. Any excuse to send in the soldiers in order to 'keep the peace'—the government will grab it. Remind them of Carter's war against the Ijebu. Some of their elders were eyewitnesses to what happened to the Ijebu. Ìsarà may not be so fortunate this time—not like that war, which we fought outside our borders. The soldiers will come in. Ask people who live in and around garrison towns and they will tell you what evil that means. It is a question of who the people want; let the people decide it. Use the right language to them. Ìsarà has never been subjugated in all its history. If we use our own hands to open the gates to an army of occupation, our ancestors will curse us from their graves."

"And their children. And unborn generations," echoed Efuape.

"All right, all right. You don't have to preach at me. I was the one who first denounced the violence, wasn't I?"

"Of course," agreed Soditan. "I was merely making suggestions because, you see, you must find the right way to talk to those stubborn old men. If you go there and speak grammar, they won't listen to a thing, least of all our man Agbari Iku—that's if he can still hear a thing. But you try reminding them of the judgement of their ancestors, etc. Make them see THE CURSE already hanging over them like a dark cloud over their roof—drought, famine, plagues, even Hitler dropping down from the sky on satanic parachutes . . ."

Mollified, Sotikare even permitted himself to join in the laughter. "You should have been a lawyer," he spluttered.

"No, no, preacher," Ogunba corrected him. "I have always said his place is really in the pulpit."

Sipe opened up the dishes and passed his hand over them with a flourish. "Bless this food o lord for christ's sake amen do we eat this congealed mess now or never?"

As they moved to take their places at the table, Ogunba touched Soditan on the arm and unobtrusively drew him a little distance away from the others. "I sent my cousin to Sagamu—to the hospital. He returned with news that two of the injured have since died. The doctor is a family friend, so I have sent back word that he should keep it quiet for as long as possible. I have not told anyone. And he'll bring back news of the council's decision. He has my motorcycle so he should be back with the first light of dawn."

And then it was the turn of a neglected Christmas and New Year spirit to intrude with a reminder of the season, which had vanished from their minds under the pace of events now moving the sleepy town closer to the brink of civil strife. It took the form of Wemuja, dressed in a two-tone cowboy affair, complete with shimmering tassels down his long yellow sleeves and aquamarine pantaloons. On his head was perched a purple conical-shaped paper cap and around his waist was a silver-studded belt complete with leather holsters and chrome-plated toy pistols. Only his face was anything but festive. He came into the room and stopped dead, confused by the presence of Soditan's friends, who had paused in various stages of transferring food to their mouths or masticating. They all stared at the apparition in amazement, looking at Soditan for some kind of explanation. Only Efuape turned his back on the eruption, burying his face in his plate.

Wemuja swallowed rapidly, his precipitate entrance—and whatever it portended—totally overwhelmed by the gathering. Soditan decided to help him out, before the paper hat, which he had now taken off, was shredded in his powerful fingers.

"What is it, Wemuja?"

"I . . . er . . . sir, Head Teacher, sir, we heard. We heard the news where we were playing band. I came right away to let you know, Brother Babatola was my friend. I have people, sir, in the motor parks. I can get fifty of them together even if I go there tonight. And I have the railway people. They never forget me. I can take Pa Node's lorry and go and collect all of them to come here. If you want, I am ready to go now."

Soditan smiled. "Thank you, Wemuja. I assure you we will need your timber lorry very soon. I already have plans for you to go to Sagamu. But not yet. I will let you know when."

The master driver's face relaxed into a satisfied grin, swiftly followed by a spasm of anguish as he remembered what had caused his presence there. "Thank you, Teacher. What these people have done, God will not forgive them. Man will not forget and God will not forgive. Good-night, sirs."

And he turned on his heel and left the house. Only then did Sipe look up from his plate, shamefacedly. Akinyode took one look at him, darted a glance at the figure of Wemuja slowly disappearing into the dark. He shook his head, and his eyes returned to Sipe and framed the question. Sipe nodded sheepishly.

"Guilty. He saw it in my mail-order catalogue and begged me to order it for him. Cost price, I swear. No commission."

It was routine work to Goriola, who had carried out this chore a thousand times in his career and in hundreds of households. His gangling figure was a familiar sight in Ìsarà, as it was—albeit on different weekdays—in Ode, Ipara, and a few clusters of cottages in between. Thursday was Ìsarà's day, though not with strict regularity. Sometimes Goriola would disappear for a month or more; a fellow worker had been taken ill or had gone on leave, and he would cover his beat in Isonyin or even as far afield as Igbajo. No matter, sooner or later his figure rose above the hilltop on a Thursday, perched on his gleaming bicycle—he always stopped just before entering a village, and gave the crossbars, the handlebars, even the spokes, a careful wipe, taking off every speck of dust. Then he took out the bicycle lamp from its protective nest in the saddlebag—even though the lamp was never required, unless sometimes on the very last mile or two of his journey home, and then only if he had stopped on the way to quench the thirst which came with his pedalling exertions. The lamp slotted in position, he pushed his bicycle up the hill and freewheeled down on his first target. His route was chosen carefully to ensure that his first appearance in town did not involve any unseemly exertion.

It was the children who usually first spotted the khaki pith helmet framed against the sky, followed shortly by a youngish face which was set in a conscious official-duty sternness. It pronounced every household guilty until proved innocent. Next followed a disproportionately long neck which, everyone remarked, must have been his main qualification for the job of sanitary inspector. It enabled his face to peer round tight corners, pry underneath beds and into cupboards, reach between rafters, and negotiate awkward shelves. Then followed a bristling white collar, its flaps nearly as wide as those of an *abetiaja*. En route, it had been protected by a white-dotted red bandana carefully tucked into the space between the collar and the neck. The collar was held together by the fattest knot ever seen in Ijebuland, while the maroon tie itself covered nearly all the exposed sector of the shirt and vanished into the regulation khaki jacket with gleaming brass buttons, bearing the crest of His Majesty's Government. Goriola's shorts were so wide that they appeared to be abbreviated versions of the local *kembe,* and the feet that rested authoritatively on the bicycle pedals were encased in white canvas shoes whose soles were holed through six years of careful usage.

When the children saw him, they set up a cry: *"Wolé-wolé! Wolé-wolé!"*

It was a signal for the women of the household to rush about as if suddenly stung by bees. Chasing the carelessly discarded leaves and other debris in the compound, scooping up the neglected excrement of a child, and screaming at older children to check that the waterpots had been covered up. Brooms flashed up and down the wall corners, darting into the rafters and slapping furiously at windowsills. Indigo-pots in the yard were covered up—never mind what the teacher once said, that mosquitoes never bred in dye-pots, how could they? The pots, half-sunken into the ground, were quickly covered up by flat iron sheets and wooden planks, while efforts were made to throw fresh earth on the indigo puddles and trickles formed by drips from the hanging cloths. In the dark corners of houses where the waterpot was stored for coolness, the damp on the floor was wiped dry, the water itself keenly probed for evidence of mosquito larvae—the very worst crime in the sanitary inspector's manual. Any suggestion of a wriggling motion and the pot would be emptied, the telltale larvae stamped into earth.

Goriola never hurried. His practice was to vary his choice of the first victim from visit to visit, and he would sometimes prop up his bicycle against one house, only to walk through the passages to begin his inspection at another. And he began by ensuring that his own appearance was beyond reproach. "A sanitary inspector," he would say, "must firstly pass his own inspection sanitarily." He saw to it that his rather willful shirt collar had both flaps in place beneath the lapel of his jacket, then walked round to the saddlebag, took out a notebook to which a pencil was attached by a string, then struck a pose which he had consciously adopted from his hero, the head teacher, who had obtained the position for him in the first place. The young sanitary inspector would stand stock-still, then turn slowly round in a complete circle, carefully surveying the neighborhood and deciding, it seemed, which would be the first doorway to receive his frame. His mind made up, he caught the dangling pencil in one swift move, wetted the lead point between his lips, and wrote down the name of the selected houseowner. This ritual never varied. Faces peeked at him from behind half-closed doors and windows, spied on him from the dark entries into the rutted passages, and even, in the case of children, looked down from treetops. Nothing moved on the outside of houses—it was too late for any careless occupant to start sweeping over dogs' faeces, tins, and food scraps which had been unhygienically ignored. In the interiors of houses, however, all was frenzied activity. Goriola's ritual, he would privately admit, was a last-minute concession to lazy housekeepers. After the five minutes' grace thus provided, any delinquents could expect no mercy. Notebook, summons, court, and fines. Knowing that he had to compensate for his youthful appearance—at twenty-nine he still looked like a twenty-year-old—he developed various strategies to bolster his authority in face of the patronising pleas of mostly older delinquents. One of them was the reputation for never rubbing out an offence once entered in his notebook, which acquired for him the name of Mr. No-Gbebè. The ex-Ilés, however, had long bestowed on him a name more suited to his appearance and also closer to his own name. He did not mind; on the contrary it made him feel a special relationship with the teacher's select circle of Ìsarà's indigenes.

On this unusual Thursday, there were no children to announce his appearance. He coasted downhill as usual and pressed down the chrome-plated bicycle stand with his foot. He sensed something different in this familiar neighbourhood but could not really place it. He shrugged it off, proceeded to execute his slow-motion rituals, and marched, somewhat thoughtfully, towards the Rokodo compound. He knocked, then frowned. There was none of the usual rustle of last-minute whispered instructions, flying brooms, and scurrying feet, no furtive scraping of congealed food from the bottom of a forgotten pan or pot. Goriola turned his gaze in the direction of the other houses, caught a face or two in the act of rapidly withdrawing, and was somewhat reassured. If there had been an untoward happening, such as a death in the household, one of the neighbours would have come forward to inform him. So he knocked again, this time announcing himself:

"Wolé-wolé. Emi ni o, Mr. Goriola."

Receiving no answer still, he reached over the gate and found the wooden stop, lifted it from its slot, and entered the passage between the immediate houses, which led into an open space. The compound was empty; a quadrangle of silent walls receded behind covered verandahs and houseposts; closed doors and windows confronted him. The Rokodo compound looked completely deserted. Goriola shrugged, flicked up the notebook with a much-practised gesture so that the pencil landed on the pad, against which his thumb pinned it, then proceeded to inspect what he could in the open compound.

The indigo-pots were grouped around a sparsely leaved *odan* tree, which appeared itself to be the centre of the compound. He smiled grimly as his gaze instantly took in three pots which were wide open. There was worse. The entire household gave the appearance, almost, of a place that had been hastily abandoned. A charred cooking-pot lay tilted on an open-air hearth near one of the houseposts, while a mound of rubbish decorated the far corner, under the eaves, as if an effort had been made to sweep up the compound, but for some reason the pile had been overlooked. Goriola picked his way through baskets and other litter of a normal, busy enclosure, walking towards the cluster of half-buried pots that had first attracted his attention. He ducked under a dirty *agbada* which hung from a cross-pole, and then his nose crinkled in disgust at the spectacle occupying the space between the trio of open pots—a potsherd; it could be the usual offering one found at crossroads, or perhaps it was a special *etutu*. He wondered, for the first time, if the *odan* tree was a household deity whose festival was perhaps being celebrated on that day. The potsherd contained some whitish food which could have been *lafun* but was so liberally covered with palm oil as to defy any certainty. There were also kola nuts, split open; a giant snail, impaled through the shell and through the potsherd into the ground; cowries; a quantity of black powder in a tin. Three *ado* tied together with a palm frond completed the picture, except for nine *onini*—the inspector counted them very carefully, wondering what coins from the white man's mint had to do with such a primitive offering.

Pondering whether or not this mess, which was already attracting a swarm of flies and ants, should also be entered in his notebook among his list of offences against household hygiene, Goriola turned away and caught sight of his reflection on the still surface of the indigo fluid. Tucking his notebook under his armpit, he seized the chance to adjust his tie and smoothe down the lapels of his jacket. That objective attained, he restored the notebook to his hand and stood still for some moments, inspecting the result. He remained in that position for longer than he had planned. The quiet of the compound slowly seeped into him. Perhaps the reflection of his helmeted face, framed against the sky, across which a few wisps of clouds idly floated, and the exertion of the five-mile ride to Ìsarà also aided the creeping lethargy. Goriola became lost in thought; the seconds lengthened into minutes. And then he experienced, he thought, a momentary hallucination. Another face had appeared behind his and, in a flash, yet another. But all thoughts of hallucinating vanished when he felt a touch on the nape of his neck which was different from the feel of his accustomed sweat-soaked bandana. And swifter than thought was the cold feel of water enveloping his head—preceded by a *plop* as his helmet fell into the dye-pot—and he knew that his head was forced again and again into the dark depths of the dye mixture. When he came up again for air, Goriola screamed. It was answered by a blow to the side of his face which sent him sprawling backward to land on the votive potsherd, smashing it and leaving a wide red swathe on the back of his khaki uniform.

Goriola was not a strong man, but he had the advantage of height, and, for once, his uncoordinated body became an advantage. As more men poured out from the various doorways and the seemingly silent, empty compound became animated with screams, curses, blows, and the tearing sound of his precious uniform, Goriola fought for his life. From the heart of the nightmare that appeared to engulf him, a government employee on official duties and in broad daylight, he succeeded in making out a few coherent voices.

"I told you they would come."

"This one is only their spy. Grab hold of his arms!"

"You're done for, foolish *ami*. You think we all sleep in Rokodo House?"

"The *etutu* drew him like a pig to slaughter. You saw it, didn't you? He got here and he couldn't move."

"No. He was uttering incantations to render it useless."

"Get the rope. Knock him on the head if he won't keep still."

Goriola struggled like a maniac, screaming for help at the top of his voice, both to neighbours and to Jesus, son of God, yet praying silently to wake up from what he still hoped was a nightmare. He felt his clothes ripped off piece by piece, his baggy shorts were already in shreds as his assailants sought to pin him down, clubbing him, while his head did its best to dodge the blows and the blood from his wounds mingled with oil from the smashed potsherd. It was when he saw the flash of a cutlass in the hands of one of these unknown assailants, however, that he found himself suddenly possessed of a superhuman energy. Flinging off the two men who clung to one arm pinioned behind his back, he leapt up, crashed unseeing through all the human obstacles around him, and fled through the gates of the compound, indifferent to the array of missiles that flew after him— pots, pans, stones, a hoe, which caught him in the small of the back, the snail, which flew past him to land on the gate as his hand found the latch . . .

Once outside, Goriola hesitated, unable to decide which way his safety lay. Then he saw a group of sober-looking men, neatly dressed, coming down the same hill he had so calmly ridden down some moments earlier. He turned uphill towards them. Sotikare, Ogunba, and Opeilu saw the half-naked madman rushing uphill at them and stopped in their tracks. It was Ogunba who first recognised the un- lucky sanitary inspector.

"Hen! It's Young Gorilla!"

Sotikare stared hard but shook his head. "Goriola? Impossible."

The fugitive also recognised them, stopped, and stared at them imploringly, his jaws trembling from their roots in a futile effort to explain, or perhaps to ask them to explain, what was happening to him. Finally there emerged a rasping "Save me, please. Save me." Opeilu pulled him gently behind them as the crowd poured out from the Rokodo compound after their victim and soon came up to where they stood; there were nine or ten wild-looking men, none of whom the three friends could recognise.

Above their shouts Sotikare succeeded in making himself heard.

"Have you people gone mad? What do you think you are doing? And who are you?"

A babble of voices ensued. With great difficulty the small group was however able to make out their accusations. This man had been caught spying and uttering incantations in the Rokodo compound. Indeed, they were now certain that he had "left something" there.

After all, he was within the compound a very long time; he could have buried it anywhere, before he moved to the centre, where he could be seen. The passage between the gates and the open space, for instance—nothing would satisfy them unless he went back with them and uprooted what he had buried in the ground. Oh yes, they were waiting for him. They had waited all night for Jagun's people, who they knew would be coming to avenge Ba'tola's death. They had sent away all the women and children and laid an ambush for the fools. It was lucky for them they didn't come at night—to be dealt with as one deals with burglars and other night-marauders. They waited until morning, then sent their spy, this shivering object, who deserved to be castrated. He was burying charms and uttering spells over the indigo-pots and the "protection" they had themselves placed there against enemy forces. Anyone who thought he could walk into Rokodo House, disguising himself as a sanitary inspector, as if he was dealing with children—

Sotikare interrupted. "Where is Chief Odubona himself?"

The assailants stopped and seemed to really look at the three men for the first time. They became somewhat wary and appeared to turn to one among them, as if to identify him as their spokesman. The hefty, cicatrixed individual pushed his way forward.

"And who is asking for Agunrin?"

Sotikare's party eyed him carefully, shifted their gazes from one to the next, then exchanged glances with one another. "You people are not from here," Opeilu remarked.

"So what? We are Erinle's people from Ode."

Opeilu nodded slowly. "I see. And Erinle asked you to come from Ode to guard his house in Ìsarà."

The man grinned. "In Ìsarà, the king cannot have relations from neighbouring towns?"

"Of course, of course," Ogunba said. "For all we know, Erinle may even have relations in Hausaland. But is the Agunrin home? It is he we were coming to see. We have a message from Lagos. This man here"—and he pointed to Sotikare—"is from Lagos courts. He has a message."

The attackers seemed to pull back. They looked at one another. "What are you going to do with that spy? We caught him red-handed, didn't we?"

"I have just told you. This is Mr. Sotikare, court clerk from Lagos. When we have seen Chief Odubona, he will decide what to do about those who attack a government official."

The spokesman's voice took on an aggressive whine. "But we caught him breaking into the house. He thought it was empty—"

"You could have killed him," Opeilu reminded them. "You were trying to kill him."

"Where is the chief?" Ogunba repeated.

The spokesman shrugged. "We were only told to watch the house. But I heard someone saying they had to go to a meeting at Olisa's place. That is all we know."

"Go back to the watch you were given," Sotikare ordered. "The people of Ìsarà don't want you on their streets. Bear that in mind."

For some moments both groups did not move. By now the street was filled with clumps of people, standing silently, keeping wary watch on the scene. The dark countenances of the men betrayed little emotion, but the ominous way the sleeves of several *agbada* hung down left no doubt about the presence of hidden weapons, waiting to be produced if matters came to a head. For a long moment, only the continued anguished panting of Goriola punctuated the silence. It was difficult to tell on which side the hidden weapons would be drawn, so uncommitted appeared the expressions of the watchers. There were many more who remained behind their doors, lurked behind walls, and crouched in the warrens of those compounds, awaiting a signal, no matter what form it took.

Finally the men from Rokodo House turned at the prompting of their leader, walked back to the compound, and closed the gate. Opeilu gave a sigh and turned to the man they had just rescued.

"Ah, Mr. No-Gbebè, what a thing to happen to you in our Ìsarà!"

"What is going on, Mr. Opeilu? Just tell me what is going on?"

Ogunba stared at him in surprise. "Where do you live that you haven't heard?"

"Heard what? Is it not the same Ìsarà to which I've been coming on inspection since . . ."

Opeilu took his arm. "Come on. We'll take you to the clinic . . ."

"My bicycle . . ."

"I'll get it," Ogunba volunteered, and walked down the hill towards the machine.

"My helmet is also in there." And then he appeared to become aware of his appearance for the first time. He turned his arms over and over, staring at them, then at his half-naked and bleeding body. "Look at me! Look at me! Look what they did to me."

"Come on. Forget your helmet for now. We'll get treatment for you. Didn't you know that Ìsarà is at war? The fight for the throne is out in the open."

"Yes," Sotikare added. "And there is no time to lose. First the battle on the farm—so many wounded, and Ba'tola dead. And now this, right in the heart of the town."

"When Jagun hears of this . . ."

"Maybe he shouldn't—at least not yet."

"How will you prevent that? You saw those looking on. They were eager for blood. In a few moments it will be all over Ìsarà. People will start arming themselves . . ."

"Then we can't waste any more time. The Agunrin is the one we must tackle. He has the longest memory, and that is what fuels the violence. Memory can be a dangerous thing in a stubborn old man."

Ogunba returned, wheeling the bicycle. "Can you ride?"

The battered inspector tried to flex his limbs. The action produced only a groan and Ogunba stopped him. "Try to get on the saddle. We'll push you to the clinic."

They assisted him onto the saddle; then, with two of them holding the handlebar on either side and the third pushing from the rear, they set off for the clinic, filled with sober reflections. They had reached the crossroads at Orelu quarters when Opeilu stopped and turned to the patient, whose face was now visibly swollen on one side.

"Young Gorilla, I know it is hardly fair to ask this of you, I mean, after what you've been through. But if you could bear your pain for just a short while longer—"

Sotikare interjected eagerly. "Just what I was thinking. We should confront Olisa with this. His fellow elders should see the work of his hands with their own eyes."

Ogunba nodded slowly and turned to Goriola. "I wish it had not happened but . . . and you are not even of Ìsarà . . ."

Goriola shook his head to disagree, only to hunch his shoulders from the pain. He half-raised his hands towards the source of pain but stopped just short, afraid even to touch himself. So he attempted to grin, producing at best a grimace. "I have been through the worst already." His tongue appeared to work on the inside of his cheek for some moments. "Wait," he said, and he turned his head to one side and spat. A gob of blood flew out, together with a tooth. "I thought so. Anyway, you can't really say I am not now part of Ìsarà, because that is my blood on that soil. And I don't think it is all palm oil you will find on the ground where I fought those ruffians just now. Only, I . . . I . . . think you may . . . have to . . ."

Sotikare caught him as he fainted. "Poor Gorilla," Ogunba murmured as they stretched him out by the roadside. He jumped on the bicycle and pedalled furiously to find Efuape and the only car accessible to them in Ìsarà.

That the meeting should take place in Olisa's house and not in the Rokodo House was more than sufficient hint of the futility of their mission, if they chose to be discouraged. The three emissaries were buoyed, however, by a sense of their role in the making of history. Where else, for instance, in the entire history of the Yoruba, had a king been chosen by the spectacle of two main contenders seated in an open field, their supporters lined up behind them, visible to all the world? Of course, there had been the earlier murky passages of intrigue, of pressures and treacheries, even of bribery. But that in the end it should come down to what, in effect, was a simple open election? Why, even the legislative council of the nation, now undergoing its fifth decade of experimentation, did not allow such a broad participation of the people. Akinyode could be forgiven, Ogunba argued, for comparing the moment with the era of the Greek *demos*. If the Oyo people had thought of the example which Ìsarà was now about to set, the Kiriji wars, with all their attendant suffering, destruction, and the final humiliating European intervention, would have been avoided.

Not for nothing, however, was the Olisa known—though somewhat uncharitably—as the *asin*.* His ruse to empty the Rokodo House was impelled by the need to keep Agunrin Odubona a virtual prisoner, inaccessible to the opposition except under his control.

* A species of rodent, small but poisonous.

Odubona, agreed by most to be over a hundred years old, was not known to have uttered a word in human hearing for the past ten years of his life. Old and gnarled as the bunched open roots of the *odan* tree, he was the last surviving tome of Ìsarà, and indeed of Ijebu, history from before the settled phase of missionary incursion. He lived with his memories, a still-active but closed circuit within the tight-skinned independency of his head. The Olisa was his sole link with the present; he translated reality to him, and even this, for Odubona, was already more than a healthy intrusion upon his peace.

Erinle, the king-elect, would not appear. To meet with mediators or representatives of the Jagun faction would be to admit that he was not truly a reigning king. And for even greater safety, Olisa, who was painfully aware of Erinle's low level of tolerance for such conflict, had sent him off to Abeokuta, where he had taken refuge with the Sodade family. There he was safe from pleas and summons, from do-gooders and peacemakers who would weaken his resolve and compromise the Olisa's masterful strategies. The lone spokesman for the Rokodo House was thus Agunrin Odubona, Agbari Iku, whose stature however transcended any one ruling house but was indeed the collective will of all of Ìsarà. To be seen with Odubona, night and day, to ensure that the word was spread throughout Ìsarà and beyond that Agunrin had actually "sought shelter" under his roof, was a decisive blow, he felt, for any challenger to his choice.

The sitting room had been carefully arranged, the reception planned to the last detail. Agunrin alone would speak for the Rokodo, and Olisa chuckled loud and long at the ploy. No one could then truthfully report to the Akarigbo or the white Resident that the Rokodo had refused the path of peace. No one would accuse them of not listening. The emissaries would talk to the venerable but dumb. When they had finished their speech, he, Olisa, would rise as regent, thank them, assure them that, as they themselves had witnessed, their father had listened intently to what they had to say. When he had digested their message thoroughly, he would send for them again and give them his reply.

Olisa installed Agunrin in a high-backed chair against the wall to the left of the doorway, so that very little light fell on him. If he fell asleep, no one would notice. Agunrin could sleep on a stool or bench without once falling off or losing his balance, even in advanced age.

Let these white-educated peacemakers talk their heads off; they might as well speak to his iron-and-bronze *ogboni* staff and hope for a reply. But he could say to all Ìsarà, to the Awujale, the district commissioner and other interfering busybodies: As the regent I was present when our Baba gave them audience. No one seeks peace with more fervour than a man who has suffered through wars in defence of the soul of Ìsarà. The rest is up to the other side, who refuse to listen to reason . . .

The callers had also agreed on their own strategy. Opeilu would speak first. It had not taken much to persuade him, on arrival, to replace Soditan, who reluctantly agreed that he was disqualified from such an arbitration role because of the open partisanship of his father. Efuape was adjudged to be no diplomat—even by himself. Opeilu frankly enjoyed the fast-growing reputation he had acquired as a dependable mediator, impartial, deferential, inspiring trust; had the Bishop of Lagos himself, the Right Reverend Vining, not employed his services to settle the odd dispute here and there among his wayward flock? His personality suited the role—nothing flamboyant; his voice deferred naturally to the sullen mumbles of the elders. And afterwards, between kola nuts and a calabash of wine, there were produce tips to be extracted from him. What were government plans regarding cocoa, for instance? Would the price go up? Were companies buying up kernels? Dried peppers? How would the war affect the thirst for palm oil? On his part, Sotikare exuded official menace, the quiet, spectacled surrogate for the hovering presence of the white men's courts, baliffs, police, and even jailers. Least desired, even to Olisa's faction, was the threat of another expeditionary force, the tramp of alien soldiers, this time on Ìsarà soil, home, perhaps, after severe mauling from that man Hitler and eager to take out their humiliation on the innocent heads of the Afotamodi . . .

None of the elders present had forgotten the consequences of the stubborn pride of the Ijebu in the past. The old man who now sat passively listening, his cheeks collapsed into each other with loss of flesh and teeth, a veritable death mask, the Agunrin Odubona, had fought in nearly every battle and skirmish on the Ibadan–Lagos route through the latter decades of the nineteenth century. Beneath his shaven skull, gleaming with *shea*-butter, an active memory recalled the days when, as a young emissary from Ìsarà to the court of the

Awujale in Ijebu-Ode, he had instigated the resolve that no mission-ary-educated youth should be allowed to return and settle on Ijebu soil. The Egba and other inland peoples were free to absorb them and ruin their customs and beliefs; they were at liberty to corrupt their children and desecrate their ancestral shrines with the manners of returnee slaves who wore European suits and ties, smoked ciga-rettes, and walked shamelessly in public with their wives, even hold-ing hands. Such habits had to stop at the gateway into Ijebuland. His fingers, now turned into dessicated claws, still tingled with recollec-tion of the numerous raids in which he had participated on that crucial route into the interior, controlled by the Ijebu. What terror had they not unleashed, aided by their ferocious allies, the Mahin!

The Egba had ruined everything. Their *ifole** had not gone far enough—every Christianised dwelling should have been gutted! Even if the Saro were their returnee brothers, freed on the high seas by the white men and replanted in that faraway place called Sierra Leone, they should simply have embraced them, loaded them with gifts, and sent them back. Did they not see right away that these sons had changed? They were no longer the same flesh and blood that was spirited away. They had become conceited, contemptuous of their past. They settled in that new place, mingled with the white people, and became successful. Good for them. But they should have stayed in their white settlements and sent money home, returned from time to time for reunions, even festivals, but not to settle! This was the plan adopted by the Ijebu, faced with the menace of pollution. That was the wisdom they adopted, and how right they had been proved . . .

"The rains of the past season cannot be sucked back into the sky, no matter how much farmland was eroded away. And anyway, do we also give back the harvest we have reaped in the meantime? We know the trouble that man Carter caused us . . ." Opeilu's voice fell harmlessly on his ears until the name Carter grated upon his hear-ing . . .

Kata-kata! Agunrin's skull-face permitted itself a small toothless grin, which Sotikare saw and misinterpreted, thinking that Opeilu's

* A resistance campaign against colonial/missionary presence—literally: house-smashing.

quiet speech was working in the right direction. No, Agunrin was merely remembering the day he finally came face to face with Nemesis—though he did not know it then—in the person of Carter. When that aggressive presence was announced, Agunrin turned round to his elders and said, "Ah, here comes Kata-kata," and the name had stuck from then on. Even the Awujale would say, deliberately, "Ah, Mister Kata-kata—ah, sorry, Mr. Carter," and his audience chamber would erupt with laughter. Agunrin's face turned grim. Yes, Kata-kata had had the last laugh. His predecessor, Moloney, had proved easier to handle, although he was quite a cunning fellow. Was he not the one who sent one Denton to the Awujale with a bribe of a thousand pounds? Just sign here on the paper, his agents said, just sign here, we promise you no one will know about it. Mind you, nobody really got to the bottom of the truth. Did Awujale Tunwase really take that money? Certainly his chiefs rejected the presents which the Denton man tried to offer them in public, and that was what began the trouble. The emissary went back to the king of England, so they said, and claimed the Ijebu had insulted his king. Well, what of it? Had the man not insulted their own king by his conduct? Trying to bribe the paramount king of all Ijebu to sell out his people just to let in the white man and destroy their lives. Was that not the father and grandfather and great-great-grandfather of insults?

*"Eyin re bare eni . . . eyin r'ologbon eni . . . eni boje l'aiye wen."**

Yes, this young man made sense but where would these people stop? How many years now since Kata-kata brought war to Ijebu? Forty? Fifty? And was this Odemo they wanted to inflict on Ìsarà not their way of finishing off what they began forty years ago? Was it not enough that the missionaries now strutted through the proud land, their churches and schools everywhere, their products mincing on feet suffocating in thick socks and leather through their council halls? Was it not enough that they had to obey laws imposed on them by Kata-kata and his black servants? Must they now permit one of these godless ones to come and sit on the throne of Ìsarà?

"Akinsanya will abide by your wishes, the wishes of the people of

---

* You are our elders . . . you are the custodians of our wisdom . . . ruin must not come to Ìsarà in your lifetime.

Ìsarà. He knows the white man but he belongs to Ìsarà. He has sworn to preserve the ways of Ìsarà while carrying our voice to the highest councils of the land, and beyond the seas. . . . The Ibadan, Egba, the Ekiti, the Ijaiye or Oyo never defeated us in war. They will not now mock our defeat at our own hands."

Yes, he had been one of the four Agunrin who took the peace offering to Kata-kata in Lagos. Four Ogboni went with them, three Pampa, and eleven Parakoyi. The man had demanded a powerful delegation to bring the humiliation of Ijebu to him and sign a treaty which declared the routes open to every Christian riffraff and company agent. Ten sheep they took, a small bag of *iyun,* but what was the result? It only boosted Carter's pride, and what a tongue-lashing he had given them! Insults. Abuse. And then, most daring of all, his soldiers had pointed guns at them and ordered them to put their thumbs on the paper. What was in it? They could not read it. And anyway they did not care. Their mission, which he, Agunrin Odubona, had agreed to, and only with the greatest reluctance, was to present their peace offering and assure Kata-kata that no one had wished to insult his king. But after the man's speech, had everything not simply scattered? Even the most appeasing of the Awujale's delegation swore that the man had gone too far, and not one of them would put their hands to the wretched paper.

"So you see, our fathers that you are, we urge that you accept the Resident's proposals. . . . Let all of Ìsarà gather together, every man, woman, and child behind the man of their choice."

Yes, as Kata-kata wanted us to do. Throw open all our roads, the lagoons, the rivers, our ancestral pathways, to the desecration of aliens. Why not our bedrooms and our daughter's thighs? Yes, why not? A "Lagosian" king sitting on Ìsarà's throne, just as those two so-called Ijebu from Lagos had been called in to do what we would not do. Well, they claimed to have Ijebu blood in them but in what nightmare of the Afotamodi was a name like Otumba Payne ever conceived? Or Jacob Williams? And were they not the two Lagos dwellers whom Kata-kata brought in to sign the paper which they, the emissaries of the Awujale, would not sign? And they had dared break the kola to celebrate the treachery. Abomination upon abomination! They, the mincing spawn of tainted Ijebu blood, had not only signed, for Ijebu, the paper that the emissaries would not touch, they also had taken the kola nut and broken it. For this white man who dared come to their own land and order them not to collect toll from Christian travellers and traders!

"No one is urging you to accept anyone as the new Odemo. We merely urge a peaceful way."

Peace. Yes, they always say that. The missionaries brought peace. Their god was the prince of peace, they said. Yet their bishop from Ibadan, that Togiwe*—if only Ijebu-Ode had cut off his head!— Togiwe came and provoked them. Deliberately. Pity he had not tried it in Ìsarà! Right from the gates of Ijebu-Ode he began to preach. He insulted their worship, cursed their gods, damned their king, and predicted the end of the "heathen" Ijebu. Yet they let him go. Well, maybe they were right. That preacher had been sent in as a troublemaker. He wanted the white man to say this time that not only his king but his god had been insulted. Then he could come in finally with his army. Well, that did happen in the end. So, they might as well have cut off his head and denied him the joy of their defeat. Peace! They told him that Togiwe kept dancing in the marketplace, dancing on one spot like a man a snake has bitten, dancing before the gateway of Ijebu-Ode even as the crowd booed him, dancing with his book held high in his hand, waving it round and round like a flag before an attack. Why are you dancing? the people asked him. Is the man insane? And he told them he was dancing on the spirits of their pagan forefathers, on the bones of our heathenish gods . . . screaming obscenities at the Ijebu-Ode people. But they only laughed at him and let him go. Yes, they let him go! They forgot one thing he preached. Yes, an Ìsarà trader coming home from Lagos had witnessed the scene and he rushed home to warn them. Christianised too and wearing trousers and tie like the others, but he had not fully lost his soul. He was no traitor, like the others. And he said Togiwe had pronounced a famous curse on them, conjuring in the name of one Newton and so betraying the secret of their future plans: "The sword of steel goes before a sword of the spirit." And the trader rushed home, more fearful, he confessed, than he had ever been in his life. And was it not he, Odubona, who had been sent to accompany the trader to the Awujale with the message: "Did you hear what

* Tugwell.

that Reverend Togiwe said? Well, a war that trumpets its advance does not kill even the lame. We are ready in Ìsarà. Send word to Ode, Ipara, Odogbolu, Isoyin . . . As for the Mahin, they need no urging. Ibadan should know that we have no animosity against them, but now is the time to choose. Either they expel the missionaries or they will get no more salt, and no more ammunition, either. And if they want our friendship, they should send Your Highness the heads of Togiwe and his companion Harding, the man of ill omen." Yes, that was Ìsarà's message to their fellow Ijebu.

"Ìsarà has been fortunate. Our fathers, uncles, are still living, who fought in the last war, but it was fought away from our borders. We have never known the tramp of aliens on our soil. Agunrin Odubona, I bow my head to you, you are the veteran of veterans, *ogbologbo ajagun;* if there is anyone in this town who knows what it means fighting against the white man's soldiers . . ."

Yes, let such a man come forward and stand before me, the old man's aggressive cheekbones challenged, while his cheeks sucked in air like an antique pair of blacksmith's bellows. Kata-kata brought Hausa soldiers, he even sent for soldiers, they learned later, from the Gold Coast. They had all heard of the Ashanti, fierce, stubborn warriors; perhaps there were some of them among Kata-kata's army—the Ijebu did not care. They showed the invaders that there were warriors also in Ijebuland. The defeat was bitter, but then, it was not for want of resistance. The Egba had long since caved in. The Ibadan thought they had scores to settle—well, it would soon be their turn. As for the Ondo, whom they had also urged to carry out their own *ifole*—how sad that all these people proved so deaf, so blind to their own fate. Even the Ijaw, with whom the Mahin had so much in common. They were river people like the Mahin; the Mahin carried out their trade with them over the same waters, they even shared some customs. Yet the Mahin reported that the Ijaw all but worshipped the white man and his ways. What was it that made some so different from the others? Had those Ijaw also been corrupted by Lagos and Saro returnees like Otumba Payne and all the others? People who actually put their hands to paper which their own fathers would not touch? Was this Akinsanya not part of that breed? A king should be like a huge *iroko,* casting a protective shade over all his subjects. Who ever heard of such a tree being nourished on foreign soil, then transplanted home on the eve of coronation? Was this how the white men chose their kings?

". . . that is all we urge on you, with all deference due to you as our father. We have not come to preach the virtues of one man against the other. Let the people choose their own king. It is the new way of doing things, and the government in Lagos has given this plan its blessing. So has the Awujale . . ."

The Agunrin's head jerked up violently, and sounds issued from his throat. The effect on the hearers was startling, like the scratch of grinding stones on which coarse sand has been sprinkled.

"Aaa-wu-ja-le!"

The Olisa ceased abruptly to affect boredom. His ears prickled and the hairs rose on his skin. Ten years at least, that voice had not been heard. He turned in his seat, his gaze transfixed by this figure, whose voice even appeared to command the timbre of an ancestral mask.

Again Agunrin spoke: "Aaa-wu-ja-le!"

Ogunba it was who broke through the paralysis that had taken hold of the chamber. In a shaken and uncertain voice he said, "It is so, Agunrin. I met the Awujale myself. And the Akarigbo has summoned Remo Council and their decision has been taken. What Olisa has done was fully condemned, and Erinle was fined twenty-five pounds. He has also been forbidden to parade himself in the king's regalia."

But the ancient warrior did not appear to have heard. His eyes seemed to be on the verge of bursting out of their sockets, and as if impelled by a force greater than could possibly emanate from his wiry yet weakened frame, he spat out the name of his paramount king: "Aaa-wujale Tunwase!"

Mystified, even alarmed, glances flew across the room. Olisa spoke slowly. "Baba, Tunwase is long dead. This is a new Awujale on the throne of Ijebu-Ode."

Apprehensive eyes remained trained on the ancient warrior as he thrust forward his trunk, like a snake about to strike, or a bird taking off from a leafless tree branch at an acute angle, to spike an insect on the wing. They watched him change course abruptly, reach for his *ogboni* staff propped against the wall beside him. He pulled himself up slowly, his hand hovering over the bronze *edan* which formed its headpiece. His fingers twitched convulsively as they grasped it, stopped there some moments, then slid slowly down the iron stem while his body sank, ever so slowly, into his earlier seated posture.

*"O ti fo n'oju!"**

The *ogboni* staff came to rest on his right shoulder. His hand continued its slide downwards until it was stopped at the knee, still clutching the stem. His head fell towards his shoulder, coming to a gentle rest against the staff. His heart then ceased to beat.

Jagun came out of *osugbo* some moments later, summoned by violent knocking on the outer gate. He took one look at the dishevelled messenger, who sought to regain his breath and transmit the weighty news he had brought from Olisa's house. Jagun raised his hand to silence the messenger.

"I know. Take the news to the other chiefs."

The messenger saluted him and ran off. Jagun adjusted his shawl, raised a grim face to the sky, and walked homewards. It had been a long night, spent in solitude in the house of divination. His expression was that of a man who regretted a task accomplished, but knew that it was all for the public good.

Wemuja stood regally before the gates of Node's compound in the very early hours of dawn and, from his vantage, surveyed the city of Ìsarà still folded in a silence of sleep. Countless times he had stood thus, but today, even the barely visible outlines of the cottages wore, it seemed, a special garb. A sheen from some of the newly installed corrugated iron sheets provided the only illumination, creating false contours that made the village curl in upon itself, like a fat caterpillar, waiting to be nudged awake by his giant feet. At such moments, the only being lawfully awake in the whole of Ìsarà—he did not count the night guards—waiting for his apprentice, Alanko, to complete the ritual washing of the Commer, when he would then take over command of the monster and ride out of the dormant domain, Wemuja felt that he was the true king of Ìsarà. He stuck his unlit pipe between his teeth, nodded, and announced to the dewy air: "This life, it is good."

He took in huge, luxurious gulps of the fresh air and turned to-

---

* It is smashed beyond redeeming.

wards the shack of Dekola, the blacksmith. The smith was not an early riser, but his apprentice would be crouched by now against the forge, blowing embers awake from a cloak of cinders. Wemuja's route to the stream where the Commer took its morning wash lay past the forge. Since he discovered this, he made a ritual of stopping by the forge, picking up an ember with the heavy pair of tongs, and lighting the half of a Bicycle cigarette which he had saved from his last smoke the night before. Its usual storage was behind his right ear, even when asleep. The apprentice had learned to expect him, and Wemuja always found the door unlatched. The lorry driver's exotic appearance more than made the boy's day. Every visit, he picked up the tongs and held out the glowing charcoal to his visitor's cigarette stump, first greeting him with a quick semi-prostration. Today, however, the apprentice was stumped; never before had he seen Wemuja with a pipe this early in the morning. Wemuja relieved him of the tongs, dropped the proffered coal, and fished in the furnace for a more suitable lump for his pipe. Squinting over the bowl to drink in the admiration of his sole observer, he drew in air and soon the pipe was smoking smoothly. He handed back the tongs and then astonished the boy further by fishing in his pockets for two *onini*, which he handed over to his server. Patting him on the head, he said, "For *saara*. On behalf of the king to come."

Until his figure was swallowed up in the dark the boy stood at the door, staring at his hero turned philanthropist. Wemuja strolled downhill, seemingly oblivious of the new raptures he had engendered in the soul of a burgeoning lorry driver. When he got to the stream he received Alanko's greeting with studied condescension, gestured that he open the bonnet for inspection. He checked the radiator, oil, and battery level with more than his usual gravity, wiped his fingers on the grease-cloth offered by his assistant, and walked round the vehicle, kicking the tyres to test their pressure. Satisfied, he climbed into the driver's seat, checked the gear to ensure that it was disengaged, then nodded to Alanko, who had taken up his position at the front. At the fourth crank, the engine roared to life. Wemuja depressed the throttle, let the engine roar for about a minute, eased it off gently, and listened intently. His eyes were shut in concentration as his body sensed the tiniest vibrations of the vehicle. Alanko had meanwhile drawn out the crank, rushed to the side to await the next order, which would normally be to remove the wooden blocks from beneath the rear wheels. To his surprise, however, Wemuja merely gave the engine one final roar and turned off the ignition. He then took off his scoutmaster's hat from its hook behind the driver's seat, adjusted it over his eyes, and settled back into his seat as if he meant to indulge in a little more slumber.

Alanko waited some moments, wondering what to do. Finally he asked: "Oga, we no go start?"

Wemuja removed his clay pipe from his mouth, tipped his hat fractionally up in his practised Rod Cameron manner, and said, "Today we are not carry timber."

"A-ah. You mean we no dey go anywhere at all?"

Wemuja looked down at him as if at a retarded child. "Who say we no dey go somewhere? You no see me fill de tank yesterday?"

Alanko scratched at the arid tufts on his head. "But just now you say . . . all right, if we no carry timber, wetin we go carry?"

"His'ry," Wemuja replied. The tone was the nearest he could muster to match Opeilu's, whom he had overheard the previous day. "We dey go carry his'ry."

And with that he pushed the hat fully over his eyes, a gesture which Alanko normally associated with those afternoons when Wemuja doused his energy long enough to permit himself a brief siesta.

Alanko gave up, returned the crank to its hole in the engine to await whatever moment was appropriate for setting off to carry history. Before he could follow his master's example, however, and snatch a few moments rest, a pair of headlamps swung round towards them from the direction of Losi, picking out the harsh grains and laterite veins of the hillsides before settling into the farmed flat stretch on the borders of the stream. Its lights sailed over browned strips of plantain leaves, lumpy green kola-nut pods, grazed the low-lying cocoa plantation, and raised new speculative thoughts at the sight of those lustrous pods, swollen to twice their normal size in the artificial light. The contrast between this outlying belt around Ìsarà and the built-up higher ground was never more insistent than at dawn when a swathe of ground mist rose, a suspended girdle, neatly dividing the two. Tangled among parasites, the euphonious *aso-*

*feiyeje** merely affirmed the sheer extravagance of the fertile basin, for it seemed that only a soil which was truly generous, even prodigal, could name such a fruit for birds alone. It was the cocoa pods however which set Efuape's brain at work all over again, until he rebuked himself, wondering how he could even think of business at such a time. A day like this, he counselled himself, should be reserved for giving thanks to God and praying for his support in the momentous undertaking. Row after row of the gold-flaunting dwarf trees leapt in and out of the headlamps and not once again did Efuape permit himself to dwell on the tonnage rate of cocoa on the world market. When he pulled up beside Wemuja, however, his wayward mind recalled that the timber man had once remarked on the rich texture in the higher soil of Ìsarà, similar to that of his village in Edo. And there, a small-time chief had become a virtual millionaire from his red-brick factory . . . well, later, muttered Sipe, son of Efuape.

Wemuja whipped off his hat as the car pulled up behind the Commer and gave his best scoutmaster salute.

"All set, are you?"

"Good morning, Mr. Sipe. We all standing by."

"Good." Sipe came out of the Morris holding a torch. He climbed onto the back of the lorry, directing the light at the platform. "You are sure it will be steady on this thing?"

"We are going to nail it down well, Mr. Sipe. And then we use ropes which hold down even timber."

"Of course," Sipe conceded, feeling more reassured with that information. He was helped down by the two men and he stood thoughtfully for some moments, trying to make his mind up about their next movements.

"All right," he decided, finally. "You go ahead to Sagamu. I still have to call at Odogbolu. See that you supervise the carpenter yourself. Because it is not even morning, don't you imagine that he won't be drunk."

Wemuja laughed. "Trust me, Mr. Sipe. I am not bad carpenter myself. If necessary I take hammer and nail and do the job."

"As soon as I finish in Odogbolu, I'll join you. Then we proceed to Lagos together."

"All right, sir. Safe journey."

* Fruit for the birds' delight.

"You too, drive most carefully. We have more than enough time."

Wemuja grinned. "I know what today is, Mr. Sipe. I just tell Alanko myself, I said, we are going to carry his'ry."

Efuape's tone was a teasing rebuke. "We-mu-ja! I thought you were supposed to be a man who could keep secrets."

"Me, Mr. Efuape, do you doubt me? Ask him yourself if he know anything. He was asking questions, but even though he is my assistant, do I tell him anything? I just say to him, we are going to carry his'ry full stop, so shurrup and don't worry me. That's him standing there, ask him if you don't believe me."

Efuape laughed and slapped him on the shoulder. "All right, all right, I was just teasing you. Not that it would have mattered. After all, you are both heading out of Ìsarà."

"You mean he can tell me now, sir?" Alanko chipped in.

"If he wishes. He is your master, after all."

Efaupe drove off, hoping to find Onayemi.

If anyone had told him twelve hours earlier that he would divert his journey through Odogbolu at an unholy predawn hour, Sipe would have retorted that there was no more time for any diversionary antics. True, the main tasks had been accomplished, but there still were possible slips, as Opeilu continued to caution them, "twixt the lid and the cup," which brought Soditan on the offensive as usual, insisting the word was "lip," not "lid"—until they were both persuaded to leave the argument to the next dictionary that could settle the dispute. Both made sense, Efuape arbitrated, but of course, "a saying is a saying and some are born incurable pedants."

"Let us go over the arrangements once more," Opeilu pleaded. "No slips, no regrets—and that is original! We are agreed there are not too many crayfish sellers, so their group should merge with others in the dried or smoked fish line, be it *apasun, ebolo, panla* etc., etc.—let them form one group. The other change is the dyers' guild. They will now join the procession after it has passed the Koranic school. Everybody got that? Regarding the hunters, they have now been supplied. They have sufficient gunpowder to restart the trade war our Odubona lost to the missionaries last century. . . ."

Soon Sipe was alone in the fast timber forests through which the rudimentary road had been driven—by the enterprising Ijebu, he reminded himself with satisfaction. The snag over the Ibadan road still rankled in his breast, but was that not one of the hopes he had set on Akinsanya's ascension? Yes, a strong man who would stand up to the Alake, never mind that the Alake was far higher in royal ranking. Saaki was like Daodu, he would battle for any rights he believed in. No browbeating this trade unionist by anyone, black king or white colonial servant. Over the Morris's noisy interior, he chuckled to himself—that Yode, he concluded all over again, he surely was a close one. Sly even. Imagine concealing from everyone all this while that he too had consulted the Spirit of Layeni—or some relation of that shade, never mind how distant.

"But I did not conceal it," Soditan had protested. "You never asked me. It simply never came up."

The death of Agunrin intrigued them. Yet what should be strange about the death of an old man, reputed to be over a hundred? True, there was the small detail of his voice, which, everyone recalled, had dwindled progressively into a hoarse, uneasy whisper that sometimes appeared to have journeyed from the depths of a densely forested gorge, then given up altogether. That was at least ten, maybe twelve, years ago. Then the eerie moment when the old man found his voice—or was it his? No one remembered any longer how the warrior's voice had sounded either in his prime or in advanced age. But even the man of Lagos, Sotikare, had admitted that it made the hairs on his arms stand on end. As for Opeilu, his stomach ulcer ran riot and had to be sedated with six wraps of *eko* taken with *ekuru* and palm oil stew from which all trace of pepper had been excluded.

Agunrin Odubona's death lured them all out of the straightforward rules of scheming and intrigues and, for Sipe especially, came a reawakened interest in the project he had merely suspended. In turmoil after the warrior's death, the House of Rokodo had no more will to resist plans for a peaceful show of strength—and Ogunba had given full credit to the powers of Jagun.

"He had a hand in it. He removed that silent obstacle."

Dinner the last night at Sipe's house marked the end of a week-long intensity of furtive motions and rehearsals. Now there was nothing to do but await daybreak and unfold their unabashedly emotion-harvesting designs. From *osugbo,* the nightly throb of heavy drums reminded them that the rites for Odubona's funeral were not yet over; conversation was easily dominated by his death, the first such experience for the three emissaries—to witness the passage of a soul. With the exception of Opeilu, the others were also mortality virgins, but more contentious was the actual manner of Odubona's exit, given the grim pronouncement of Jagun when he withdrew into seclusion.

"I would have been better persuaded," Sotikare scoffed, "if your Jagun had exerted this so-called power on Olisa. That old man already had both feet in his grave."

"I don't know," Soditan countered. "It's only common sense to strike at the weakest point in an enemy's defences. Olisa was tougher material. Maybe Jagun needed a whole month to—call him home."

"Stop playing the devil's advocate," Sotikare said irritably. "Do you realise what you're all saying? You are accusing an innocent man of murder."

"No-o-o. Conspiracy with Nature perhaps . . . an acceleration of her tempo . . ."

"How? How? Tell me how. By poison? Did he even move near him? No. Your supposed murderer locks himself away in seclusion and—yes, does what? What exactly does he do?"

"We don't know. No one here says he does."

"Ha! Yet you persist in suggesting that Jagun did it!"

"May have done it," Efuape corrected him.

"No." Ogunba shook his head stubbornly. "I believe he did it."

"Then you must be able to say how he did it."

"There are more mysteries in this world, Horatio . . ." Efuape intoned.

"Oh, go away!"

". . . than are dreamt of in your legalisms."

Sotikare shook his head in despair. "If only Reverend Beeston knew how much he wasted his time."

"Why do you say that? Didn't his own Shakespeare also believe in ghosts and charms, etcetera?"

"You're right." Soditan nodded. "So, Duncan's castle or Odogbolu shrine, what's the difference?"

Sipe pricked up his ears. "Odogbolu? What do you know of Odogbolu?" His voice was tinged with suspicion, as if Soditan's remarks had been a subtle dart in his direction.

"What shouldn't one know of Odogbolu? Where else in Nigeria would you find spirits which actually *read* English?"

"Oh, come on . . . !" Sotikare began.

"This is not hearsay. I can personally testify to it."

"Where? When? Do you seriously mean . . . ? How did you . . . ?"

Soditan raised his hand. "One at a time, one at a time. It was—let me see—yes, some four or five years ago. With Efunsewa, before he went overseas. He asked me to accompany him."

"So what happened? Go on, go on, what happened?" Efuape was by now on the edge of his seat. Soditan laughed.

"Hey, look at Sipe! Why are you so excited?"

"Never mind Sipe. Just tell me what happened!"

"It was simple really. Efunsewa wanted to know how he would fare in the U.K. What to do and what not to do, what to take . . . the usual stuff. The medium had instructed him to write everything down on a piece of paper. So, we entered the shrine. The medium—he remained invisible throughout—told him to put the paper under a piece of stone. He did. Well, I know you won't believe this, but the voice—it came from behind those walls—answered all his questions one by one. In the very order in which they were asked. He read out the questions—not exactly read but he summarized them pretty well, and replied to them."

Sotikare snorted.

Ogunba tweaked his nose at him. "It's true. I was present the second time."

Opeilu was alarmed. "You mean you risked it a second time? Oh. Maybe you recited Psalm—"

"What risk? It was all straightforward. The first time it was a bit frightening, I must admit. The atmosphere of the place . . . it was intimidating. But I had resolved to go back. In fact I made the appointment before we left—you have to, you know. Some periods are simply not appropriate. I prepared my own list of questions."

Opeilu's eyes twinkled. "Was he right about which of them you would marry?"

The dinner table broke out in laughter. "Maybe Morola had already nailed him at the time," Sotikare suggested.

"Or how many he would end up marrying." Sipe began to tick off an imaginary list. *Obiren alaran.* Indirect Speech . . ."

"Hm! Ola-rumpus!" Opeilu chuckled long and loud.

"Then the floral codes—Bougainvillea . . ."

"A-ah, that was a thorny affair . . ."

"Bachelor's button. Cana Lily . . ."

In his best baritone, Sotikare began to sing, "Behold, the lilies of the field . . ."

Soditan's lips went prim and he folded his hands across his chest. "Right. Finish off the story yourselves."

They cajoled him. He relented. "Only, don't let me have any more of this pot calling the kettle black. You, Sipe, especially. *Oo l' enu oro.* "*

Sipe threw up his hands. "Why pick on me?"

"Just you shut up. Now where was I?"

"You went back with Ogunba."

"Right. And if you really want to know, I asked the obvious questions any young man would ask. Would I be successful in life? Would I go to the U.K. or not? Should I invest my money in stocks and shares or start up a business of my own?"

"Hypothek and Creditbank," Efuape grumbled aloud. "Sabotage by the ghost of Roger Casement, R.I.P."

Soditan continued, as if he had not missed a beat. "And of course, teaching—do I stick to teaching? Is Sipe a reliable friend or is he the devil in disguise?"

"I knew it. I knew that was coming. . . ."

"I haven't given the answers yet," Soditan protested.

"I don't want to hear. No, I don't want your made-up answer."

"Ogunba can back me up."

"Sure he will. Which party would the housefly endorse if not the one with the sores?"

"Thank you, Mephistopheles. Now I shall tell you all what Yode truly asked," Ogunba said. "Seriously. Are you ready for it?"

Ogunba's demeanour arrested their attention. He was not joking. In any case, Ogunba rarely told stories. He would laugh at them but he seemed incapable of actually inventing a story for laughs. So they watched him cautiously. Whatever it was he tried to recall struck them as a long-hidden puzzle, teased out by this recent occurrence which, like the other, he could not explain.

"It is true," he said at last. "Yode's first question was: Would he be

---

* You haven't the mouth to comment.

successful in life." His frown deepened further. "And you know what the medium replied, it was very strange. He said, Find Asabula."

There was silence, then Sotikare spoke. "Asabula. But isn't that Yode's correspondent—no, the name of his town?"

"Minus the *t*, yes," Opeilu observed.

"Yes." Ogunba nodded. "I heard it distinctly. Asabula, not Ashtabula."

"A half-literate spirit after all," Sotikare mocked.

Efuape remained undeterred; he tried to work out a meaning. "Axabula . . . asabula . . ." He shook his head. "So much easier work making something out of those Italian names." He tried again. "Asabula . . . Sakabula . . . abula . . . are you sure you got the intonation exactly right?"

"Allowing fully for the ghostly echoes . . . definitely Asabula."

"So it could not mean 'the hawk has facial marks?' "

Soditan smiled. "We thought of that."

"We thought of every possible twist. Nothing made sense."

"Why should it?" demanded the court clerk. 'Oracles speak in parables, don't they? Maybe it has no more meaning than 'Abracadabra.' Have you thought of that? 'Abracadabra' in ancient Odogbolu dialect, now fallen into disuse." And his stomach heaved with chuckles.

Opeilu had remained thoughtful. "It could be mind-reading, you know. There are some genuine mind-readers among our herbalists and *babalawo*. That unseen medium was probably all-seeing. He watched and studied you from the moment you entered, reading your minds."

"But that's the point," Ogunba explained. "We returned to Abeokuta the same day, trying to puzzle out the word all through the journey. We were so exhausted, so we parted company at the gate—I wanted to go to bed right away. I had hardly pulled off my shirt when Yode came running up to my quarters, screaming my name. He was waving a letter in his hand, an overseas letter."

"No, don't tell me," Sipe began.

Yode nodded. "That is God's truth. I saw the mail on my table as soon as I stood in my doorway. Lying on the top was this overseas letter, the very first from Wade Cudeback. It was the first time I had ever heard of Ashtabula. So you see, that name did not yet exist in my mind. It was not there for the medium to read."

An unusual sound had begun earlier outside, a low rumble that rose and diminished in intensity, a purr from a feline throat, not menacing at first, almost soothing in fact. Opeilu was the first to hear it, and he raised his hand for silence. It drew nearer and nearer, seeming to retreat, then swelling in volume until it took on the semblance of a warning of thunder, only steadier, smoother, carefully controlled. They looked towards the door, then at one another. The earlier possibility, that this could be an unusual motor engine, had been dismissed. Each one had a feeling that he had heard it before, that it signified something, but the memory had become faint, tenuous. As the now powerful roar transferred, it seemed, from the outside dark and encroached on the lit interior space they occupied, booming against the rafters and circling their heads, its meaning broke through the distance of childhood and, one after another, sheepish grins appeared on their faces.

"Have we really become such total expatriates?" Sipe lamented.

"*Oro.* Imagine that! I no longer recognise the voice of *oro.*"

"Well, how often did we hear it, even in those early days?" Sotikare paused, troubled. "But why . . ."

"Odubona's death, of course. The grand climax, I suppose."

"Which may last all night," Sotikare grumbled, rising. "Me, I am off to bed."

"Keep your head down," Soditan advised. "Don't let *oro* snatch it off into the night."

"You worry about yourselves," Sotikare shot back.

"Yode is right," Sipe agreed. "We'd better see you home. *Oro*'s wind may sweep you into the darkest void from where there is no return. We will wake up in the morning and look in vain for our court registrar. Vanished. Gone with the wind."

"Is it me you are trying to scare?"

"No, no," Soditan reassured him, taking his hand, while Efuape seized the other. "In fact, what we shall do is take you right to Igbo'ro and leave you there. When *oro* returns at dawn and finds a stranger at his very doorstep . . ."

"I said I was going home. I prefer my own bed."

"*O ya.* Let's carry him. . . ."

They hooked their arms firmly under his armpits, and hoisted him over the doorstep and into the night. Their laughter overwhelmed the now-retreating noise of the bull-roarer. Sipe stood on the doorstep, shouted advice to the struggling Sotikare. "When *oro* tries to seize you for breakfast, just send a *habeas corpus* to Lagos on its wind. . . ."

In the contrasting silence which enveloped the house after their departure, even Sipe conceded a faint unease. He ensured that his windows were shut and his door firmly bolted. He hesitated as his hand reached for the kerosene lantern, then laughed at himself. Before turning down the wick, however, his eyes went to the calendar and he was startled to recall what day of the month it was. Under the pressure of events he had forgotten all about the "consultation." Only two more days, and then the appropriate opening would be gone.

There was still time, fortunately. A detour through Odogbolu, see Onayemi and authorise him to reopen negotiations with the Spirit of Layeni. Enough time to team up with Wemuja in Sagamu, carry out his mission in Lagos, and Onayemi would then meet him at the gates of Ìsarà with the answer to the new question which so stubbornly occupied his mind. Sipe smoothed out a notepad and unscrewed his catalogue-order fountain pen. A smile of satisfaction (and virtuousness) wreathed his face as he tried to imagine the sigh that would be wrung from his erstwhile trading partner when he unfolded the notepaper and found, instead of the agreed theme of a business shopping-list, a single question which read:

"Will S. A. Akinsanya, popularly known as Saaki to his friends, the trade unionist currently living in Denton Street, Ebute Meta, will this Akinsanya be Odemo of Ìsarà?"

He read it over more than half a dozen times. He was about to put it away, intending to give it a very last lookover before setting out early dawn, when a sudden fear struck him and he again unsheathed his pen. Before "Odemo" he now inserted the words "the next," smiling with self-satisfaction at his narrow escape. He, Sipe son of Efuape, was not the man to permit ambiguity to any spirit of Odogbolu, literate or illiterate, and in whatever language.

And, just for good measure, he underlined "the next."

That Pa Josiah, that hard-laterite embodiment of the stubborn core of Ìsarà, should panic, even for a moment before his breakfast, only affirmed what even children sensed as they rose from their sleeping-mats: a tension in the very air of Ìsarà, a complication of their normal Christmas and New Year treats and larks, and the open faces of the grown-ups. Iya Ajike, Node's wife, had risen early and discovered that Wemuja was missing. Then she called out to Alanko and found he was also gone. There had been no plans for transporting timber, and even if there had been, such plans would have been cancelled on a unique day. So she rushed to Mariam, and both invaded Josiah as he cleaned his teeth on the chewing-stick. For Mariam, it was a welcome excuse to intrude on Josiah. She had tried and failed to see him for over a week, and an urgent matter weighed on her mind.

"Wemuja?" Fear, anger . . . it was impossible! And yet that was where his thoughts leapt instinctively; he did not even have to think about it. Wemuja was the only stranger in town. Agunrin was dead and his funeral rites approached their conclusion. *Oro* had wailed its famished circuit through the night, sending shivers through women and making children pull coverlets tighter round their heads. Josiah had never been part of *oro* cult but that did not mean he did not know where *oro* fed, and on what. . . .

And then Josiah cursed himself for a fool and told the women to go home. There was nothing to worry about. He had recalled all the to-ings and fro-ings and conspiratorial sessions between his son and Efuape, and, of course, Wemuja. He knew that it all had to do with bringing Akinsanya to Ìsarà but he did not bother himself with their plans. Wemuja's dawn disappearance obviously had something to do with their furtive schemes; what a state he must be in to think that anyone would dare touch Wemuja! Or even that *ekan* weed he called his apprentice. His mood improved almost immediately; he shook his head and took some snuff to restore his nerves.

Mariam lingered after the departure of Iya Ajike. "I think you should call on Iya Agba. I know you have been busy with affairs of the town but I saw her yesterday. She did not seem to know me. I think she is fading."

"Tonight. I shall see her tonight."

"Don't leave it till too late. . . ."

"I said tonight, after the meeting. Do you think I have not had enough to do without going to watch her funeral antics?"

"I am going to cook her food now. I shall tell her you will be along later. Pray she may recognise you when you get there."

Through a bright red mist, that speciality which Ìsarà shared with few other towns or villages in the South, the late *akuro* farmers began to drift homewards from their farmsteads, anxious to arrive early to take their places where their loyalties lay. Rumour was their travelling companion, rumour welcomed them into town. Under the curfew imposed by *oro*—was anyone still foolish enough to think that Agunrin's death was natural?—a faction had sneaked into Ìsarà charms-potent *igun* men from Badagry. Under cover of the noise of the bull-roarer, the drums of *gelede* had sounded and its masks beamed a discriminating sorcery through the critical roads and passageways of Ìsarà. When the District Officer stepped on Ìsarà soil, he would find that he was defenceless against the alien spell. He would perform just what the faction demanded of him. He would see three but would count three hundred, see a tree and attempt to enter it as he would his own house. Seasoned as Ìsarà was in her own ways with the forces of rain and wind, of earth and sky, and the secret words that bound them together, the *igun* were in an otherworld class by themselves; nothing could stand against their invocations. And the secret departure of Efuape's two-vehicle motorcade at such an unearthly hour had also been observed. So the Olisa faction warned their supporters to be alert. It only confirmed what had long been suspected, that Jagun would import a private army to drive Erinle from Ìsarà. When the District Officer arrived, he would find only one candidate and his supporters. The alien stalwarts keeping guard within Agunrin compound now paraded their own street openly, diverting all human traffic to other routes—no hostile shadow was to fall on the walls of the main figures of the contest. Even the children's tin-can masquerades vanished from the streets, but their glad rags, it seemed, had been transferred to treetops. For there they were, high among the branches of Ìsarà's scattered baobab trees, leafless, strips of clothing where *oro* had perched at night. And the women did not look up at them, while the older children pointed them out to the younger ones and narrated dire tales of their efficacy, skirting the trees or turning back to find another route.

The field of contest, the open grounds in front of the Native Administration court, were prepared early by prisoners brought in a station wagon from Sagamu. They came with hard-back chairs and a baize-covered table, with soft-cushioned armchairs and an awning where the District Officer's party would sit and listen to both parties. They were supervised by a foreman from the Public Works Department under the watchful eye of their prison guards. The guards' were not the only eyes that watched.

Olisa's clutch of *onisegun,* his medicine guards, watched from one side, silently muttering incantations, gesturing towards treetops and rooftops, in the direction of the moist valley and even at their feet. From time to time they made motions of spitting in the wind in all directions of the compass. Jagun contented himself with strolling vaguely past the field from time to time, putting on an unconvincing show of minding any business except the present. Only the most watchful eye could see a movement of his lips when he drew parallel with the dais, but all could see that he took off his shawl from the left shoulder, let it drag on the ground for a few steps before slapping it back into place. His gestures with the fly whisk went beyond merely brushing off troublesome flies, but no one could really accuse him of any sinister devices.

The sun rose higher in the sky. The Native Administration police with blue-dyed baggy shorts, red cummerbunds, and brown fez caps had begun to take up positions when a cloud of dust announced the approach of yet another vehicle and derailed all the self-conscious, guarded motions of the populace and their division into clans. Even the motley guards momentarily lost their alertness. Never before had a three-legged monster appeared on the streets of Ìsarà. The motorcycle half was ridden by one of their own people, but the low-slung pod which shuddered on elastic springs contained a white man in safari suit, complete with pith helmet. The combination came to a stop by the dais, and the policeman dismounted. Olisa's medicine guard retreated, moving backwards slowly at first, then turned homewards in a precipitate rush to spread the news. Olisa, in council with Erinle, nodded grimly. So the news was true after all. Moments later another emissary arrived with a report that removed any lingering doubt. The policeman had been overheard; he had asked for directions to the head teacher's home. Olisa turned to his *onisegun* and told them to prepare charms to deflect the now inevitable bullets; the contraption was undoubtedly the advance guard of reinforcements which Sipe Efuape had sneaked off at dawn to obtain.

Josiah's scouts were even swifter. When they told him a policeman and a white man had asked the way to his home, he dragged out his son and, ignoring his protests, marched him off to his mother's house to hide. "At least wait here until we find out who they are. You forget Erinle has been staying in Abeokuta; he could have plotted something against you there. Why should a white man come looking for you today of all days?"

It did not make sense, yet it was possible. "By the way, watch out for anything strange in Iya's behaviour. Your mother was talking some nonsense about her not recognising people anymore."

Akinyode could only insist that Ogunba be informed at once, and resigned himself to spending a few hours under his grandmother's roof. He found her asleep and tiptoed past her mat, praying fervently that she would not put on her funeral performance for him when she awoke and found him tamely seated there.

When Josiah returned to his house, the motorcycle and sidecar were parked by the door, surrounded by milling children and a few grown-ups. The policeman kept them at a respectful distance.

"Your visitor is inside," a neighbour informed him.

"Whose visitor?" he snapped. "The one your grandfather sent me?"

But first he took the precaution of peeping through his own window. There, seated in his favourite chair, looking totally at ease as if he had lived there a hundred years, was a man so pale, even to hair, including the hair on his skin, that he seemed to have been moulded from cotton fluff. A few freckles on his forearms were the sole exception. Yet he looked sturdy, was probably of his own height. He sweated abnormally, constantly mopped his face and the back of his neck. Josiah would have assessed him harmless but for one curious fact. The stranger had brought a notebook with him and there he was, making notes. It was this that Josiah found alarming. The man inspected the interior of his home with unnatural intensity and, as any feature struck him, put down something in the book. It confirmed Josiah's worst fears and he turned and fled, muttering to himself as he heard the amazed cries of the excited crowd:

"Take him home since you are so fond of uninvited guests."

Now he had to find Jagun wherever he was.

Yode waited but no one came. An hour passed, then two. He had not even brought his pocket watch. He was grateful for one thing, however; although his grandmother had stirred once and even muttered in her sleep, she did not wake up. Perhaps he would be spared her show altogether. He moved stealthily around the cottage, hoping to find even a neglected Bible with which to occupy his time. There was nothing. He stood by the window, looking at the sky. The source of drumming that broke the silence was easy enough to identify—it came from the direction of Ago Aro, from where Erinle would emerge with his supporters, chant and dance towards the field, exuding confidence and hopefully attracting waverers to his side. The teacher felt a twinge of pity for Erinle, so confident was he in the outcome of that afternoon's gathering. Had the regent himself not committed the unspeakable folly of writing to Akinsanya and conceding that he, Saaki, enjoyed the greater support? Yet he wanted him to step down for Erinle "in the interest of Ìsarà." For Olisa had sought to remind Saaki that Ìsarà was not Abeokuta, it was not Lagos, it was not even Ondo. Ìsarà had always gone her own way, protected her own ways. What Ìsarà needed was a king steeped in its oldest traditions, not one who hobnobbed with city operators and alienated civil servants and fired angry letters at the white men. Ìsarà simply wished to be left alone. Wily Saaki . . . he had promptly dispatched a copy of the letter to the Resident.

In the isolation of the cottage, Ìsarà and its frantic manipulations of the past few days seemed suddenly remote. Indeed, before he had spent the first hour, Akinyode found himself sinking into the illusion that this was an unseasonal visit after all. Nothing was happening, or else nothing was happening here, it was all—elsewhere, it was another time. He was again alone in Ìsarà out of season, where nothing disturbed his peace beyond the munch of grass tufts between the gums of indolent sheep and goats, transfixed in wall corners by solid shafts of heat.

With a twinge of guilt, his mind went back to his other home, to Morola and the children. How soon did the midwife predict the expected child? Well, at least the illness was over. She would miss this Ìsarà New Year, but then, it really had not been much of a New Year. The next would be different, that would really be a double celebration if all went well today—which it must. It had to. Ìsarà needed Saaki. It was no generation thing. After all, even Jagun, indeed Apena, Ladega—a number of Olisa's fellow chiefs were, if anything,

more fanatical on the choice. And his popularity was not in question
. . . especially with women, Yode added, wondering why no one had
remembered that but chose instead to saddle him with that reputation. No matter. It meant also that kingship would suit him—at least,
that aspect of the palace image. For the rest, the real challenges,
well, the ex-Ilés had accompanied him this far, they would remain
with him the rest of the way, keep him on his toes. Abeokuta was too
far ahead in every way. He faced the truth squarely—Ìsarà was still
backward. What the ex-Ilés needed was a focus for all their schemes,
someone with a real vision—well, at least the drive, the experience
of organising. Between them they would provide the vision. . . .

Akinyode turned round at a new sound. His grandmother had sat
up on the mat. He could not explain it, but at that moment he was
seized with a terrible premonition and he leapt in her direction,
kneeling down beside her in the same motion. Almost at once she
tilted slowly sideways. He caught the bundle of twigs that her body
had become and let it down gently, straightening her limbs and then
closing her eyes.

For a long time he knelt there, staring at the form turned lifeless
before his eyes. Then he pulled the coverlet over her body, and
covered up her face.

Akinyode rose, let his eyes journey round the room. It had always
seemed so small, so sparse, and now it was truly empty. He tried to
gauge his feelings and found only a simple sadness, no lacerating
anguish, only a sense of a freshly untenanted space in his concerns
and thoughts of that home which was Ìsarà. He wondered how it
would affect his father, but he knew that he would never reveal the
extent of his bereavement, except perhaps to his friend Jagun.

Over the heated air now came unmistakable sounds of *sekere*,
pierced by bugle notes. Again, Erinle's. They all knew he had
brought a royal bugler from Abeokuta, as if that would make up for
his loss of the unsurped regalia, or the paucity of heads he would
muster to his side. But what could be the nature of events which
brought a policeman and a European to seek him out? Was his father
right? Something cooked up with intriguers from Aké? Was the
Alake taking sides? Or was it some powerful Olisa supporters from
Lagos?

He glanced again at the stilled bundle on the mat, indulged his thoughts in wondering if she was ever aware that the Odemo she knew was long dead and another, and perhaps a different era, was now in the making. What, anyway, did all that matter to her? She would meet her Odemo over there, wherever there is, and maybe they would look down on the current performers and shake their heads, patronisingly. They had been through it all. Akinyode walked to the window again to see how high the sun had risen. If it was not three o'clock, it would be very close. Their tryst had been planned for three, at the very spot where the motorcade had moved off in the morning. Perhaps Sipe had already arrived. And Saaki. Yode strained his ears to catch any motor sounds but realised that even gunshots from that area would be blanketed by the thick vegetation on the intervening slopes. He shut the window, unlatched the door, and looked out carefully. Locking the door behind him, he slipped into the lesser-used paths and skirted the town towards 'Gborobe stream.

Wemuja's appearance was loudly incongruous. He had changed into his cowboy suit topped by the scoutmaster hat and was grooming a spotless white horse as one born to the job. He saw the dubious expression on the head teacher's face and hastened to reassure him.

"These are just my job clothes, Mr. Yode. A man has to suit to the part, that is my belief, especially on an occasion like this. I am the one looking after the chief's horse."

"Have the others arrived?" Yode was anxious to know. "Efuape, Mr. Akinsanya . . ."

"All present and correct. They went into *igbale*. . . ."

"What *igbale?* What do you know of *igbale*, you just-come Edo alien?"

Wemuja laughed aloud. "Mr. Teacher sir, *egungun* is coming out today. Royal *egungun* is coming out and then we will know who is who in this Ìsarà town. So the masquerade has gone to dress up, and if you want to know where, it is that former maternity clinic which has been taken over, and that is now the headquarters. I have been resting the horse after its journey. . . ."

"Better go and tell them I am here."

Wemuja's mouth opened in astonishment. "But they are waiting for you over there."

"No. Tell them—just tell Mr. Efuape I am here. Tell him to come quickly."

Wemuja caught something in the tone of his voice and became anxious. "Anything wrong, Mr. Yode? Any trouble in our absence?"

"No. At least, we don't quite know what it is. . . ."

Wemuja's face had changed to dark clouds. "If it is those Olisa people again, Teacher, I have told you to let me—"

"No, no, no. We don't really . . . look, just you go and find Sipe. . . ."

An approaching motorcycle drowned out his remaining words. It was Ogunba's young cousin who had been posted as lookout on the road from Lagos. That gave the ex-Ilés' rally at least two hours' notice, since lunch had been planned for the commission at the Residency, where they would also spend the night after completing their task in Ìsarà. Everything appeared to be on schedule so far, so the meeting might actually begin as planned.

"They arrived half an hour ago," young Ogunba reported. "I waited until they actually started lunch."

"Well, our group seems to have shifted base," Soditan began, but a squelch of tyres on the soft road announced the approach of the Morris. Sipe leapt out, his eyes blazing with excitement. "Where have you been? Where have you been hiding your head?"

"You changed the arrangements. When did you switch to the clinic?"

"We had to. What else did you expect us to do? We couldn't very well invite your guest into the heart of this jungle."

"What guest?"

Sipe looked stumped. "What guest? Isn't he here yet? He left Lagos hours before we did. He said he would go ahead of us."

"Sipe, who are you talking about?"

Efuape held his head. "Oh my God, he's missed the way. By now he's probably in . . ." He stopped abruptly. "No, he couldn't have. A policeman drove him, we found one who was once stationed at Ode. Your man rode in the sidecar."

"Oh. A sidecar has been reported, yes. . . ."

"Then he's here. How come you haven't seen him?"

"Seen who? I fled. Baba thought they had come to arrest me."

"Arrest you? What for? Wait, wait, wait a minute. Are you telling me you haven't caught up yet with your friend Cade Woodenback . . . or whatever he calls himself?"

"Wooden . . ." The teacher stood stock-still. "Who did you say?"

"You know, your friend, your pen pal."

"Here? Wade Cudeback?"

"That's him. He arrived on the mail boat over a week ago but he'd taken ill in the high seas. So he stayed with the Education secretary while recovering."

"But, but, how—"

"Let me finish. He began enquiries about how to reach you, and Melville Jones contacted Saaki. That's all. The man isn't fully himself yet but he insisted on setting off when he heard you were here."

But Soditan only repeated, "Wade Cudeback! Within the protectorate?" And then as a light broke through his mind, he shouted, "Ho! He must be sitting in Baba's house this very moment!"

Sipe's mind stayed on the stolidly practical. "Then let's make a start. We shall simply pick him up along the way, with the rest of the procession."

And so, with only minor variations, the centenary pageant that had floored the librettist, Akinkore, in Abeokuta was replayed through the troughs and serpentine streets of Ìsarà. Spirited as Olisa's procession attempted to be, it proved no match for the sheer spectacle of the Jagun faction, led by what Sipe dubbed their secret weapon, the thoroughbred Bahia, his white-maned head tossing above the hill from where Goriola normally made his grand descent, until his mishap.

A moment stayed with the rider. It would remain with him throughout that day. As he was assisted onto his horse on the blind side of the hill over which they would first appear to the carefully installed groups, his mind rehearsed the routes and functions which had been mapped out for him and he was struck by the elaborateness of planning, and the prodigal resources expended for this contest. As the folds of his *agbada* were carefully draped over the horse's flanks and over the horn of the chased saddle, his face fell in unaccustomed humility and his voice broke slightly.

*"Ha! Emi re wuwo l'owo wen to 'we?"**

They saw that he was overwhelmed. Akinyode, however, looked

---

* Ha! Is it I who weigh so heavy in your hands?

his cousin in the eye and spoke for all: *"Si ko je k'Ìsarà wuwo n'owo re."**

Akinsanya nodded slowly, his far gaze a solemn pledge. Then he brightened up abruptly, hitched up his shoulders, and kicked the sides of his horse, impatient to begin. Wemuja wrapped his stubby fingers round the horse's bridle, and the procession moved forward.

Saaki's face, a black sun against the sky, was topped by an *abetiaja* of stiffened white damask, its triangular flaps bristling above his ears in severely symmetrical folds, their tips at right angles to the ears. No one had, until then, seen an *agbada* made entirely from *èye etù*. The huge embroidered robe shimmered in soft contours with the motion of the horse. Wemuja, self-appointed equerry, obeyed his instructions to the letter. Dressed now in a simple *buba* and *soro,* with *ikori* cap, he brought the horse to a halt at the very crest, while groups of hidden supporters poured out from every side to swell the triumphal entry. Saaki raised his extra-long whisk and acknowledged the tumultuous greetings, his face eclipsed from time to time by huge *sekere* tossed ever higher by the competitive musicians.

Across the heaving rump of the stallion, Efuape and Soditan winked at each other and smiled with satisfaction at this first detonation of the hidden caps. This part of the affair was assured. The rest was in the hands of the commission. And perhaps right within the pocket of my *buba*? Sipe asked himself. For hidden beneath his *agbada* was a sealed envelope from Onayemi, and he found that he feared to open it, to come face to face with the prediction of the Spirit of Layeni!

The route had been deliberately chosen, boldly past the Rokodo House, but only after that faction had left for the meeting place. The symbolic defiance was sufficient, there was no need to mar the resplendence of their progress with unseemly scenes. Yode answered the question in Wemuja's look, nodded, and they proceeded slowly down the hill.

Akinyode Soditan turned his attention to Saaki's ramrod figure on the horse, yes, this was indeed homecoming. But would he truly "return to sender"? The tasks were daunting. Beneath the finery that surrounded them, the teacher was only too aware of bodies eaten by yaws, a fate that seemed to overtake an unfair proportion of Ìsarà

* You simply ensure that Ìsarà weighs heavy in your hands.

inhabitants. The children's close-cropped heads did not all glisten in the sun; tracks of ringworm ran circles through stubs of hair. The mobile clinic which served Ìsarà and other towns in Remo district was infrequent. Sometimes, an expectant mother would deliver her baby on the roadside, having set off too late to reach the maternity clinic at Ode. Within that crowd, Akinyode's eyes caught sight of a goitre round a woman's neck, the size of a pawpaw; he knew the woman. The ex-Ilés had once gathered funds to send her for an operation in Sagamu but she would have none of it. If anyone was going to cut her up, let it be done, she said, within Ìsarà. Dysentery took the lives of far too many infants, even before they were weaned. It was a symbolic reminder, the clinic that had closed down for lack of staff. It was a good thing that Sipe had turned it into the headquarters from which Saaki would make his bid for the crown. There was no running water; not one faucet had ever been installed in Ìsarà. The streets, swept abnormally clean for this day, were often like the interiors of far too many homes which remembered the feel of brooms only at the approach of Goriola. . . . Ah, yes, Saaki's shoulders might look straight enough; Akinyode saw them already bowed under the load of expectations. "Am I that heavy in your hands?" he had exclaimed with touching gratitude. It is Ìsarà, Saaki, which, alas, will weigh heavy in your hands. Must. And you dare expect no gratitude, only more demands, more expectations, and miracles, yes, nothing short of miracles. But no gratitude. That emotion, Akinyode felt often, did not exist in Ìsarà dialect.

And yet despite that suspicion, and in spite of the divisions and present bitterness, Ìsarà had that sense of community, quite unlike Abeokuta. When their procession joined up with Olisa's at the meeting place, with a wide space between to proclaim the division to the wide world but not, he hoped, to enshrine it, all of Ìsarà would be there, a feat which would be impossible in Abeokuta. Indeed, where in Abeokuta could one find a band of ex-Ilés who could so routinely scheme in concert towards the day they would massively "return to sender"? No, Abeokuta was too vast, its ex-Ilés had no knowledge of Ìsarà's poverty, no instinct of the "sender" as that mutely demanding, irritating entity from which they had all dispersed. The rockland city of the Egba was a kestrel with outspread wings, Ìsarà a wood-pigeon scrambling out from the shell of time. . . .

Battered by the noise, but inwardly elated by the result of weeks of careful planning, Soditan's mind took refuge in many directions. He was dying with curiosity to see his fellow teacher who had travelled thousands of miles across the seas—for what? An obsessive interest in that "dark continent" he had merely read about? Or was it a general thirst for knowledge? Knowledge at first hand, that impossible teacher's ideal? Well, whatever he sought here, this was one outing to beat General Montcalm's ghost fields, the Reversing Falls, and Salem's witching house all rolled in one. . . .

Wade Cudeback! Soditan stopped so abruptly that the group behind bumped into him and propelled him forward. Yes, of course, there was such a difference. Cudeback travelled for pleasure, not necessity. But Ìsarà was bereft of choice; she pushed out her sons and daughters, firstly to be trained, then to earn a living. The aridity was all-embracing; Ìsarà could not provide a living. The starkness of it shook him. He knew a few other peoples with that itinerant reputation—the Ogbomosho, for instance. Anywhere along the coast of West Africa, you would find them there. So perhaps to a lesser degree, were the Ijebu. He could not speak for the Ogbomosho's reason for self-dispersal but he knew now, for a certainty, what made the Ìsarà such exiles. There were no factories, not even small businesses, no institutions, nothing of note that would draw in the curious or make the existence of the indigenes a productive adventure.

Did Akinsanya know this? His *abetiaja,* its sharp triangular ends still stiffly parallel to the ground, began to look more like a chunk of the cactus which Ìsarà's hardy soil sprouted on odd hillocks and in the occasional backyard. The teacher made a note to pass this on to him as warning—not that Saaki was likely to forget his mission. Still, it might come in useful. If Saaki slackened or tired, or began to live only for the pleasures of position, it would be time to vary the ancient saying for him—an *abetiaja* is never made of velvet, and no one compelled you to wear it.

And it soon became clear that the homage was cast wider, that it embraced more than the rider. As often as a group surged forward to touch the horse, or Saaki's robes, a figure, or groups of two or three, emerged quietly at Soditan's side, beaming or giggling, manifesting their personal forms of pride and gratitude, sometimes, a claim of simply belonging.

"Do you still remember me, Teacher? You trained me at . . ."

It became routine, every few steps. Faces he had not seen for years, they had responded to the summons by telegrams, by couriers, grapevine, and newspaper notices, even by episcopal circulars—there were several ex-Ilés who had taken the cloth. Opeilu simply took them in charge. Some arrived that very day, in time to swell the ranks; the ex-Ilés had cast their nets far and wide. Some faces merely shouted "Teacher" from within the crowd and waved until he responded and they were satisfied that he had recognised them. Others raised up their children above the milling heads for him to see. And there was Mrs. Esan standing slightly apart, nodding with quiet satisfaction. He waved a grand approval towards the triumph of her *èye etù* on Saaki's back. Their discussion ran through his mind and he felt himself warmed by an inner glow, acknowledging that, as if by accident, he had stumbled on the secret of fulfillment.

Could it be—he returned to the shrine at Odogbolu, to the medium whose enigmatic pronouncement had defied all understanding—could this be what it all meant? Ask a foolish question and you get a foolish answer? When you ask a spirit if you'll find success in life, you should first tell it what you mean by success. That game played on you by grown-ups as a child: Go to your Uncle So-and-so and bring me some *arodan . . .* and the child goes to that uncle, and the uncle shakes his head dolefully, no, he has no *arodan.* But he encourages you to try his friend, who probably has it. That friend, alas, only regrets that he lent his last piece to his brother, so to the brother you proceed . . . then his cousin . . . until at last—don't say you heard it from me but—try your next-door neighbour, who returned from *arodan*-land only yesterday and is sure to have plenty on him. On to Mr. Next-door-neighbour, who exclaims, But your father has just dropped by to pick up the last bit! Somewhere along the way, certainly by the very end, you discover yourself that *arodan* is just a nonsense word, that there is no such thing, and another lesson is implanted. Well, maybe spirits also play games with humans, especially those who pester them with foolish questions. . . .

Node had been brought out to watch the parade. Mariam stood by his side, among the women and children of his household, Node, on whose timber lorry the horse had ridden from the home of the Santeros and whose blessing could only be conveyed by Mariam. Saaki halted briefly, bowed and silently pledged to obtain one of the wheelchairs in use in Lagos General Hospital for the paralysed man. Then to the gate of *osugbo* amidst gunshots, swelled at every passage by tens of newcomers.

Jagun waited with the *osugbo* elders to sacrifice a ram and smear its blood on the horse's forehooves. They entered the last stretch of crude terracing, the horse's hooves raising hard clacks, as if to counterpoise the optimism of the cheers. Then to Josiah's home, Ile Lígùn, where bowls of water were thrown on the ground before them. An hour or so earlier, the mystery of the strange caller had been explained to Pa Josiah, so he now stood side by side with the guest and the rest of the ex-Ilés against the three-legged transport that had brought him from Lagos. Wemuja did not need to be told; he tugged at the bridle and the horse came to a halt, the crowd nearly impossible to control as they sought to catch a glimpse of the intruder from over and beyond the seas who had come to seek out an Ìsarà son— and on such a singular day! Did it augur well? The feeling was—it had better!

As he set eyes on the visitor, Soditan was mildly disconcerted to find that the white teacher in no way resembled his handwriting, neither did he emit the slightest aura which evoked the places and adventures he so richly conveyed in his letters. Saaki gave Wade Cudeback a massive wink as Soditan stepped forward to shake hands with him. The Ìsarà teacher had decided on the form of greeting he would use for this encounter. It would certainly raise a laughter of approbation from the ex-Ilés and his guest, break the ice and set everyone at ease. But Wade Cudeback beat him to the salute: "Teacher Soditan, I presume?"

In the few seconds of grace provided by the knowledgeable laughter, Soditan thought rapidly. His response, he would later acknowledge, emerged in spite of himself. Astonished, he heard himself say, and with a feeling of inner composure:

"Welcome to Ashtabula."

WOLE SOYINKA lives in Abeokuta, Nigeria. His other works include *Aké: The Years of Childhood,* which was chosen by *The New York Times Book Review* as one of the twelve best books of 1982; *Mandela's Earth and Other Poems; The Man Died;* and *Death and the King's Horsemen.* Wole Soyinka received the Nobel Prize for Literature in 1986.